MUIRHEAD LIBRARY OF PHILOSOPHY

An admirable statement of the aims of the Library of Philosophy was provided by the first editor, the late Professor J. H. Muirhead, in his description of the original programme printed in Erdmann's *History of Philosophy* under the date 1890. This was slightly modified in subsequent volumes to take the form of the following statement:

'The Muirhead Library of Philosophy was designed as a contribution to the History of Modern Philosophy under the heads: first of Different Schools of Thought—Sensationalist, Realist, Idealist, Intuitivist; secondly of different Subjects—Psychology, Ethics, Political Philosophy, Theology. While much had been done in England in tracing the course of evolution in nature, history, economics, morals and religion, little had been done in tracing the development of thought on these subjects. Yet "the evolution of opinion is part of the whole evolution".

'By the co-operation of different writers in carrying out this plan it was hoped that a thoroughness and completeness of treatment, otherwise unattainable, might be secured. It was believed also that from writers mainly British and American fuller consideration of English Philosophy than it had hitherto received might be looked for. In the earlier series of books containing, among others, Bosanquet's *History of Aesthetic*, Pfleiderer's *Rational Theology since Kant*, Albee's *History of English Utilitarianism*, Bonar's *Philosophy and Political Economy*, Brett's *History of Psychology*, Ritchie's *Natural Rights*, these objects were to a large extent effected.

'In the meantime original work of a high order was being produced both in England and America by such writers as Bradley, Stout, Bertrand Russell, Baldwin, Urban, Montague, and others, and a new interest in foreign works, German, French and Italian, which had either become classical or were attracting public attention, had developed. The scope of the Library thus became extended into something more international, and it is entering on the fifth decade of its existence in the hope that it may contribute to that mutual understanding between countries which is so pressing a need of the present time.'

The need which Professor Muirhead stressed is no less pressing today, and few will deny that philosophy has much to do with enabling us to meet it, although no one, least of all Muirhead himself, would regard that as the sole, or even the main, object of philosophy. As Professor Muirhead continues to lend the distinction of his name to the Library of Philosophy it seemed not inappropriate to allow him to recall us to these aims in his own words. The emphasis on the history of thought also seemed to me very timely; and the number of important works promised for the Library in the very near future augur well for the continued fulfilment, in this and other ways, of the expectations of the original editor.

H. D. LEWIS

MUIRHEAD LIBRARY OF PHILOSOPHY

General Editor: H. D. Lewis
Professor of History and Philosophy of Religion in the University of London

The Analysis of Mind BERTRAND RUSSELL 8th impression
Clarity is Not Enough by H. D. LEWIS
Coleridge as Philosopher by J. H. MUIRHEAD 3rd impression
The Commonplace Book of G. E. Moore edited by C. LEWY
Contemporary American Philosophy edited by G. P. ADAMS and W. P. MONTAGUE 2nd impression
Contemporary British Philosophy First and second series edited by J. H. MUIRHEAD 2nd impression
Contemporary British Philosophy third series edited by H. D. LEWIS 2nd impression
Contemporary Indian Philosophy edited by RADHAKRISHNAN and J. H. MUIRHEAD 2nd edition
The Discipline of the Cave by J. N. FINDLAY
Doctrine and Argument in Indian Philosophy by NINIAN SMART
Essays in Analysis by ALICE AMBROSE
Ethics by NICOLAI HARTMANN translated by STANTON COIT 3 vols
The Foundations of Metaphysics in Science by ERROL E. HARRIS
Freedom and History by H. D. LEWIS
The Good Will: A Study in the Coherence Theory of Goodness by H. J. PATON
Hegel: A Re-Examination by J. N. FINDLAY
Hegel's Science of Logic translated by W. H. JOHNSTON and L. G. STRUTHERS 2 vols 3rd impression
History of Æsthetic by B. BOSANQUET 2nd edition 5th impression
History of English Utilitarianism by E. ALBEE 2nd impression
History of Psychology by G. S. BRETT edited by R. S. PETERS abridged one-volume edition 2nd edition
Human Knowledge by BERTRAND RUSSELL 4th impression
A Hundred Years of British Philosophy by RODOLF METZ translated by J. H. HARVEY, T. E. JESSOP, HENRY STURT 2nd impression
Ideas: A General Introduction to Pure Phenomenology by EDMUND HUSSERL translated by W. R. BOYCE GIBSON 3rd impression

Muirhead Library of Philosophy

EDITED BY H. D. LEWIS

ESSAYS IN ANALYSIS

ESSAYS IN ANALYSIS

BY

ALICE AMBROSE

LONDON: GEORGE ALLEN & UNWIN LTD
NEW YORK: HUMANITIES PRESS INC

FOR

CJ, AJ, SG

B29
A5

PRINTED IN GREAT BRITAIN
in 11 on 12 point Imprint type
BY UNWIN BROTHERS LIMITED
WOKING AND LONDON

PREFACE

Over the years in which these essays were written I have kept constantly before me the model of procedure in philosophy which Professor G. E. Moore gave me in the three years I was his pupil at Cambridge University. Moore devoted himself steadfastly to the clarification of problems, employing his great powers of analysis in renewed attempts to clear away confusions which were obstacles to their solution. I have tried to the best of my abilities to follow the example set by his standards. Some of the problems dealt with in these essays have in part been determined by his interest in them; other problems stem in part from another great thinker who was at Cambridge during those years, |Dr later Professor) Ludwig Wittgenstein. His original insights into the nature of philosophical problems and theories have been for me an intellectual compass. What he taught us seemed to me then, as it does now, revolutionary and vastly promising for a subject whose problems, as time has shown, have no exits. There can be no doubt that his conception of philosophy lights up the labyrinth of language in which the philosopher wanders. His conception gives us a perspective in which the intractability of philosophical controversies finds an explanation and which promises the dissolution of the problems. The fundamental thesis of Wittgenstein's later work is that the exit from a philosophical problem is the clear understanding of its nature. The view that philosophical positions are verbal structures with a false scientific facade is destructive of the treasured illusion that philosophers are in search of truth. But it compensates in full by improving our understanding of a time-honoured intellectual phenomenon. The careful reader will note that the papers in this book do not equally represent application of Wittgenstein's conception. This is because my own understanding of Wittgenstein's later work grew with the years.

My indebtedness to Morris Lazerowitz will be evident throughout these studies. His own consistent theme has been that philosophical theories and their supporting arguments are radically different from what they appear to be, and this has helped my understanding of Wittgenstein. It has contributed in substantive ways to the treatment of problems I consider here; and in more intangible ways as well I owe him very much indeed.

Three of the essays in the present collection have not appeared before in print. These are: 'Invention and Discovery', 'Unknowables and Logical Atomism', and 'Factual, Mathematical and Metaphysical Inventories'. One paper is in an ambiguous position: 'Finitism and "The Limits of Empiricism" '. This paper is an extensively revised version of a paper of the same title appearing in *Mind*. For permission to reprint the remaining essays I am indebted to the editors of the following journals and books:

Mind, The Journal of Philosophy, Proceedings of the Aristotelian Society.

Philosophical Analysis (edited by Max Black), Cornell University Press; *Metaphysics: Readings and Reappraisals* (edited by W. E. Kennick and Morris Lazerowitz), Prentice-Hall, Inc.; *The Philosophy of G. E. Moore*, The Library of Living Philosophers, Vol. IV (edited by P. A. Schilpp), Open Court Publishing Co.

Northampton, Massachusetts
June, 1966   ALICE AMBROSE

CONTENTS

NOTE

The papers in this book which have been previously published originally appeared as follows:

1. 'Proof and the Theorem Proved', in *Mind:* a Quarterly Review of Psychology and Philosophy. Vol. LXVIII, N.S., No. 272, 1959.
2. 'Self-contradictory Suppositions', in *Mind*, Vol. LIII, N.S., No. 209, 1944.
3. 'Wittgenstein on Some Questions in Foundations of Mathematics', in *The Journal of Philosophy*, Vol. LII, No. 8, 1955.
6. 'On Entailment and Logical Necessity', in *Proceedings of the Aristotelian Society*, Vol. LVI, 1956.
7. 'Wittgenstein on Universals', in *Metaphysics: Readings and Reappraisals* (edited by W. E. Kennick and Morris Lazerowitz), Prentice-Hall, Inc., 1966.
9. 'Linguistic Approaches to Philosophical Problems', in *The Journal of Philosophy*, Vol. XLIX, No. 9, 1952.
10. 'The Problem of Linguistic Inadequacy', in *Philosophical Analysis* (edited by Max Black), Cornell University Press, 1950.
11. 'The Problem of Justifying Inductive Inference', in *The Journal of Philosophy*, Vol. XLIV, No. 10, 1947.
12. 'Three Aspects of Moore's Philosophy', in *The Journal of Philosophy*, Vol. LVII, No. 26, 1960.
13. 'Moore's "Proof of an External World" ', in *The Philosophy of G. E. Moore*, The Library of Living Philosophers (edited by P. A. Schilpp), Vol. IV, Open Court Publishing Co., 1942.

PROOF AND THE THEOREM PROVED*

In his *Remarks on the Foundations of Mathematics* Wittgenstein writes: 'One would like to say that the understanding of a mathematical proposition is not guaranteed by its verbal form, as is the case with most non-mathematical propositions.'[1] The point of this comment, or at least an important point, comes out in the account he gives of mathematical proof, in particular of the connection between the proof of a statement and the meaning of the statement. This account has difficulties, which Wittgenstein has himself pointed out, but the resolution of which remains obscure. I shall not pretend here to present how he intended to circumvent these difficulties, as this would involve me in doubtful interpretation and extension of what he has said. What I wish to do in this paper is to elaborate the difficulties inherent in his description of proof and to indicate where it is, and where it is not, possible to escape them.

I begin with his account of the connection between a proof and the statement proved. As is well known, he frequently asserted that 'if you want to know what a mathematical statement means, look at its proof'. The concluding expression of a sequence of expressions constituting the statement of a proof derives its sense from the proof, and it does not have that sense apart from the proof. This means that what one understands at the end of a proof is different from what one understood by the same sentence at the beginning. Concretely, if 'There are no odd perfect numbers' is proved, one's understanding of the sentence expressing it will differ from one's present understanding. Similarly for the unproved statements 'Every even number is the sum of two primes', 'There are infinitely many pairs of primes of the form

* Reprinted from *Mind:* a Quarterly Review of Psychology and Philosophy. Vol. LXVIII., N.S., No. 272, October 1959.
[1] P. 147.

p and $p + 2$'. Wittgenstein's account of the connection between the proof of a statement and its meaning is supported by his claim that in advance of proof we do not know what it is like for the statement to be true, since we cannot describe what it is like to establish its truth. A problem in mathematics for which as yet there is no solution 'is like the problem set by the king in the fairy tale who told the princess to come neither naked nor dressed, and she came wearing fish net. He did not really know what he wanted her to do but when she came thus he was forced to accept it. His order was of the form: Do something which I shall be inclined to call neither naked nor dressed. It is the same with the mathematical problem: Do something which one will be inclined to accept as a solution; though one doesn't know what it will be like'[1]. Being unable to describe a possible solution—since this would be to give it—he took as a reason for saying we do not know what it is like for the statement in question to be true, and this in turn as a reason for saying we do not know its meaning, and that proof gives it its meaning. To put his point alternatively, an expression in the interrogative does not have the sense it has once the answer is provided; proof 'provides it with content'.[2]

The following series of questions discussed by Wittgenstein[3] illustrates his thesis: Is there a 6 in the first thousand places in the development of $\frac{1}{7}$? Is there a 2 in the infinite development? Are there two 2's? Are there three consecutive 7's in the expansion of π? In the case of the first two questions mere continued division is an adequate method of giving the answer: that there is no 6 in the first thousand places, that there is a 2 at the third place and hence in the infinite development. But suppose that in the process of calculating one discovered periodicity. The question concerning a 6, and its answer, according to him now has a new interpretation, namely, that there is no 6 in the period. The interpretation is provided by the new method of answering it, a calculation embodied in the formula *Remainder = dividend* (which is not merely a calculation yielding several repetitions of the same group of numbers). This method also shows that there cannot be two 2's in the development. But in the case of π there is no method for showing either that there must be three 7's or that there cannot

---

[1] From lecture notes taken in 1934–35.
[2] *Ibid.*   [3] *Ibid.*

be; there is as yet no operation comparable to the division which yields a 2 at the third place in the development of $\frac{1}{7}$ nor any rule comparable to *Remainder = dividend* which precludes a pair of 2's.

Because the rule for expanding π determines what occurs at *each* place in the series it might appear that the ground for the decision was already there, and that we could decide between the existence of three 7's and the existence of no such triple had we the omniscience to survey an infinite expansion. But omniscience cannot surmount the logically impossible.[1] Nor could it settle the question by its grasp of the rule of expansion: 'Even God can determine something mathematical only by mathematics. Even for him the mere rule of expansion cannot decide anything that it does not decide for us. We might put it like this: if the rule for the expansion has been given us, a *calculation* can tell us that there is a "2" at the fifth place. Could God have known this, without the calculation, purely from the rule of expansion? I want to say: No'.[2] If, then, omniscience fails both to survey the infinite expansion and to see what the rule must or must not yield, and hence fails to settle the question regarding π, the situation is not to be described as one in which there is something to know which we do not know. Rather, there is as yet no calculus for it.[3] The ground for the decision has yet to be invented.[4] Were this question to become decidable it would change its status: 'For a connexion is made then, which formerly *was not there*'.[5] Before the mathematics has been invented which will provide a decision this question does not make sense—just as 'in an arithmetic in which one does not count further than 5 the question what $4 + 3$ makes doesn't yet make sense' . . . though 'the problem may very well exist of giving this question a sense'.[6]

There is something curiously opaque about Wittgenstein's assertions concerning the connection between proof of a proposition p, sense of the sentence 'p', and understanding 'p'. The difficulties inherent in his account are apparent, and he has himself

[1] This I have argued in 'Finitism and "The Limits of Empiricism" ', *Mind*, Vol. XLVI, No. 183.
[2] *Remarks on the Foundations of Mathematics*, p. 185. (New York: The MacMillan Co, 1956.)
[3] Lecture notes, 1934–35.
[4] *Remarks on the Foundations of Mathematics*, p. 138. [5] *Ibid.* [6] *Ibid.*, p. 140.

mentioned them, while leaving their resolution obscure. I shall now detail them, so that it will be clear what difficulties must be got round and what clarification is required. First, if a question lacks content because nothing in the body of mathematics developed so far is capable of yielding the answer to it, then apparently the question must already be answered in order to be called a question.[1] To *what* question does the proof provide an answer? Wittgenstein admits that 'to say it is the proof which gives sense to the question is absurd because it misuses the word "question" '.[2] 'Answer' is in the same case. If an interrogative expression puts no question, then there is nothing to which anything one demonstrates is an answer. Further, if 'a mathematical proposition has no sense before being proved true or false',[3] then what has the mathematician proved? Proof neither provides an answer to the question set nor establishes that a *given* proposition has a truth-value. The proposition the mathematician attempts to prove, if there is one at all, is not identical with the proposition proved, which is to say that he does not prove what he sets out to prove. For if proof *gives* sense to an expression, then prior to proof the expression did not have *that* sense. That sense which exists only as the result of proof, cannot be described as 'what was to be proved'. No proof should conclude with the words 'Quod erat demonstrandum'. This means that what one understands at the end of a proof is different from what one understood by the same sentence in the beginning. Either one understands nothing at all before knowing the proof or one understands something different after knowing it. Further, if the expression concluding the sequence of sentences expressing the proof gets its sense from the proof it would seem to follow that there could not be two proofs of the same proposition. Wittgenstein was aware of these paradoxical consequences: '. . . ought I to say that the same sense can only have *one* proof? Or that when a proof is found the sense alters? Of course some people would . . . say "Then the proof of a proposition cannot ever be found, for, if it has been found, it is no longer the proof of *this* proposition" '.[4] His rejoinder is: 'But to say this is so far to say nothing at all'.[5] 'Of course it would

---

[1] Lecture notes, 1934–35.
[2] *Ibid.*
[3] *Ibid.*
[4] *Remarks on the Foundations of Mathematics*, p. 164.
[5] *Ibid.*

be nonsense to say that *one* proposition cannot have two proofs—for we do say just that.'[1]

This is not in the least helpful. The puzzle remains. Perhaps it will be useful to see that whatever point Wittgenstein had in mind cannot be expressed by the words 'proof gives "*p*" its sense'. Suppose we ask 'proof of what?'. Is it intelligible to be told: Proof *of p* provides '*p*' with sense? Clearly it is nonsense to say that proof that a proposition expressed by '*p*' has a certain truth-value makes '*p*' express that proposition. It will be observed that the language used to assert a connection between proof of *p* and sense of '*p*' is in what one might call the 'mixed mode' of speech. Language referring to a proposition turns out to be language which should refer to a sentence (or *vice versa*). That is, 'proposition' or 'statement' is used ambiguously, now to mean 'sentence', now to mean 'sense of a sentence'. '*p* is necessary in language L', 'a statement *s* is meaningful if it can be verified or falsified', are similar examples of the same mixed use of language. The first expression can be satisfactorily replaced by ' "*p*" expresses a necessary proposition in L', but the second when rendered unambiguous clearly fails to express a criterion of meaningfulness: '*s* is meaningful' requires *s* to be an expression, '*s* can be verified' requires that *s* be what the expression means. The situation is similar with 'proof of a statement gives it sense': 'statement' is ambiguous. And when rendered unambiguous the claim becomes: an expression acquires meaning when one establishes the truth-value of what it already means.

I see no way to interpret Wittgenstein's assertion so as to make it a sensible description of a deduction. However, I think a reconstruction of it can be given which correctly describes certain pieces of mathematical reasoning, misleadingly called proofs, as giving meaning to an expression. Further, it is possible to remove the paradox in his claim that what one understands by the terminal sentence of the sequence of sentences expressing the proof is different from what one understands before it takes its place in such a sequence. I should like to consider this latter point first. To this end it will be enlightening to note certain facts about sentences expressing necessary propositions, i.e. the kind of propositions figuring within mathematics.

[1] *Remarks on the Foundations of Mathematics*, p. 92.

Consider the sentence: 'It is logically impossible for a heptagon to be constructed with straight edge and compass'. The fact that this sentence expresses a necessary proposition implies that the phrase 'heptagon constructed with straight edge and compass' does not serve to describe any figure. If the phrase did have a descriptive use, then it would describe something which would falsify a necessary proposition. This fact about the way language is used prevents the sentence from saying anything falsifiable. That is, the sentence expresses a necessary proposition *because* its empirical verbal correlate, ' "heptagon constructed with straight edge and compass" has no descriptive use', expresses what is true.[1] This is not to say that it *asserts* that its verbal correlate says what is true, else the necessary proposition expressed by 'No heptagon is constructible with straight edge and compass' would be the same as the empirical proposition about the use in our language of the phrase 'heptagon constructed with straight edge and compass'. But neither is it about a sort of figure, heptagon constructible with ruler and compass, the existence of which it asserts to be impossible. If it were it would be precisely similar to the proposition that it is impossible for iron to be melted in boiling water. 'Iron melting in boiling water' denotes the kind of occurrence which would falsify the proposition; it *describes* what is declared to be impossible, a conceivable state of nature. If then such a sentence as 'It is impossible for a heptagon to be constructed with straight edge and compass' is not about a kind of thing which it declares to be impossible, what do we understand by it? What do we know? The sentence does not *express* any fact about the use of words. Yet all that is left for one to know in understanding it is such a fact. There is no inconsistency between these two claims about the sentence, for what is known in understanding it is not the same as what it expresses.[2]

This account can be brought to bear on the question as to what the mathematician understands when he is in the position of having to ask, 'Does "*p*" express something true or something false?', e.g. 'Does "There are no odd perfect numbers" express a truth or a falsity?'. To raise this question about a sentence which

---

[1] For the detail of this description of sentences expressing necessary propositions, see M. Lazerowitz, *The Structure of Metaphysics*, pp. 265–271.

[2] *The Structure of Metaphysics*, p. 270, where this distinction is discussed.

does not terminate any sequence of sentences expressing a demonstration is to betray ignorance of whether its descriptive part, e.g. 'odd perfect number', has a use. And in this circumstance he can justly be said not to understand the sentence. Prior to finding out whether its descriptive part has a use he does not know what the proposition is which is expressed by it, whether an impossible one or a necessary one. To know the truth-value of what is expressed by a sentence terminating the statement of proof is to know *what* is expressed. This seems to me good reason (although no such reason may have been in Wittgenstein's mind) for saying that one understands after proof, i.e. once one has a sequence of statements constituting proof, something different from what one understood beforehand.

It may seem paradoxical to assert that, properly speaking, we do not understand a sentence for an *a priori* proposition whose truth-value we do not know, whereas we do understand such a sentence as 'It is impossible to construct a heptagon with straight edge and compass'. To assert this is to emphasize the difference between the two cases, in particular, to emphasize what we do *not* know in the case of 'There are no odd perfect numbers'. What proposition this combination of words asserts we do not know, nor therefore whether 'odd perfect number' has or has not a use. In the case of 'heptagon constructible with straight edge and compass', proof shows that it is to be excluded from our notation, as denoting no figure, and we can hardly claim to have understood by it the same concept as before this was shown, or for that matter, that we understood this *combination* of words at all. We *can* claim to understand 'There are no odd perfect numbers' if understanding it comes to nothing more than knowing the combination of words to be grammatical and understanding the individual words. To claim this is to emphasize the similarity between the two cases. It does not matter whether we describe ourselves as understanding a sentence in both sorts of cases so long as we note the difference which proof effects in what we know. For to signalize this difference by asserting that only after proof do we understand a sentence in effect merely restricts the scope of the word 'understand'. The claim seems paradoxical because it seems to deny a fact rather than to bear on our use of language.

Let us now consider Wittgenstein's assertion that proof gives sense to a mathematical statement. As has been seen, the expression 'proof gives sense to "p" ' is nonsense if 'proof' is understood in the sense of a straightforward deduction. But there are procedures in mathematics which are called proof and which have the air of being demonstrations but whose work is actually to give meaning to an expression. These may have been in Wittgenstein's mind when he said this. Consider Cantor's proof by means of his diagonal procedure that the set of real numbers is non-denumerable. Of this Wittgenstein says: It 'does not shew us an irrational number different from all in the system, but gives sense to the mathematical proposition that the number so-and-so is different from all those of the system. . . . Cantor gives a sense to the expression "expansion which is different from all the expansions of the system" by proposing that an expansion should be so called when it can be proved that it is diagonally different from the expansions in a system. . . . These considerations may lead us to say that $2^{\aleph_0} > \aleph_0$. That is to say: we can *make* the considerations lead us to that. Or: we can say *this* and give *this* as our reason.'[1] The last three sentences are particularly important. They give one an idea as to what he had in mind in saying 'One would like to say: the proof changes the grammar of our language, changes our concepts. It makes new connexions. (It does not establish that they are there; they do not exist until it makes them.)'[2] 'A proof induces us to make a certain decision, namely that of accepting a particular concept-formation.'[3]

Let us now consider several simple examples. It is usual to find in textbooks an *argument* for equating a° with 1. To quote from N. J. Lennes's *College Algebra*: 'Since $a^m \div a^m = a^m/a^m = 1$ and also $a^m \div a^m = a^{m-m} = a^\circ$, it follows that $a^\circ = 1$ for all values of a.'[1] The comment made by Lennes upon this bit of reasoning is significant: 'Hence we will adopt the following definition: $a^\circ = 1$.'[4] This comment makes explicit what the role of the 'proof' is: to justify the introduction of the expression '$a^\circ = 1$' and to give it meaning. For the definition given of an exponent, as the number of times an expression is used as factor, i.e. is multiplied by itself, provides no meaning for the expression 'a°'. That is, the definition does not make a° a member of the power series a^n, for it does not

---

[1] *Remarks on the Foundations of Mathematics*, p. 58   [3] *Ibid.*, p. 122.
[2] *Ibid.*, p. 79.   [4] P. 40.

define 'a^n' for $n = 0$. Without the reasoning, 'a^0' and '$a^0 = 1$' would lack sense. What is set out as a proof that the *proposition* $a^0 = 1$ is *true* is in fact a reason for giving use to the *expression* '$a^0 = 1$'. Similarly, the 'demonstration' that any number different from zero cannot be divided by zero and that zero divided by zero may represent any number whatever provides the reason for excluding the expression '$a/0$'. Most often a justification for introducing or excluding an expression in mathematics is not presented as such, but rather is presented as a piece of reasoning showing something to be true or false. Thus, $a^0 = 1$ is 'proved' to be true, division by zero is 'proved' to be impossible. A decision about language, a linguistic innovation, is often concealed by the form of words in which it is introduced, i.e. by the language of demonstration of truth or falsity. The idiom natural to the doing of mathematics is that in which expressions are used rather than mentioned, and it is often not as clear as in the examples above that the reasoning adduced is a justification for a decision with respect to an expression rather than a proof of the truth or falsity of what is expressed by it. For example, it is said that in order to ensure that linear equations and equations of higher degree always have solutions the domain of numbers was extended by the addition of negative integers, rationals, reals, and complex numbers. This way of putting the matter conceals the fact that extension of the domain of numbers consisted in introducing new symbols and a use for them which assured meaning to the expressions '$a + x = b$, $b < a$', '$ax = b$, a not a factor of b', '$x^2 = a$, a not an integral square', '$x^2 = -a$'. The latter expressions and the expressions '$-(a - b)$', 'b/a', '$\sqrt{a}$', '$\sqrt{-a}$' simultaneously acquire meaning. To say that prior to the introduction of negative integers $a + x = b$ did not always have a solution suggests that the expression '$a + x = b$' was meaningful even when $b < a$; actually it was not.

It is instructive to compare the so-called proof that $a^0 = 1$ and the proof of the Fundamental Theorem of Euclid: If a and b are any two positive integers there exist integers q and r, $q \geqslant 0$, $0 \leqslant r < b$, such that $a = qb + r$. Here there are two cases to consider: (1) a is a multiple of b, (2) a is not a multiple of b, where (2') $a > b$, (2") $a < b$. In case (1) the theorem is verified, r being 0. In case (2') a must lie between two consecutive multiples

21

of b: qb and $(q + 1)b$; whence there is an integer r, $0 < r < b$, such that $a = qb + r$. In case $(2'')$, $q = 0$ and $r = a$. Q.E.D. The deduction here moves between strictly delimited concepts—positive integer, the relations greater than, less than, equal to, the operations of addition and multiplication. No concept-word undergoes an extension of meaning in the course of the proof. The proof merely makes explicit what the initial concepts imply: it is analogous to a calculation, say to that which shows a 6 in the product 13×13, where once the rules are accepted one is not free to operate arbitrarily. In such cases it is appropriate to speak of discovery of a mathematical fact.

How is it with the so-called proof that $a^\circ = 1$? Wittgenstein's claim that 'a proof is not found but constructed',[1] that 'a proof induces us to make a certain decision, namely that of accepting a particular concept-formation',[2] fits this case. Keeping in mind that when a sentence expresses a necessary proposition a certain expression has no use, consider the equations '$a^m \div a^m = a^{m-m} = a^\circ = 1$'. To accept '$a^m \div a^m = a^\circ$' as expressing a logical necessity is to accept a reason for refusing a use to '$a^\circ \neq 1$'. And the decision to accept it mathematicians might not have made, just as Descartes refused to describe $x^2 = -1$ as having a solution, or $x^3 + x^2 + x + 1 = 0$ as having three roots. No such freedom of decision exists in the course of the proof of the Fundamental Theorem of Euclid. In equating a° and 1, under the guise of a proof explicating the concept of exponent, an additional rule for the use of 'a^n' is argued for. And the acceptance of the reason is expressed in the non-verbal idiom as 'proof that $a^\circ = 1$'. This it appears to me illustrates how Wittgenstein's claim that proof gives sense to an expression is to be construed. Mathematics in such a case can appropriately be described as invention.

The point can be brought out by means of a distinction made by M. Lazerowitz[3] in describing two different activities of philosophers which go by the name of 'analysis', and which have their analogue in mathematical deductions: what he calls actual analyses and 'conversion' analyses. As has been argued, a necessary proposition, in which an analysis eventuates, sets out in the non-

[1] Lecture notes, 1934–35. [2] *Remarks on the Foundations of Mathematics*, p. 122.
[3] 'Moore and Philosophical Analysis', in *Studies in Metaphilosophy*. (London: Routledge & Kegan Paul, 1964.)

verbal idiom the criteria for the usage of an expression. Actual analysis, as contrasted with 'conversion' analysis, merely makes explicit those features in virtue of which an expression is in accordance with established usage applied (this, of course, without entailing any factual statement about usage). But a conversion analysis calls attention to verbal analogies in order to justify extending, or contracting, the use of an expression, or eliminating an expression altogether. This it usually does under the guise of mere explication, as though the usage it in fact proposes is a matter of record.[1]

Consider the necessary truth that $x^3 + x^2 + x + 1 = 0$ has three roots, $-1, +\sqrt{-1}, -\sqrt{-1}$. Had a different decision been made about this and similar equations—had the decision been to say it had but one root—then we should not say it is true that there are three. And that mathematicians made the decision they did rested on accepting a linguistic innovation: on giving '$\sqrt{-1}$', or 'i', a use. The term 'i^2' was *defined* as -1, and the symbol '$a + bi$' (where 'a' and 'b' denote real numbers) was so defined as to obey the commutative, associative, and distributive laws of addition and multiplication holding for real numbers. That is, the expressions '$(a + bi) + (c + di)$', '$(a + bi) \times (c + di)$', etc., were given a use, a use so similar to '$a + c$' and '$a \times c$' that the invention of complex number symbols is described in the non-verbal form of speech as an *extension* of the field of real numbers. With this, the simple expressions '$x^2 = -1$' and ' "$x^2 = -1$" has two roots' have meaning. Further, *every* quadratic equation $ax^2 + bx + c = 0$, the roots of which are $-b \pm \sqrt{(b^2 - 4ac)} / 2a$, could be said to have roots both when $b^2 - 4ac \geqslant 0$ and when it is < 0. 'Every quadratic equation has two roots' *came* to express a necessity; that is to say, that it expressed a necessity did not derive from already accepted rules for the use of words, but from an extension of the use of 'root'. Similarly, '$a^n = 1$, for $n = 0$' does not record an analytic fact backed by the definition of 'exponent'. If it did, mathematicians would not have been at liberty to accept the definition and deny that for $n = 0$, $a^n = 1$. Nor, had complex numbers fallen under

[1] See M. Lazerowitz, 'Moore and Philosophical Analysis', op. cit., for an illustration from philosophy: his analysis of 'Causation is nothing more than invariable conjunction'.

23

the concept of 'root' analytically, would they have been at liberty to decide whether the definition of 'root' as 'value of x satisfying $x^2 = -1$' covered $\pm \sqrt{-1}$.

The point I wish to make is that in cases such as those cited, and doubtless in many cases of theorems connected intimately with a notational innovation, what is presented in the form of demonstrative reasoning for a conclusion is actually a justification for a linguistic alteration. This fact renders harmless the puzzling consequence of Wittgenstein's assertion that proof gives sense to a statement, namely, that the mathematician does not prove what he sets out to prove. For in these cases he does not set out to establish the truth-value of a given proposition. To suppose he does is to be misled by the language of demonstration he uses. Where a proof proceeds by an actual analysis the language of demonstration does what it appears to do: it states the reasoning for a proposition's truth, whereupon we know that some expression, e.g. 'integer not representable uniquely as a product of primes', has no use. But a conversion analysis, which is also presented in the form of proof, does something else. When Kummer is described as having invented ideal numbers which he proved were uniquely factorable into primes, the description conceals what his reasoning in fact did. It put forward an additional rule for the use of 'number uniquely representable as a product of primes' and induced others to accept it. Similarly, when Hamilton is said to have discovered quaternions for which he 'showed' that $i \times j \neq j \times i$, it would be less misleading to say that he justified a new use of '$\times$'. Agreement by mathematicians that the reasoning has justified a certain usage is usually signalized by their saying that such-and-such has been proved. Sometimes the use is either not accepted or not agreed on. Weyl's requirement that an existence proof construct that which is said to exist covertly recommends in the non-verbal mode of speech that 'There exists . . .' be used only when a method of construction can be given. The opposing positions over the 'validity' of non-constructive proofs of existence theorems is in fact a dispute over the latitude to be given 'There exists . . .'.

To sum up, I have placed on the assertion 'proof gives sense to a mathematical statement' a construction which makes it unobjectionable as a claim about certain pieces of reasoning misleadingly called proof. My explanation of the sense in which we can be said to understand by the terminal expression of a sequence of expressions stating a proof something different from what we understood by it originally holds *a fortiori* of these so-called proofs.

2

SELF-CONTRADICTORY SUPPOSITIONS*

Fermat made the 'conjecture' that for all integers n, $2^{2^n} + 1$ is prime. In his review[1] of M. Lazerowitz' paper,[2] Professor Alonzo Church says of this: '. . . since, by calculation, $2^{2^5} + 1 = 641 \times 6700417$, the conjecture is logically impossible, but it would hardly be said to follow that Fermat never made any conjecture on this point'.[3] His statement is intended as a criticism of the view that self-contradictory expressions are meaningless, since it would seem to follow from this view that any expression in number theory of the form 'Suppose p', where p is shown by a negative instance or by a *reductio ad absurdum* proof to be impossible, could express no conjecture at all because it has no meaning. Professor Church holds that expressions such as 'for all n, $2^{2^n} + 1$ is prime' have 'an intelligible meaning for anyone with a knowledge of elementary arithmetic and algebra'[4] even though they state something impossible. That this is the case he thinks follows from the fact that they function within expressions of the form 'Suppose p'.

Whether or not self-contradictory expressions[5] are to be classified as meaningful I do not wish to discuss here. In fact I think that this question has no answer, in the sense that it is not a part of the analysis of ' "p" is a self-contradictory expression' that it is either meaningful or meaningless. In any case I shall leave this question aside to discuss the claim Church makes in connection with self-contradictory expressions 'p' of the sort he

---

* Reprinted from *Mind:* a Quarterly Review of Psychology and Philosophy. Vol. LIII., N.S., No. 209, 1944.

[1] *The Journal of Symbolic Logic*, vol. 5, no. 2, p. 81.

[2] 'Self-contradictory Propositions', *Philosophy of Science*, vol. 7, no. 2.

[3] *The Journal of Symbolic Logic*, op. cit., p. 82.   [4] *Ibid.*

[5] I shall use this term to cover not only expressions of the form $p \cdot \sim p$ but such expressions as "There is a third root to $x^2 = 4$'.

cites from number theory that if they are meaningless one has made no supposition at all in saying 'Suppose p is true', that is, that it is a necessary condition for the existence of a supposition about p that 'p' be meaningful. This is the thesis from which he argues to the meaningfulness of self-contradictory expressions. For it is a fact that in mathematics suppositions of what is self-contradictory are made. Church's thesis, together with this fact, entails that self-contradictory expressions have meaning. Now it is the case that in *ordinary* discourse the use of 'conjecture' and 'supposition' is so connected with the use of the word 'meaning' that to express a supposition by 'p' entails that 'p' has meaning. With any meaningless expression 'suppose' could never be sensibly used, for example, we could not sensibly say 'Suppose 'twas brillig and the slithy toves did gyre and gimble in the wabe'. No supposition is possible, for there is nothing (no meaning) with regard to which a supposition is being made. Hence if the mathematical use of 'suppose' is the same as the ordinary one, Church has produced an argument showing Lazerowitz' claim to be wrong. What I wish to show in this paper is that there is a mathematical usage of 'suppose' such that use of the expression 'p' in the sentence 'S supposes p' does not imply that 'p' has meaning. This is not to argue that in connection with such a usage 'p' is meaningless, but only that from the fact that in mathematics suppositions of self-contradictions are made it does not follow that expressions for such self-contradictions are meaningful. Thus, although nothing is thereby offered in defence of the view that self-contradictory expressions are meaningless, Church's reason for saying they have meaning will be shown to be mistaken.

It is tempting to object to Church's argument on the ground that it is impossible to make a supposition with regard to what is self-contradictory, in which case it would no longer be open to Church to argue that self-contradictory expressions have meaning from the fact that they are used to express something supposed. One might agree that if an expression 'p' is meaningless, 'Suppose p' expresses no supposition, and then go on to maintain that it is in fact the case where p is self-contradictory that no supposition about it can be made. Ordinary usage lends plausibility to such an assertion. For if one were to ask someone to suppose that his house were both white all over and red all over, the reply would

27

be that this cannot be supposed. The same considerations prompting one to make such a reply might be held to obtain in cases where one introduces a *reductio ad absurdum* proof by asking that something self-contradictory be supposed. Now I do not wish to make objection to Church's argument on any such ground, but I shall set out the considerations leading one to hold that in mathematics no supposition with regard to what is self-contradictory can be made, because Church's claim and these considerations are infected by a common error. When it is clear what confusion results in the paradoxical claim that in mathematics nothing self-contradictory can be supposed, I think it will also be clear that the same confusion is responsible for Church's arguing that self-contradictory expressions are meaningful.

It is the very great differences between *reductio ad absurdum* arguments in which 'what is supposed' is self-contradictory and those arguments in which it is not which tempt one to hold that nothing self-contradictory is ever supposed. It will therefore be useful for making one see what is wrong with arguments leading to this conclusion to consider two such arguments, A and B, the one from number theory and the other from ordinary discourse:

A. Suppose there is a rational number $\frac{s}{t} = \sqrt{2}$ (s and t relatively prime).

   Then $s^2 = 2t^2$, which implies that s is even: $s = 2n$.
   (If the square of a number is even, the number itself is even.)
   Since $s = 2n$ and s and t are relatively prime, t is odd.
   Since $s^2 = 4n^2$, whence $2t^2 = 4n^2$, or $t^2 = 2n^2$, t is even.
   Thus t is both even and odd.
   But this is impossible.

   $\therefore$ There is no rational number $\frac{s}{t} = \sqrt{2}$.

B. Suppose that the earth is a perfect sphere.
   If this is true, a pendulum will make the same number of swings per second everywhere on its surface.
   But the number of swings varies at different points.
   $\therefore$ The earth is not a perfect sphere.

The general form of these arguments is as follows: (For the

28

purpose here it is not required that the form of A, which is more complex than that of B, be exhibited in detail).

A. Suppose p is true.
$p \rightarrow q . \sim q$.
But $q . \sim q$ is impossible.
∴ p is impossible.
∴ $\sim p$ is true.

B. Suppose p is true.
If p, then q.
But q is false.
∴ $\sim p$ is true.

The formal analogy between these two arguments is clear. If now we delineate their differences we shall see how easily one finds oneself committed to denying that any supposition in A could ever have been made. Each conclusion, $\sim p$, is the formal negative of what one is asked to suppose, but in the one case, B, what follows from all the premises taken together is the mere matter of fact falsity of p, while in the other, A, what follows from the single premise p is its own self-contradictoriness. That the latter does follow *shows* that p is self-contradictory, whereas in B it is only shown that p's falsity is a *consequence* of certain premises, and the possibility of p's being true still remains. It is logically possible, i.e. it is not self-contradictory, for the earth to be perfectly spherical. But it is impossible that there should be a rational number $\frac{s}{t} = \sqrt{2}$. The supposition that the earth is perfectly spherical, i.e. a supposition contrary to fact, presents us with no puzzle. It is logically possible for what is in fact false to be true and for what is in fact true to be false, and hence it is unquestionably possible to suppose either one or the other. It might appear to be proper to give an analogous description of the premise of A, 'There is a rational number $\frac{s}{t} = \sqrt{2}$'. This statement might be held to have, in fact, the property impossibility, so that in supposing it to be true one would simply be supposing something contrary to fact. But it is not a matter of empirical fact that p ('There is a rational number $\frac{s}{t} = \sqrt{2}$') has this property. Impossibility is a necessary, or intrinsic character of it, i.e. it is logically impossible, or inconceivable, that it should not have it.

29

It is this consideration which tempts one to raise the question, Can one suppose that what is impossible is true? Is this not the same as supposing that a property necessarily belonging to the premise p of A does not belong to it? If p is impossible, can one conceive that it is not impossible—as one seemingly is being asked to do in being asked to suppose p is true? One feels impelled to answer that if p could not conceivably be other than impossible then to suppose it is true is itself impossible—in which case we have in A no supposition at all.

A somewhat different characterization of contradictions, which is connected with their characterization as impossible, likewise makes one feel, after having made the deduction A from premise p, that it is impossible one should have done so. This is the commonly accepted description of self-contradictions as 'inconceivable'. The form of the conclusion in A, namely, $\sim p$ *is true*, suggests that we have here, as in B, one of two alternative possibilities, that either alternative *could* be the case. But the conclusion of A is necessary; it is a truth to which no alternative is conceivable.[1] That is, its opposite, p, is such that it could not conceivably be the case. We do not know what it would be like for it to be true—it is 'logically inconceivable'. The puzzle arises when we consider what we are being asked to do in being asked to suppose a self-contradiction is true. Are we not being asked to conceive something which is inconceivable? Is this not logically impossible? But if it is logically impossible, then it is logically impossible that a supposition in A has been made.

I think there can be no doubt it is a mistake to think these arguments show that nothing self-contradictory can be supposed. If they did, we should have to say that when a mathematician in a *reductio ad absurdum* proof says 'Suppose p', where p is self-contradictory, he is using the word 'suppose' improperly. But no argument can show that this well-established mathematical usage is wrong. If a usage is currently accepted, something must be wrong with arguments which purport to show it is improper. It seems to me that the mistake in arguing that this mathematical

---

[1] C. I. Lewis and C. H. Langford, *Symbolic Logic*, p. 24. It should be clear that in saying this there is no disparagement of anyone's capacities for conceiving. There is no comment here about anyone's capacities as there is in 'He can't conceive of a better world'. (New York & London: The Century Co., 1932.)

use, illustrated in proof A, is improper results from assuming that 'suppose' means the same as in argument B. From this assumption it is inferred that 'suppose' in context A is improper. But this consequence merely shows the arguments for its being improper are wrong, and the correct conclusion about what the arguments show is that the uses are different. That this is the correct conclusion, and that the mistake in the arguments given lies in assuming the opposite I shall try now to make clear.

The gist of the considerations resulting in the paradox that in proof A no supposition is being made is that one cannot consider the possibility of p's being true unless p is possible nor conceive p's being true unless p is conceivable, and that one is being asked to do just this in being asked to suppose p, no matter what the context is. Thus 'Suppose p' is taken under all circumstances to entail 'Consider the possibility of p's being true', where the latter is understood to involve knowing what it would be like for p to be true. This analysis of the nature of a supposition clearly eliminates the possibility of supposing what is self-contradictory. The question is whether the meaning of 'suppose' bears this analysis in all contexts. There is no doubt that in argument B the word 'suppose' is so used that in supposing p one is entertaining a possibility. There are a number of contexts where the usage of 'suppose' can properly be described in this way. What is supposed is a possible state of affairs, and what is inferred[1] from what is supposed is also a possible state of affairs, e.g. that the pendulum would make the same number of swings everywhere on the earth's surface.

That there is some similarity between the uses of 'suppose' in the two arguments A and B is obvious—were it not for the similarity we should not be puzzled about the possibility of making a supposition in A after seemingly having made one. One important respect in which the uses are similar is that in both A and B we say 'suppose p' as a preliminary to deriving consequents. In both cases we derive consequents from what we say we are supposing. But in another respect the use of 'suppose' in A is very different from that in B: we cannot describe 'the

---

[1] It is to be noted here that the consequence said to be inferred from the supposition does not *follow* from the supposition, i.e. the connection between supposition and consequent is not one of logical entailment.

supposition' that there is a rational number $\frac{s}{t} = \sqrt{2}$ as consisting in consideration of the possibility of there being a rational number $\frac{s}{t} = \sqrt{2}$, for once we do this we are led to denying that there is any supposition to describe. But what this fact should show us is not that a supposition cannot be made but that the nature of the supposition in such a context as proof A is very different. It is correct English, and it expresses something true, to say that in proof A one supposes there is a rational number $\frac{s}{t} = \sqrt{2}$. It then remains to be seen what it comes to to make a supposition of this sort, and how supposing a self-contradiction in the course of a mathematical demonstration differs from what we do in ordinary life in making suppositions. What we do in ordinary life is illustrated by the usage of 'suppose' in argument B. This usage is such that to suppose p entails knowing what it would be like for p to be true. Where we do not know what it is like for something to be the case, e.g. for a given person to be both alive and dead, we should say it was impossible to make any supposition to this effect. But the mathematical usage in connection with a self-contradiction p is such that to suppose p does *not* entail knowing what it is like for p to be true. When Fermat conjectured that for all integers n, $2^{2^n} + 1$ is prime, it is not the case that he knew what it would be like for this to be true but just did not know how to prove it. He did not know what it was like for all numbers of this form to be prime, as the disproof of this proposition shows. But he did conjecture, and hence conjecturing in such a case cannot entail what it does in non-mathematical contexts.

If we examine the function of suppositions within the arguments of which they are the first step, and the function of the arguments with respect to them, we shall have further reason for distinguishing between the usages of 'suppose' in arguments A and B. In demonstrations in number theory such as A, in contrast with arguments like B, it is clear from the preceding discussion that certain ways of describing the function of the supposition p are precluded: The supposition is not a preliminary to determining which possibility of p is realized, since p does not have each of **two** possibilities. If p is possible, its negative will be impossible. Nor can supposing p be described as conceiving something the impossibility of which it is the function of the deduction to disclose: if it is conceived, it is possible. Without doubt the deduction shows that p is impossible, but it could not show that what was conceived is impossible. It looks then as though in making a supposition one has before one, prior to inventing the disproof, only what one utters or writes down.[1] One is unable to *see* anything about its use. For example, one is unable to see prior to disproof whether it does or does not make sense to say every equation of the form $x^2 = a$ has a rational solution. I understand Wittgenstein to have made a similar point in lectures, and I quote from notes the following discussion explicating the contrast between suppositions figuring in mathematics and in ordinary life:

'To make a supposition would normally be to have some kind of picture of the kind of thing that is being supposed. If I suppose that this room is higher than it is, I can say it will be difficult to heat, that it will look so-and-so; and these are consequences which are other than the picture which corresponds to the supposition. But if I say, Suppose there were a proof that so-and-so, I have nothing at all. What comes after that, and what I then say, is all the supposition consists of. I might say there is nothing behind my statement but only something before it, namely, the use made of it. In the case of the room I have one picture which represents it, and other things which are its consequences; but with the proof I have nothing but "Suppose we have a proof", and what comes after partly describes what my supposition consists in. This shows that what we call a supposition in mathematics is entirely different from what we call a supposition in ordinary life.'

I want now to say something about the statement, 'What comes after [the supposition] and what I then say, is all the supposition consists of'. For this is, I think, intended to make the point that one has no knowledge of the supposition distinct from what the deduction provides,[2] and thereby to call attention to the function of the demonstration. In argument B we conceive a possible state

---

[1] From notes of lectures by L. Wittgenstein, 1934–35, taken by Alice Ambrose.   [2] *Ibid.*

of affairs when we suppose the earth is a perfect sphere, and in saying, 'If this were so, a pendulum would make the same number of swings per second everywhere on its surface', we draw a consequence not logically entailed by the supposition, which is another conceivable state of affairs. Clearly in A we are conceiving no state of affairs, nor is the consequence logically entailed by 'There is a rational number $\frac{s}{t} = \sqrt{2}$', namely, 't is both even and odd', another conceivable state of affairs. How then are the deduction and its functions to be described? It is important to note that we should never construct an indirect proof on a supposition for which it was obvious to inspection that it was self-contradictory. We should never say anything which was explicitly of the form, 'Suppose both p and $\sim p$'. Were we to do so the deduction would be pointless. The point of such a deduction as A is to show us that our supposition is impossible; by resulting in the consequence $q \cdot \sim q$ it makes us understand something *about* our supposition. 'Suppose p' is used as the starting point of a process which makes us see something about p. And what we see about p enables us to see that any use of p in a direct proof of the truth of any other proposition is precluded. It also enables us to see that any such expression as 'Measure off exactly $\sqrt{2}$ yards of cloth' does not make sense.

Now it might be held that quite often an ordinary inference from an empirical hypothesis is also intended to aid us in determining something about our supposition, namely, whether it is true or false: we derive consequences as a preliminary to seeing whether the hypothesis is or is not in conformity with fact. But it is clearly not the deduction which determines this about the hypothesis, namely, that it conforms or fails to conform with fact, but experience. All the deduction in these cases does is to produce consequences which can be tested. Only experience can show one what is true, or false. By contrast, what is impossible deduction by itself shows. Furthermore, arguments such as B, unlike A, are not intended to show anything about the modal properties of the supposition. For both $\sim p$ and p in this case each quite plainly have the same modal property, possibility, and can have only this one.

If I have succeeded in showing that the use of 'suppose' in such

34

arguments as A and B is different and that ignoring this fact by taking the usage in B as the paradigm to which any legitimate usage must conform is responsible for arriving at the consequence that no self-contradiction can be supposed, we are in a position to see what makes Church argue from the fact that a self-contradiction p is supposed that the expression for p, in whatever language, is meaningful. It has been pointed out that the ordinary use of 'suppose' is such that supposing p entails knowing what it is like for p to be true. This is to say that the ordinary use of 'suppose' is connected with the ordinary use of the word 'meaning': 'S supposes p' entails 'S knows what it is like for p to be true'; and if S knows this, then whatever expression S uses for p must have meaning. In this sense of 'meaning' it is correct to say one could not know what it was like for p to be true if 'p' had no meaning. The question is whether the mathematical use of 'suppose' is similarly connected with 'meaning'. Church prejudices the issue in saying that the self-contradictory expression, 'for all n, $2^{2^n} + 1$ is prime', 'has an intelligible meaning for anyone with a knowledge of elementary arithmetic and algebra'. For one might know arithmetic and algebra and still deny that it had meaning. I want to hold, not that it has no meaning, but that the mathematical use of 'suppose' is such that to express a supposition by 'p' does not imply that 'p' has meaning. And I think that because Church takes the mathematical use of 'suppose' to be the same as the ordinary use he argues that supposing or conjecturing p requires that whatever sentence is used to express the supposition has meaning. That is, the same kind of confusion is responsible for this claim as for the claim that nothing self-contradictory can be supposed.

In the sense of 'meaning' in which 'p' has meaning only if it *could* be known what it is like for p to be true, a self-contradictory expression in mathematics has no more meaning than a Lewis Carroll rhyme. The use of 'suppose' and 'conjecture' which is connected with expressions having meaning in this sense, i.e. the ordinary use, is such that it *is* impossible to suppose a mathematical self-contradiction. One could no more suppose that he had five marbles of which he gave away six than suppose a surface was both brown and green all over. For in neither case could one know what it would be like for these propositions to be true. Neverthe-

35

less it is obvious that in mathematics it is possible, in *another* sense of 'suppose', to suppose what is self-contradictory, and clearly this possibility does not rest on knowing what it is like for what is supposed to be true. Thus in the sense in which ' "p" has meaning' entails the possibility of knowing what it would be like for p to be true, it cannot be held that in mathematics expressing a conjecture by 'p' implies that 'p' has meaning. Hence when Church urges that in making a conjecture of p it must be the case that the expression for p has meaning, he can only be right if the sense of 'meaning' differs from the ordinary sense just explained, that is, if there is a sense corresponding to the mathematical sense of 'conjecture' which differs correspondingly from that associated with the ordinary sense of 'conjecture'. This sense must be such as to make the term 'meaningful' applicable to self-contradictory expressions. For to hold, as Church would, that it is correct to say self-contradictory expressions in mathematics have meaning, is to say that 'meaningful' has application to mathematical expressions for self-contradictions (just as admitting that it is proper English to say 'self-contradictions are supposed' comes to admitting that 'supposition' is applied to self-contradictions). If Church could point out instances in mathematics in which 'meaning' had a commonly accepted application to such expressions, that would be sufficient to establish that there is a different sense of that term. In this event Church could show that Lazerowitz denied meaning to self-contradictory expressions in mathematics only because he had failed to note this non-ordinary use of 'meaning'.

The question thus arises whether Church can point out in mathematics a common use of 'meaning' to describe self-contradictory expressions. Exhibiting such a use would enable him to make his point, that self-contradictory expressions do have meaning. It would be an extremely simple way of doing this and it would provide a conclusive answer to any *argument* brought forward to show that they do not have meaning, just as pointing out a use of 'suppose' in connection with mathematical self-contradictions is a simple and completely conclusive way of answering an argument that self-contradictions cannot be supposed. If anyone were to agree with Church's view that what is meaningless cannot figure in the expression of a supposition and then go on to deny what Church takes for granted, that it is correct to say 'S supposes p', where 'p' is self-contradictory, it seems plain what his reply would be: 'But mathematicians constantly suppose what is self-contradictory. There is no difficulty in doing that.' This reply is the most natural one to make. It tells us that it makes sense to apply 'supposition' to self-contradictions, and thereby settles any question about the possibility of supposing what is self-contradictory, by appeal to usage. And if to the claim that self-contradictory sentences are meaningless it were possible to reply that 'meaningful' is constantly applied to such sentences, then the question as to their meaningfulness would be settled in a similar manner. Pointing out current usage would obviate the necessity of arguing for the claim or of meeting, by argumentation, any argument against it. The curious thing is that Church does not employ this simple method of establishing that self-contradictory expressions have meaning, but resorts to *argument* instead. That he does this is important. For it shows, I think, either that it is not possible to establish his view otherwise, or that he himself does not find it possible to establish it otherwise. I do not believe he resorts to it simply because he *prefers* the method of argumentation to the method of exhibiting cases in which the word 'meaningful' is applied to self-contradictory expressions. I believe the latter method is not open to him. Whether it is or not, i.e. whether the word 'meaning' has an established usage in the language of mathematics, Church is in a better position to know than most people. But I should doubt that it did. Here and there one finds the expression 'meaningless', e.g. 'division by zero is meaningless' (whence '$\frac{2}{0} = x$', or '$2 = 0$', is meaningless). And something like an equivalent of it occurs in *reductio ad absurdum* proofs when it is said of the contradiction deduced, 'but this is absurd'. These examples would seem to indicate that mathematicians do sometimes characterize self-contradictory expressions as meaningless, and that not all of them would agree with Church that such expressions have meaning 'for anyone with a knowledge of elementary arithmetic and algebra'. But the fact that disagreement could arise amongst people equally conversant with mathematical usage shows that it is not yet a settled convention to describe self-contradictory expressions as meaningless. And it is not usage, i.e. not a settled convention, to describe them as meaningful. Cases of describing them thus, if any exist, are too infrequent to permit of their use by Church to establish his view. Moreover, as just pointed out, there are also cases, even though infrequent, of describing them as meaningless.

Now if the view that self-contradictory expressions have meaning cannot be established by citing common applications of the term 'meaningful' to them, can an argument (from the fact that self-contradictions are supposed) succeed? Argumentation sometimes is but an alternative way of proving a point. But here an argument is offered because the alternative method of direct substantiation (by appeal to usage) is not available. Church's argument is intended to show that the description 'meaningful' is correct. But an argument will show a description to be correct only if there is a *possibility* of citing a commonly accepted application of the descriptive term. So long as one finds it necessary to *argue* that self-contradictory expressions are meaningful because usage of the term 'meaningful' as a description cannot be exhibited, the view cannot be correct.[1] Under these circumstances argument will not show self-contradictory expressions *are* meaningful, although argument might convince one of the appropriateness of so describing them. If mathematicians were to become convinced of this, i.e. were to introduce the word 'meaning' as a description of any supposition-expression and make it common usage, then Church's argument would establish his view. For then there would be a possibility of citing an accepted application of the term, and argumentation would not be forced upon one as a substitute for direct establishment by appeal to usage. But in advance of its being common usage to describe self-contradictory expressions as meaningful, no argument can show the description to be correct. For no description is correct in advance of its being commonly accepted. Further, even though it were accepted usage to call these expressions meaningful, anyone who did not know this and who thought it was not possible to establish the view that they are meaningful by citing usage, would be wrong in thinking that under such circumstances argument would establish it.

---

[1] By this I do not mean it is *in*correct. I should say it was neither correct nor incorrect.

It is clear that if 'meaning' has no established use in mathematics as a description of self-contradictory expressions, the fact that one uses the expression 'Suppose p', where 'p' is self-contradictory, will imply nothing whatever about the meaningfulness of 'p'. To hold that 'Suppose p' has meaning only if 'p' has meaning will be correct only if there is a mathematical use of 'meaning'. What mistake then has Church made? It looks as though he has noted in connection with ordinary empirical propositions p that use of the expression 'Suppose p' implies that 'p' has meaning, that he has taken 'suppose' to mean the same in mathematical contexts, and has then gone on to maintain that to make a supposition about any mathematical proposition p requires that the expression for it has meaning. From this it would seem to follow that the sense in which a mathematical expression has meaning will be the same as that in which an ordinary empirical statement has it. For the ordinary sense of 'meaning' will be associated with a use of 'suppose' which in no way differs from the ordinary use. In claiming for self-contradictory expressions 'intelligible meaning' Church seems to lend support to construing 'meaning' in this sense. So soon as one sees that in mathematics 'suppose' does not have the same use as in ordinary contexts, and that 'meaning' has no established use as a description of self-contradictory expressions, it becomes clear that Church's argument is wrong, and that in order for 'Suppose p' to express a supposition it is not required that 'p' have meaning.

3

WITTGENSTEIN ON SOME QUESTIONS IN FOUNDATIONS OF MATHEMATICS*

'Philosophy is a battle against the bewitchment of our intelligence by means of language.'[1] This pronouncement in Wittgenstein's posthumously published book is an index to the philosophical outlook which prompted Wittgenstein to scrutinize with the greatest attentiveness the language in which philosophers have stated their problems. Each problem is according to him the product of an obsession—a linguistic obsession that is not recognized.[2] In consequence of this the philosopher envisages his task not as the elimination of the obsession, but rather as the solution of a scientific problem. It is as if he had to find out something new, as if he faced a question of fact about which we do not yet know enough.[3] 'The real discovery', Wittgenstein says, 'is the one that makes me capable of stopping doing philosophy when I want to.—The one that gives philosophy peace, so that it is no longer tormented by questions which bring *itself* in question.'[4] The sign that this discovery has been made is that we cease to seek a *solution* of a particular philosophical problem. These problems are not the kind that have a solution, in the usual sense of 'solution'. They should *dis*solve, '*completely* disappear',[5] once clarity about our use of language is achieved.

Rather than launch into an extended discourse on method I shall try here to exhibit Wittgenstein's procedure in dealing with certain philosophical problems, and I shall at the same time expound the substance of what he had to say about them. The problems I have chosen come from the foundations of mathematics. They were treated by Wittgenstein in lectures I attended in Cambridge in 1934–35 and in the 1939 lectures on foundations

* Reprinted from *The Journal of Philosophy*, Vol. LII, No. 8, April 14, 1955.
[1] *Philosophical Investigations* (New York, Macmillan, 1953), p. 47.
[2] Lectures, 1934–35.   [3] *Ibid.*
[4] *Philosophical Investigations*, p. 51.   [5] *Ibid.*

of mathematics of which I possess notes. Initially I shall set a question which Wittgenstein did not formulate in precisely my fashion; but my formulation provides a springboard for the exposition of his treatment of problems intimately connected with it.

I shall begin with a question which parallels Kant's question about pure mathematics: How is applied mathematics possible? How is it that *a priori* propositions have an application to matter of fact? The puzzle suggested by this question is, more specifically, the puzzle as to how an *a priori* proposition, e.g. $2 + 3 = 5$, can both be true independently of matter of fact and be true of collections of two apples and three apples. If *a priori*, such that its truth-value is unaffected by any theoretically possible state of affairs, it can give no information about any actual state of affairs. How then can it be about apples? Puzzlement about this may very well have been one source of Mill's denial that '$2 + 3 = 5$' is anything more than an empirical generalization. If it cannot both be true regardless of fact and also imply a truth about apples or other observable objects—in particular about objects which do not coalesce or reproduce themselves in the course of being counted—one must discard one of the two seemingly incompatible accounts of it. Mill discarded the account of it as a necessity. And yet the arithmetic statement '$2 + 3 = 5$' seems obviously to possess all the properties ascribed to necessary truths: it can be known without recourse to experience; its opposite would be self-inconsistent; no state of affairs could possibly disconfirm it, nor would any be required to confirm it. How then can one account for the harmony between the two quite different areas of logic and of empirical fact? How is it that we can apply arithmetical calculations to physical objects, or trigonometric calculations to physical lines and angles? Is there a genuine mystery here or only a gratuitous puzzle?

The suggestion which my question makes, unlike that which Kant intended by his, is that there is a difficulty in conceiving any application of a proposition of logically incorrigible status to matter of fact—that application is impossible. The question thus has what Wittgenstein singled out as the earmark of every philosophical difficulty: the presence in its expression of the words 'cannot' or 'must', or their equivalents. These are the words which signalize a philosophical obsession. How, we ask, *can* the statement '2 + 3 = 5', whose truth is independent of experience, apply to apples, i.e. be such that the numerical equality it asserts not only tallies with, but seems to be empirically established by, a count of the members of the two sets of apples, and seems even to *predict* the empirical result of counting? As Russell said, 'We do not know who will be the inhabitants of London a hundred years hence; but we know that any two of them and any other two of them will make four of them. This apparent power of anticipating facts about things of which we have no experience is certainly surprising.'[1]

But the applicability of mathematics is not surprising to common sense. That arithmetic, geometry, and trigonometry have an application is a commonplace, and no philosopher in his ordinary pursuits questions whether mathematical propositions can apply to matters of fact any more than he questions whether motion is possible. But one cannot as a philosopher dismiss the question by an appeal to common sense. The common-sense answer to 'How can "2 + 3 = 5" imply a truth about collections of apples?', namely, 'It simply does', is true; but it is not the proper answer to the philosophical question. The proper answer should rid one of the puzzle. This, says Wittgenstein, is the business of philosophy: to rid one of puzzles which do not arise for common sense.[2] Doing philosophy according to him consists of three activities: first, seeing the common-sense answer to these problems; second, getting oneself so deeply into the problems that the common-sense answer seems unbearable;[3] and finally, getting oneself from that situation to the common-sense answer again. But the common-sense answer by itself is no solution; one must first allow oneself to be dragged into the mire and then get out of it.[4]

Were it proper to describe an arithmetic proposition as an empirical generalization having no exceptions, then its application to fact would present no puzzle. But tempting as it is to escape a difficulty in this way, I think it is clear that we should do violence

---

[1] *The Problems of Philosophy*, p. 132, 17th impression (Oxford University Press, 1943).   [2] Lectures, 1934–35.   [3] In this connection C. D. Broad's comment on common sense is worth remarking: 'Let it go out and hang itself' (*The Mind and Its Place in Nature*, p. 186).   [4] Lectures, 1934–35.

to the current usage of the term 'empirical generalization' were we to take this way out. For an empirical generalization can be falsified, and it is clear that we will accept nothing as a counter-instance to '$2 + 3 = 5$'. Mill's theory re-classifies arithmetic propositions, and furthermore, in such a way as to leave us with no proper use of the word 'necessary'.[1] For if arithmetic propositions are not necessary, we are at a loss to describe what would be necessary, just as we should be at a loss to say what would be a religious belief if the description 'religious belief' were refused to 'There is a God'. Wittgenstein says that what he does under the name 'philosophy' 'may in no way interfere with the actual use of language'.[2] 'It is not our aim to refine or complete the system of rules for the use of our words in unheard-of ways.'[3] 'What *we* do is to bring words back from their metaphysical to their everyday usage.'[4]

Let us begin then with acceptance of two facts: (1) that it is proper to describe mathematical propositions as necessary, and (2) that applied mathematics is possible. Whatever the philosophical difficulties involved, these are the facts which common sense dictates that we begin and end with. But philosophical difficulties in which it is easy to become mired do exist. I shall try to expound these difficulties as Wittgenstein envisaged them, together with the attempts he made to clarify them and, by clarification, to dissolve them. These are all intimately connected with whatever problem may be felt about the possibility of applied mathematics, though Wittgenstein did not make this particular problem central in the cluster of related problems he investigated. All of them concern the connection of mathematical propositions with experience, and in my opinion it would not be a misrepresentation of Wittgenstein to say they all arise directly or indirectly from the misleading question, 'What are mathematical propositions *about*?'.

It has sometimes been held that '$2 + 3 = 5$' is a proposition about numbers, necessarily true in virtue of the nature of numbers, whereas '2 apples + 3 apples = 5 apples' is a proposition about

[1] See M. Lazerowitz, *The Structure of Metaphysics* (Routledge & Kegan Paul), pp. 258–259.
[2] *Philosophical Investigations*, p. 49.   [3] *Ibid.*, p. 51.
[4] *Ibid.*, p. 48.

apples, which is factually true in virtue of the nature of the apples our world provides—non-generating, non-coalescing apples. We can use arithmetic to count, and to predict the result of adding two apples to three, because, so it is claimed, it is a fact about apples that they do not either vanish or multiply when this operation is performed. The application of arithmetic thus depends on whether or not certain empirical conditions are satisfied. It will be true then to say 'If no apples disappear or multiply, 2 apples + 3 apples = 5 apples', but not unqualifiedly true that 2 apples + 3 apples = 5 apples. Now Wittgenstein says that whether this is a correct account of the proposition '2 apples + 3 apples = 5 apples' is to be determined by the *use* we make of it. It is not that the use is determined by whether the proposition states a contingent truth about apples or a necessary connection between concepts. If, unexpectedly, apples increase or diminish in number when addition is performed, and we accept this fact as constituting a falsification, then our statement is experiential. But if we excuse every case in which five apples fail to be present when three apples are added to two, i.e. if no such fact is accepted as disconfirming it, then our statement is necessary. One and the same sentence can be used in either of these two ways, and of course it is a fact that the latter way is by far the more usual.

If we examine this more usual use of '2 apples + 3 apples = 5 apples', i.e. to express a necessary proposition, we shall see its proper relation to the empirical fact that apples remain discrete when added. This fact is not an empirical condition of the truth of the proposition it is used to express; rather, that this proposition applies to apples is the criterion for their having remained discrete. And if in an imaginable case it did not apply, i.e. if the number of apples counted was not five, this would be the criterion, not for the equation's falsity, but for the number of apples not having remained constant during the process of their being counted. Similarly, that the equation '2 quarts + 3 quarts = 5 quarts' does not hold for the *physical* addition of two quarts of alcohol to three quarts of water indicates something about the mixture of these substances, but the behaviour of these substances when mixed implies nothing about the truth of '2 quarts + 3 quarts = 5 quarts'. Their behaviour does imply the falsity of the statement '2 quarts physically added to three quarts yield five quarts', but it is logically irrelevant to the statement which asserts the arithmetic addition of units—as our usual use of this statement shows.

One likely source of the temptation to disregard how such a statement functions (as necessary rather than empirical) is the compulsion to ask, and to answer, the question, 'What is the proposition about?' 'About apples', 'about discrete entities', etc., are the natural answers. Similarly, 'about numbers' is the natural answer to 'What is "$2 + 3 = 5$" about ?'; and of course it cannot be denied that it is proper to distinguish this proposition from empirical propositions by characterizing it as being about numbers. But our question, according to Wittgenstein, is misleading, since we thereby treat '$2 + 3 = 5$' as analogous to empirical propositions, and only differing from them in being about non-empirical, abstract entities. Mathematics, according to this way of looking at it, becomes a sort of physics of mathematical entities, and mathematical research an expedition of discovery. This is the conception which Professor G. H. Hardy had. He writes: 'I have myself always thought of a mathematician as in the first instance an *observer*, a man who gazes at a distant range of mountains and notes down his observations. His job is simply to distinguish clearly and notify to others as many different peaks as he can. . . .'[1]

Wittgenstein says that philosophy arises out of prejudices in favour of certain grammatical forms. We try always to work from one paradigm, which operates as a grammatical obsession.[2] 'What are mathematical propositions about?' is a question motivated by the obsessional emphasis on the analogy of these propositions to empirical ones. To rid one of this obsession it has some point to say, as Wittgenstein says in a number of places, that arithmetic propositions are not about numbers, nor are geometric propositions about geometrical figures. But this is also misleading, since, like Plato's answer to this question, it seems to give information in the way in which a scientific answer does. If we wish not to be misled we shall do well to direct our attention away from the question as to what they are about to the *use* we make of them. And by examining their use the connection between their necessity and their application will no longer appear puzzling.

Now what we do when we allow nothing to count against a

[1] 'Mathematical Proof', *Mind*, Vol. XXXVIII (1929), p. 18.
[2] Lectures, 1934–35.

proposition, when we enshrine it amongst the incorrigibles and refuse to surrender it in the face of any conceivable facts is to assign to the expression for the proposition a special rôle in our language. According to Wittgenstein we have decided on using the sentence in a certain way, namely, as a rule for the use of expressions, i.e. a rule for the application of certain words.[1] To elucidate, let us consider an example similar to one he used: Suppose I multiply 25 by 17 in order to find out the number of squares in a rectangle 25 squares long by 17 squares wide. If the number of squares is found upon counting not to be 425, the result got by multiplying according to the rules, and I thereupon say '$25 \times 17 = 425$' is false, I use it to express a proposition testable by experience. But if I say it is correct regardless of what number of squares I find on counting, and use it as a criterion of the correctness of my count, I thereby make it independent of experience. And to do this is to resolve on a certain use, namely, that it shall function analogously to a rule for the use of numerical terms—for one thing, that 425 can be substituted for 25×17, for another, that the two statements, 'The number of roses I received is equal to the quotient $425/17$' and 'The number of roses I received is two dozen', may not describe the same fact. Similarly, the statement that it is impossible to construct a heptagon with straight edge and compasses functions as a rule which prevents my saying with sense, 'I drew a heptagon on the board using only straight edge and compasses'.

Mathematical propositions are *preparations* for the use of language, says Wittgenstein, almost as definitions are.[2] Note that he does not say they *are* either definitions or statements about symbols; but they function as explicitly formulated linguistic rules in fact function. Euclid's proof that a line can be bisected by a certain method serves to provide a rule for the application of 'equal lengths', and arithmetic serves to give rules for the use of number words, whereas no non-verbal empirical proposition ever functions analogously to a rule governing the use of language. If, then, the function of mathematical propositions is to govern usage it is no more surprising that they have an application than that a knife should cut. The connection between them and their application is like that between a rule for the use of an expression and the occurrence of that expression in various verbal contexts.[1] For example, 'exactly one straight line can be drawn between any two points' functions prescriptively: in understanding it we know it makes sense to say that one physical straight line, but not to say that more than one, is drawn between two points. One tends to look upon the geometrical proposition as asserting a truth about ideal lines which somehow also holds of coarse drawn lines. But the application of a geometrical proposition in an experiential context is to show, not what is true or false, but what makes sense or nonsense.[2] It obscures an important difference between empirical generalizations and their purported instances and mathematical propositions and the things to which they apply to say that both kinds of propositions show what is true, or false. Necessary propositions about ellipses and circles show that 'I cut an elliptical cake in eight equal parts' does not make sense, whereas 'I cut a round cake in eight equal parts' does. The relation of the necessary propositions about circles to the physical circle is like that between a rule and its application, not between a generalization about ideal circles and a rough approximation.[3]

This account squares with the fact that mathematical propositions do not get confirmed or disconfirmed by experience: one does not confirm or disconfirm by seeing, feeling, etc., a proposition whose use is to show what makes sense rather than to assert what is in fact true, or false. Further, there are certain puzzles about the connection of mathematics with experience which this account helps clarify. One is that mathematical propositions when applied seem to make predictions whereas, being necessary, they cannot. Suppose we say that two crystals which separately weigh three grams each must together weigh six grams, or that six two-foot boards must fit into a space twelve feet wide. If these are predictions, then they can be false. It could happen that six two-foot boards cover more or less than twelve feet, and that the two crystals weigh more or less than six grams. But '$6 \times 2 = 12$' and '$3 + 3 = 6$' are not predictions. They function as criteria for judging when the boards do not fit or the scales read five, that something *must* have happened.[4] '$6 \times 2 = 12$' does not even assure us that, unless the boards change, six two-foot boards will

[1] Lectures, 1939.   [2] Lectures, 1934-35.   [3] *Ibid.*   [4] *Ibid.*

fit into twelve feet, for the criterion of change is their not fitting. If we say they *must* fit, and cite '6 × 2 = 12' as evidence while at the same time refusing to accept any other method of showing the width of the boards, then, says Wittgenstein,[1] we are not saying anything about measurement. The burden of what we are saying is that what is called two feet is what goes six times into twelve. Were we making an experiment to determine whether six such boards will fit the space, the result would not be fixed in advance, and prediction of the result would be appropriate. The difference between a mathematical calculation and an experiment is that in fixing the rules of the calculation one fixes the result.[2]

What Wittgenstein says about the nature of mathematical propositions also has a bearing on the further puzzle, namely, that we sometimes seem to discover a fact of experience which we then go on to prove must be so. It looks as if a matter of fact has an *a priori* demonstration. Pythagoras' theorem is a case in point. But the puzzle is gratuitous. According to Wittgenstein what happens is that an empirical proposition, which experience discovers, is converted into a proposition which no experience could make us give up. The proposition which is made independent of experience is suggested by experience. For example, the proposition, 'A pentagram is a pentagon plus five triangles', is certainly suggested by experience, but it functions as a rule because we allow no method of construction to invalidate it. To see a pentagram as this composite is an experience, but as Wittgenstein says, there is no comparable process of seeing that a rule holds.[3]

Now what may appear as a surprising harmony between mathematical propositions and their application is merely due to our assigning the functions of a rule to those propositions which conform to fact, other things being equal.[4] Because the specific gravity of iron is 7.86 it would be natural and might be useful to say 'No matter what experiment shows, the specific gravity of iron is 7.86'. By this token an empirical proposition would be given a status and function like that of a rule of language. But the matter of fact does not compel acceptance of this change of status. The kind of fact which persuades us to accept it is that it is useful; and that it has applications is a mark of its usefulness. Thus, if we

[1] Lectures, 1934–45.
[2] Ibid., 1939.
[3] Ibid., 1934–45.
[4] Ibid.

had a world in which counting the members of two groups having 2 members and 3 members, respectively, *never* totalled up to 5, some other proposition than '2 + 3 = 5' would have been adopted as necessary. If circumstances made it practical to calculate differently than we do, e.g. because things multiplied or disappeared regularly upon being counted, we should adapt arithmetic calculation to the circumstances.[1] If we got different results every time we counted the squares of a rectangle 17 by 25, we should probably not say the calculation, 17 multiplied by 25, was a proof that $17 \times 25 = 425$. We might still call the calculation a piece of arithmetic just as 'it is not the case for all a and b that $a \times b = b \times a$' is a part of group theory. But we should either have different arithmetics, or we should have an arithmetic in which certain multiplications had different results. For example, as our world is now, there is no phenomenon for which '$23 \times 18 = 800$' has any use. But if these numbers were constants relating to all natural phenomena, says Wittgenstein,[2] we could imagine an arithmetic in which this multiplication, among all others, had two results. To the objection that it is in the nature of 23 and 18 to give 414, he replies that in giving a rule of multiplication we do not give an infinity of applications of it. Behind the use of a rule is a habit of reacting in a certain way. Given the rules of multiplication we do in fact agree in getting the result 414; to do this is natural. And it is this fact which makes us say this result is correct. But we can imagine having always agreed in getting 800. And if this were in fact the case, would not 800 be the *correct* result? What would it be like to say that we always had made a mistake in thinking $23 \times 18 = 800$? Our agreement, not that such and such a result *is* the case, but *in getting* that result, is what determines what is called a correct calculation. Thus arithmetical propositions, though independent of experience, are in two ways dependent upon experience: in being suggested by experience, and in having their special function rest on common linguistic habits.[3]

In the remainder of this essay I should like to examine certain things which Wittgenstein appears to be saying concerning the connection between the necessity of mathematical propositions and their origin in and application to matter of fact. He seems to be saying that it is by an arrangement of ours that, for example,

[1] Lectures, 1939.   [2] *Ibid.*, 1934–35.   [3] *Ibid.*

the arithmetic proposition $2 + 3 = 5$ tallies with the empirical result of counting two groups of 2 and 3 things, respectively, and that if circumstances were different, so that counting the members of such groups never resulted in 5, we should adapt counting to the circumstances and accordingly have a different arithmetic. That is, if circumstances were different, we should have a different necessary proposition. A proposition can be 'suggested by experience and then made independent of experience'.[1] Thus an expression which is given a special place in our language by being used to denote a necessary proposition is somehow connected with fact. I should like to examine both the hypothesis and the consequent of the statement, 'If circumstances were different we should have a different necessary proposition'; for there is an unclarity about both.

How are we to understand the words 'circumstances such that the members of two groups of 2 and 3 things, resp., never total up to 5'? One possible interpretation of these words, though I advance it with hesitation and without intending to imply it was Wittgenstein's, is the following: that the juxtaposition of two groups of objects, each of which we correctly counted as having 2 and 3 members, respectively, should result in the creation or destruction of, say, one individual, so that subsequent counting of the combined sets showed more, or fewer, than 5 objects. It is of course perfectly conceivable that something like this should happen. Wittgenstein has said[2] that if, for example, things disappeared regularly in certain ways it might be practical to count differently, that one might adapt one's technique of counting to the circumstances. Our arithmetic might then include the statements '$2 + 3 = 4$', '$1 + 1 = 1$', etc. That is, we should adopt those as expressing necessary propositions, so that in the exceptional case when our final count was 5, or 2, we should say not that these propositions were false, but that the objects must have reproduced, just as now we say, when one object put in juxtaposition with another results in one, 'the objects must have coalesced', or 'one must have vanished'. That we should say this sort of thing is a sign that we are in the two comparable cases taking '$2 + 3 = 4$' and '$2 + 3 = 5$', respectively, to be necessary: we accept nothing as a falsification.

[1] Lectures, 1939, 1934–45.   [2] Ibid., 1939.

Throughout this paper it will be noted that I am interpreting Wittgenstein to be taking arithmetic to consist of what are commonly called necessary propositions, i.e. propositions that are both non-empirical and *true*. The problem is to explain the connection of such propositions with matter of fact, with their application. Professor G. E. Moore, relying on lectures of the period 1930–33, points out[1] that Wittgenstein characterized '2 + 3 = 5' and the like as 'rules of grammar', 'treating only of the symbolism', and as being neither true nor false. This Wittgenstein undeniably did; '2 + 3 = 5' was said to be a rule specifying a possible manner of speaking or writing (which one might adopt or not). But he also stated at various times that '2 + 3 = 5' is not a definition, nor *about* the symbolism in the way ' "2 + 3" is interchangeable with "5" ' is about the symbolism, although it is used analogously to the way we use such a rule. For example, it prevents our saying such things as 'I augmented my savings of three hundred dollars by two hundred more but did not have a total of five hundred'. Moore thought he might be using such an expression as '2 + 3 = 5' in two different ways, to express a necessary proposition and to state a rule for using words or sentences, and even that when he used it in the first way it expressed something neither true nor false.[2] But it is obviously self-contradictory to describe necessary propositions as being neither true nor false; and one can find support in Wittgenstein's lectures (e.g. in his comparison of necessary and empirical propositions) for his supposing them to be *true*, though of course not true in the sense in which an empirical proposition is true. It may be no consistent account is to be had. I am going to assume that though he holds that such expressions as '2 + 3 = 5' are *used* to proscribe certain linguistic combinations,[3] he also holds that they do nonetheless express necessary truths, and hence that in a world of coalescing objects what is expressed by '2 + 3 = 4' might be a necessary truth.

Now in this hypothetical world is it proper to say we should have a different *arithmetic*—in particular, that *arithmetical* addition of 2 and 3 would yield a different result than 5? We can easily

---

[1] 'Wittgenstein's Lectures in 1930–33', II, *Mind*, Vol. LXII (1954), no. 251, pp. 298–308. [2] *Ibid.*, p. 302.
[3] Note that such might be their use without their translating into rules 'treating of the symbolism'.

conceive of '2 + 3 = 4' expressing a necessary proposition (it is easy to conceive of the involved symbols being used differently), but if we use '2', '3', and '4' as we do now, surely the meaning of some other symbol or symbols must change. The natural assumption is that '+' can no longer mean arithmetic addition of two numbers, nor '=' arithmetic equality. '2 + 3' must denote not the arithmetic sum of two numbers, but the physical combination of two sets, and '=' must mean something like 'yields'. '2 + 3 = 4' would be a shorthand for '(x). $2x + 3x = 4x$', interpreted as '2 things physically conjoined with 3 yield 4'. But it describes this world paradoxically to say its arithmetic is different from ours. '2 + 3 = 4' only appears shocking if taken to express an equality between a number and an arithmetic sum of numbers, as it does now. If '+' had a different usage in this hypothetical world, and if we also had our arithmetic for sums of numbers, the expressions '2 + 3 = 4' and '2 + 3 = 5' both could without inconsistency express necessities, although confusion might result. And if there were but one arithmetic, what we might call the arithmetic of invariant coalescence, it is misleading to say that we have made '4' and '2 + 3' interchangeable as though *in preference to* '5' and '2 + 3', since '2 + 3' has two entirely different uses when equated with '4' and with '5'. The sentence 'In different circumstances some other proposition would be necessary' suggests that were facts different we should arrange that the *addition* of 2 and 3 would necessarily yield a different result. This is unobjectionable if we reinterpret 'addition'. What Wittgenstein says is then little more than that in a different world we might have a different language. What is interesting about his statement is the claim that a difference in the language of arithmetic is influenced by the exigencies of making application of arithmetic to fact.

There is reason to suppose that what I have described as possibly illustrating a circumstance in which we might have a different arithmetic, and the account I have given of it, is not in fact what Wittgenstein had in mind. It will be worthwhile to consider an example which Professor Moore reports in Wittgenstein's 1930–33 lectures,[1] in order to note differences and to elaborate what Wittgenstein has said. In this example I think it is clear that '+' continues to be interpreted as arithmetic addition, however

[1] *Loc. cit.*, 302–304.

puzzling this may be; and this is the main respect in which it differs from the case I have discussed. I shall alter the numerals used in the lectures so as to make comparison easier. Wittgenstein supposes the following imaginable circumstances: (1) that one has the two experiences of counting first up to 2, then up to 3 in the case of two groups of apples, and (2) then a third and subsequent experience of (correctly) counting *all* the apples and finding only 4. This is imaginable because it is a mere matter of experience that one usually finds 5, inasmuch as apples do not vanish without cause. '2 + 3 = 5' makes no prophecy as to what experience one *will* have upon counting *all* the apples. But if one were to find 4 apples, the most natural comment to make would be that one must have vanished. By this comment Wittgenstein says we can only mean 'If we keep to the arithmetical rule "2 + 3 = 5" we have to say "one must have vanished" '. In analyzing this latter statement and what he takes to its consequences Moore augments the circumstances (1) and (2) above by two further ones which he supposed Wittgenstein to have had in mind as the situation in which one made the comment 'one apple must have vanished': (3) that one knows, because one has kept watch, that nothing has happened to account in any normal way for there being only 4, (4) that one does *not* know, by counting done by oneself or by someone else, that one has counted out a total of 5, so that if one said there were 5 apples in all, this would be a deduction from the fact that one had counted out 2 + 3 of them. It is important to keep circumstance (3) in mind in appraising the consequences Moore draws from his analysis of Wittgenstein's claim that by 'one must have vanished' we can only mean 'If we keep to the rule "2 + 3 = 5" we must say "one must have vanished" '.

Suppose one says there are 5 in all. Moore claims that Wittgenstein's reason for explicating 'one must have vanished' as he did, is that 'there are 5', if asserted under circumstances (1) and (4), means something different from what it would mean had one discovered by counting, rather than deduced, that there are 5, namely, B: 'One keeps to the rule "2 + 3 = 5" if one asserts there are 5 apples and violates it if one asserts anything inconsistent with saying there are 5'.[1] And this is the only thing meant by 'there are 5' in circumstances (1) and (4). Now one can keep to

<hr>

[1] *Ibid.*, p. 306.

the rule, i.e., speak correctly, without saying what is true: it can be correct but not true to say there are 5. Moore concludes that Wittgenstein's insistence on proposition B as the only thing that we mean by 'there are 5' is intended to prevent the mistake of supposing we mean 'If one sets out 2 + 3 apples then *necessarily* one sets out 5'. This proposition Moore takes Wittgenstein to suppose is false, which is to say he supposes it imaginable that one should count 2 + 3 apples and that a correct count of the total *at that very time* should show only 4. Further, Moore thinks that whether or not this interpretation of Wittgenstein is correct, it is quite certain that he held that '2 + 3 = 5' is never used in arithmetic to express a proposition from which it follows that if one counts out 2 + 3 apples one necessarily counts out 5.[1] In this case I should take it that neither '2 + 3 = 5' nor 'If one has 2 + 3 apples one has 5 apples' is a necessary proposition.

Wittgenstein has at various times certainly said things which support the account Moore has given, e.g. that '2 + 3 = 5' is 'purely arbitrary', which suggests that there is no necessity about 'If one counts out 2 + 3 apples the total is 5'. I am not now in a position to judge whether this account of what Wittgenstein held is in fact correct, although I heard the 1932–33 lectures in which there was some discussion of the example under consideration. Nor for that matter am I sure that I am correctly reporting what he said in the lectures I heard in 1934–34 and in later lectures to which I have access at second-hand. If Wittgenstein did commit himself to holding it to be imaginable that one should count out 2 + 3 apples and not at the same time have a total of 5, I think, with Moore, that he was surely mistaken. If he did, then 'If one counts out 2 + 3 apples one has a total of 5' would be an empirical proposition. But I wish to make plain that I have not supposed him to imply this and my criticism will not presuppose thinking he does.

For one thing, (a) when Wittgenstein said that '2 + 3 = 5' functions analogously to a rule of language, i.e., so that 'I counted out 2 + 3 apples but did not at that time have a total of 5' does not make sense, I took it that what does not make sense could not express an imaginable state of affairs. Further, the reason for its not expressing an imaginable state of affairs is that the truth of

[1] *Loc. cit.*, 307–308.

'the total is not 5 apples' is inconsistent with the truth of 'I counted out 2 + 3'. That is, if I did count out 2 + 3 apples it necessarily is *true* that I counted 5. It is not merely that I must engage in this manner of speaking (and say there are 5) if I am to speak in accordance with a rule. This certainly seems to me to be correct, although I am not at all sure but that Wittgenstein held what Moore reports.

For another thing, (b) what makes convincing Moore's concluding that Wittgenstein held to be imaginable a logically inconceivable state of affairs is circumstance (3) of the example. (3) is to the effect that it is *known*, because one has kept watch, that nothing has happened to account in any normal way for there being only 4 apples, e.g. it is known that none has been removed, or has flown away. Only if Moore means that knowing this implies that *none has vanished* could it be inferred that one could set out 2 + 3 apples which total up to 4. But if we *know* that none has vanished, should we say, on counting 4, 'one must have vanished'? I doubt that Wittgenstein intended this circumstance to figure in the example he was considering; rather, it seems to me that he supposed not that one knew an apple had *not* vanished, but that one did *not* know that it had, although it in fact had, by some process quicker than sense-observation could detect. When Moore says he can imagine that one really has vanished, even under circumstance (3),[1] it appears that he also is holding not that one knows none has vanished but that one merely knows none has vanished *in any normal way*, though one has in fact done so. But then it could not be inferred from Wittgenstein's example that he held that one could set out 2 + 3 apples and have *at that time* 4. Rather, if one set out 2 + 3 apples and one vanished, one would have 4. And then we should have our present arithmetic—unless '2 apples + 3 apples = 4 apples' were interpreted as a statement about physical combination.

However, Wittgenstein made a comment on the example, according to my lecture notes of 1932–33, which might well have led Moore to suppose that Wittgenstein is committed to holding it to be imaginable that one should set out 2 + 3 apples and have a total of 4. The comment was that in circumstances (1) and (2) we can *either* say 'one must have vanished' or we can '*change the*

[1] *Loc. cit.*, 309.

rules.[1] That is, we can choose either to say 'I set out 5 apples' (and thereby speak in accordance with the present rule '$2 + 3 = 5$') or to adopt the rule '$2 + 3 = 4$'—and accordingly speak correctly in saying 'I set out 4'. Moore took it that since we can speak correctly without saying what is true, it could conceivably be false that one set out 5 apples when one set out $2 + 3$. Wittgenstein's insistence that 'there are 5' only means 'If the rule "$2 + 3 = 5$" is adhered to one must say one put 5', Moore took to indicate that a proposition commonly held to be true was false, namely, 'If one sets out $2 + 3$ apples *necessarily* one sets out 5'. And if this is false it would seem that one could set out $2 + 3$ apples and not have a total of 5.

I have placed a different construction on what Wittgenstein said. Because he held that as language is used 'I set out $2 + 3$ apples but did not have a total of 5' does not make sense, I am supposing (as Moore does not) that he held that '$2 + 3 = 5$' is used in arithmetic to express a proposition from which it follows that if one set out $2 + 3$ apples one necessarily sets out 5, that is, that if '$2 + 3 = 5$' is a necessary proposition so is 'If I set out $2 + 3$ apples I have a total of 5'. And the latter *is* necessary because '$2 + 3 = 5$' expresses a necessity, as we use language now. When Wittgenstein says that under circumstances (1) and (2) one can either say 'one must have vanished' or change the rules, I take him to be saying that either we can keep to our present arithmetic, whence 'If I set out $2 + 3$ apples I have 5' would be necessary, or we can have a different arithmetic, whence, for example, 'If I set out $2 + 3$ apples I have 4' would be necessary. Thus with present arithmetic 'I counted out $2 + 3$ but did not have a total of 5' would express a self-contradiction, and *with a different arithmetic* it would be a redundancy expressing a possible state of affairs. But what is expressed would be contingent on which arithmetic we chose. Now it is rather different to think (as I believe Moore did) that Wittgenstein is committed to holding it to be possible that one should set out $2 + 3$ apples and have only 4 and to think him committed to holding that it would be possible *if* our arithmetic were different. It must be admitted, however, that the one position seems no whit better than the

---

[1] Here is a clear case of Wittgenstein's characterization of '$2 + 3 = 5$', etc., as rules. I shall use his language in expounding what he said.

other. The example seems rather clearly to use '2', '3', '4', '+', and '=' precisely as we do now: the numerals to stand for the numbers we correlate with a couple, a trio, and a quartet, '+' to mean addition (not physical conjunction, as in my first interpretation), and '=' to mean 'equals'. But if this is their use it is difficult to know what could possibly be meant by saying '2 + 3 = 4' is necessary, or by saying that if our arithmetic were different (e.g. if this proposition were necessary) then it would be necessary that if I set out 2 + 3 apples I should have a total of 4.

The unclarity about this matter makes it unclear what is meant by saying that depending on the circumstances different propositions would be necessary. I should like now to examine this claim together with the view Wittgenstein apparently held that it is a matter of choice whether or not '2 + 3 = 4' expresses something necessary (whether we have 'a different arithmetic'). According to Wittgenstein *we adopt* necessary propositions, and which ones we adopt is 'suggested by experience'. Present circumstances are such that we deduce 'I set out 5 apples' from 'I set out 2 + 3'; but we could choose to deduce 'I set out 4 apples' instead. The fact that the arithmetic in use tallies with the result of counting is presumably explained by our choice being suggested by experience. Facts do not compel the choice, but they suggest it. Other things being equal, we take as necessary the proposition conforming to fact.[1] For example, were we to say 'The specific gravity of iron is 7.86, no matter what experiment shows', we should thereby make independent of experience a proposition which experience suggests. Had we a different arithmetic presumably the difference would be explained by what is suggested by experience: in our example, by the experience of always finding 4 apples when one counts out a couple and a trio.

But now *what* is suggested by experience? That it would be useful to adopt *these propositions* as necessary? *These* propositions are first of all factual truths, empirical propositions. Hence *they* cannot be made independent of experience, i.e. *these* propositions cannot be necessary. One and the same proposition cannot depend for its truth or falsity on matter of fact and also have its truth-value quite independent of fact.

Suppose one maintains instead that because the proposition

---

[1] Lectures, 1934–35.

expressed by the sentence '2 + 3 = 4' is true as a matter of fact, this suggests making the *sentence* express something which no fact will falsify—something Wittgenstein possibly meant. The sentence, '2 + 3 = 4', which is first understood as expressing a generalization about set of things in juxtaposition or about the number one arrives at by counting a couple and a trio, is made to express something to which the behaviour of sets of things or the experience one has upon counting the total group comprised of 2 + 3 objects is irrelevant. It is made to do this by being made to serve an entirely different purpose—to function as a rule for the use of the expressions '2 + 3' and '4'. What once served to express a generalization which a different world could confute comes to serve as a guide in the conduct of language, proscribing such statements as 'I put 3 apples into a bowl containing 2, but there were in all more than 4.' The proscription, of course, is not of a falsity but of a use of language—of the use of '2 + 3 but not 4' to characterize any set of objects. What experience 'suggests' is then the *choice* of language—because such a choice would be useful.

Does this description of the change in status of the sentence '2 + 3 = 4' explain the harmony between the arithmetic proposition and the fact that 4 is the result got by counting a couple and a trio? Does it explain the connection of the necessary proposition with its application? The difficulty I find is in specifying any connection between the sentence expressing a necessity and the empirical proposition originally expressed in the same words. When the truth of the proposition '2 + 3 = 4' was verified by experience, the expression '2 + 3 but not 4' at that stage had a use, whereas at the stage where the sentence is taken to express what is necessary this same expression is thereby denied a use. And this is to say that '2 + 3' has different uses, i.e. different meanings, at the two stages. '2 + 3' means something in the one case which is inconsistent with 'not 4', and in the other case not. If the sentence '2 + 3 = 4' has different meanings at the two stages, what connection is there between the sentence for the necessary proposition and the observed fact that when a couple and a trio are counted the result is found to be 4—i.e. with the fact which verifies the empirical proposition which the sentence no longer expresses?

4

FINITISM AND 'THE LIMITS OF EMPIRICISM'*

Bertrand Russell's criticisms of the finitist position[1] as set out in my papers in *Mind* on 'Finitism in Mathematics'[2] concern in the main two topics: the condition, held there to be a necessary one, for a mathematical sentence to have meaning, and the proper interpretation of such descriptive phrases as 'the expansion of π'. The first of Russell's criticisms concerns the criterion given for determining whether a sentence has meaning. He says (p. 144): 'It seems to follow that, if a form of words p is syntactically correct, we always "know what is meant by the statement that p is demonstrated".' It is not clear whether Russell intends 'syntactical correctness' to mean mere grammatical correctness. If he does, then I wish to hold that the latter is not sufficient to guarantee that 'p' has meaning, and further, that if 'p' is to have meaning it is necessary that it (or a sentence into which it translates) appear as the terminal sentence of a sequence of sentences which set out a proof. That is, 'p' gets meaning when p is proved, or better, 'p' is *given* its meaning by the demonstration. This paradoxical thesis is given detailed analysis and criticism in 'Proof and the Theorem Proved', pp. 13–25, I shall therefore devote myself here to claims Russell makes concerning the descriptive phrases 'the expansion of π', 'an infinite number of operations', and 'the class of finite integers'.

Russell states that it is only 'medically impossible' (not logically impossible) to run through the expansion of π.[3] In 'Finitism in Mathematics' I used the phrase 'to run through the expansion of π'; and this suggests, as M. Lazerowitz has pointed out to me, that Russell and I agree on the important point regarding the

---

* This paper is an extensive revision of a paper by the same title which appeared in *Mind*, Vol. XLVI, no. 183 (1937).

[1] In 'The Limits of Empiricism', *Proceedings of the Aristotelian Society*, Vol. XXXVI, pp. 131–150.

[2] Vol. XLIV, nos. 174, 175.   [3] 'The Limits of Empiricism', p. 143.

existence of an infinite extension and disagree on the relatively
trivial point as to which kind of impossibility in involved in the
supposition that one runs through π. For the supposition that it is
impossible to run through the expansion of π would seem to
entail that there is a 'consummated'[1] expansion (comparable to a
long finite array of coexisting elements) which some sort of
obstacle, either physical or logical, prevents us from completing.
The use of the phrase 'the expansion of π', which carries with it
the air of referring to an extension, is misleading, and invites
dispute over what kind of impossibility is involved in running
through its members. The important question is not whether
anyone can in theory write all the terms of *the* expansion, which
Russell supposes to be infinitely many, but whether it *makes sense*
to talk about there being, in extension, an infinite number of
terms, and *a fortiori* of anyone's writing them down. I wish to hold
that, in the sense of an extension, there is no expansion which is the
infinite expansion of π, but that there is only a finite number of
expansion*s*. The view that π, taken as an extension, is always finite,
makes both Russell and me wrong. For it need not be impossible
in any sense to run through a finite number of terms.

Now I think Russell assumes that there is an infinite *extension*,
a, which the phrase describes but which, except for Leibniz' God
(who 'alone can accomplish'[2] an infinite analysis), it is medically
impossible to write down. It would appear that one of Russell's
underlying assumptions is that an omniscient Deity could know
a by acquaintance, and that finite minds know it only indirectly,
by the description 'the expansion of π'. It would appear that he
assumes either (*a*) that the Deity envisages a as a whole, or (*b*) that
the Deity accomplishes what he conceives a person to accomplish
whose skill 'increases so fast that he performs each operation in
half the time required for its predecessor',[3] in which case 'the
whole infinite series would take only twice as long to write down
as the first operation'.[3] If the first operation took a minute, the
whole of the infinite series would be completed in two minutes.
Russell in another place says 'classes which are infinite are given

[1] Georg Cantor's expression.
[2] *Die Philosophischen Schriften von G. W. Leibniz*, herausgegeben von C. J.
Gerhardt (Berlin 1875–90), Vol. VII, p. 309.
[3] 'The Limits of Empiricism', *op. cit.*, p. 144.

all at once by the defining property of their members',[1] the suggestion of his language being that the members of an infinitely many membered whole are displayed before our eyes. Parmenides' warning against being duped by 'the deceptive ordering of words' applies to Russell's language here. For what is 'given' is merely *the property* of the infinite set, not the members of the set defined by the property. There is no *whole* of what is infinitely many. In a trivial, vacuous sense not only the Deity but anyone whatever could run through a whole which does not exist. Russell's supposition (*a*) implies that the totality of members of an infinite set is given to the Deity in the way in which a finite selection might be presented to a person, and supposition (*b*) that the process of counting off the members one by one could be completed.

In 'Finitism in Mathematics' I said the phrase 'to run through the expansion of π' was self-contradictory, on the ground that it stood for a process of terminating the non-terminating. But this is not the important criticism, for it presupposes that 'the expansion of π' describes an infinite extension. The important thing to see is that this way of speaking is bound to confuse the function of this phrase, and many like it, in mathematical language. 'The expansion of π' does not describe an infinite extension, not because 'There is an infinite extension' is in fact false but because the phrase refers to a *law*, e.g. the law for expanding the function $4 (\arctan \frac{1}{2} + \arctan' \frac{1}{3})$. 'The expansion of π' is not a shorthand, as 'the numbers between 1 and 50' is for '1, 2, 3, . . .' And if the phrase refers to a law rather than to an extension, it has an entirely different use from a phrase like 'the numbers between 1 and 50'. To say that the expansion of π is longer than $3 \cdot 14$ is to say something utterly different from saying $3 \cdot 141$ is longer than $3 \cdot 14$.[2] It is longer because there is no end, not to an extension, but to the possibility of developing a function. That is, given any expansion E_1 of π, a longer expansion E_2 can always be constructed by means of π (understood as a law of construction). The term 'longer than' in the sentence 'The expansion of π is longer than E_1' thus is not used in its usual sense. In the usual sense of 'longer than' in which

---

[1] *Our Knowledge of the External World* (London: Allen & Unwin, 1914), p. 156.

[2] Use is being made here of what I understand Dr L. Wittgenstein to have said in lectures at Cambridge University, 1932–35.

the term applies to E_2 with respect to E_1, E_3 with respect to E_2, etc., it does not apply to π with respect to any E. Contrary to how one is tempted to picture π, 'π' does not refer to the longest extension of which the E's are partial extensions.[1] The difference between π and any E, Wittgenstein said, is like the difference between a railway train and a railway accident. The expansion of π and the expansion of π to seven places are related as a law to an extension, not as two extensions one of which is longer than the other. 'π is longer than any E' means that a function, say 4 (arctan $\frac{1}{2}$ + arctan $\frac{1}{3}$), can be developed to 20 terms, to 50 terms, *and so on* indefinitely. 'And so on' distinguishes the terminating from the non-terminating decimal, and it is not a shorthand here for an extension one does not wish to trouble to write (what Wittgenstein called 'the and so on' of laziness), nor for the longest decimal one's strength allows one to write. It is part of a law about the construction of signs, without relation to inclination or endurance.

Thus when I said that it was logically impossible to run through the expansion of π, I should have said that it did not make sense to say this. For it does not make sense to say one *runs through a law*. That it fails to make sense to speak of literally running through the expansion of π is not, primarily, because it is self-contradictory, but because one has misapprehended the function of a descriptive phrase with an unsual job, a misapprehension which has its source in the linguistic similarity of this phrase to descriptive phrases which have standard jobs, such as 'the expansion of π to seven places'. If these comments are correct, then the supposition (*b*) that a person's skill might increase in such a way that if the first operation of expanding took a minute, 'the whole infinite series would take only twice as long . . .' would also be without sense.

Some philosophers will deny the claim that the extensional interpretation of 'the expansion of π' is literally unintelligible, and I therefore wish to make some further comments about Russell's supposition (*b*). Russell looks upon the sequence of intervals required for each operation, i.e. $1, \frac{1}{2}, \frac{1}{4}, \frac{1}{8} \ldots$ in precisely the same

---

[1] In this connection the mathematical malapropism of an eminent mathematician, reported by P. E. B. Jourdain, is well worth noting: 'Representation [of a complex variable] on a plane is obviously more effective for points at a finite distance from the origin than for points at a very great distance.' *The Philosophy of Mr B*rtr*nd R*ss*ll*, p. 63.

way as upon the sequence 3, 3·1, 3·14, ..., namely, as an infinite extension. The possibility of running through the expansion of π is supposedly shown by presupposing that a person completes an infinite sequence of time intervals in the course of completing an infinite number of operations.[1] But clearly the possibility of completing an infinite sequence cannot be demonstrated by assuming the existence of a completed sequence, here 1, $\frac{1}{2}$, $\frac{1}{4}$. . . . The finitist must hold that 'the sequence of decreasing time intervals' also cannot meaningfully be supposed to denote an infinite extension. There is no objection to the hypothesis that a person performs each calculation in half the time required for its predecessor. What is objectionable is Russell's conclusion that the whole infinite series would take only twice as long as the first operation—that is, supposing the first operation took a minute, the second a half-minute, etc., that he would be *done* in two minutes. The following, which is my rough translation of an excerpt from a manuscript of Wittgenstein's on *Grundlagen der Mathematik*, is an enlightening commentary on this conclusion: 'The statement that he would be done in two [minutes] rests on a confusion between a limiting value of the sum $1 + \frac{1}{2} + \frac{1}{4} + \frac{1}{8} \ldots$ and "sum". This series is no sum. It is sensible to talk of the velocity of the [operation] so long as we don't talk of it at the point $t = 2$, since for this our calculus gives *no* value (the value $v = $ infinity doesn't exist for us: no experience is correlated with it). For every point before $t = 2$ our law gives a velocity. The wrong conclusion is in the proposition "In two [minutes] it is all finished".'

Some mathematical writers on the notion of a sum of an infinite series have shown an awareness of the unique relation of the sum to the series and of the radical difference between 'sum' as defined for the series and 'sum' as defined for a number of addends. About the series $1 + \frac{1}{2} + \frac{1}{4} + \ldots$ (whose sum Russell takes to be the total time required to complete the described calculation of π) N. J. Lennes has written as follows: 'Heretofore the sum has been obtained by adding a definite number of addends, but clearly the terms of an infinite series can never be completely added. Hence if it is to be regarded as having a sum at all, this must be defined in some new way.'[2] Lennes expresses himself in what

---

[1] Pointed out to me by M. Lazerowitz.　　　　[2] *College Algebra*, p. 113.

might be called 'the composite idiom': the first part of his statement seems to be about how the series is to be regarded, while the
second part makes it clear that a *new sense* of 'sum' is being introduced. In a typically philosophical way, a term is being redefined,
or being given a new sense, while the impression is created that
the term is being used in its old sense—with some sort of difference
being acknowledged, in the present case a difference between
an infinite series and partial series.

The unique position of the number 2 which is said to be the
sum of the series $1 + \frac{1}{2} + 1 \ldots$ Lennes remarks on as follows:
'(*a*) No matter how far the series is extended its sum will never be
as great as 2. (*b*) If k is any number less than 2, this series may be
extended sufficiently far so that its sum shall be greater than k.
Hence the number 2 sustains relations to this series which are
different from those sustained to it by any other number. It is,
namely, the smallest number which is never reached by the sum
of this series, no matter how far it is extended.'[1] This way of
putting the matter hints at, but partly conceals, the fact that the
relations 2 sustains to the series are different in *kind* from the
relations any term of the series has to the series, and that to say
2 is larger than any of the terms is to use 'larger than' in a different
way from its use in '$1 + \frac{1}{2} + \frac{1}{4}$ is larger than $1 + \frac{1}{2}$': 'larger than'
does not refer to a difference of degree between magnitudes. This
point is similar to that made concerning the relation of π to any
expansion E. With the precise definition of 'limit of a series' and
the definition of 'sum' as the limit, it becomes clear how different
a 'sum' of a series is from the sum of a definite number of addends.
It also becomes clear why one cannot speak of being *done* at time
$t = 2$ with an infinite series of addends, that is, with a series of
which (*a*) above is true.

Something should be said about Russell's claim that on a finitist
view one has no right to say there is no greatest finite integer,
because 'the proof that, if N is *any* finite integer, $N < N + 1$,
requires us to be able to deal with the whole class of finite integers,
which we cannot do [on finitist principles] unless the class is
finite'.[2] Had Wittgenstein's symbol (0, ζ, $\zeta + 1$) meant, as Russell
supposed,[2] 'Start with 0, and if you reach ζ go on to $\zeta + 1$, as

---

[1] *College Algebra*, p. 113.
[2] 'The Limits of Empiricism', *op. cit.*, p. 143.

long as humanly possible, i.e. till you die, or alternatively, until the race dies out', that is, if it meant something about persons and their capacities, then at the time of a person's death, or at the time the race ends, there would be a maximum finite integer. Thus, in one sense of the phrase 'the greatest integer', namely, the sense in which it is equivalent to 'the greatest integer constructed up to a given time', there is no disagreeing with Russell that there would be a greatest integer. However, this sense of 'the greatest integer' is mathematically trivial, and is not the sense one would suppose finitists intend, although it is only in this sense that anyone could be holding something false in holding there is no greatest integer. Finitists can hold that the greatest integer constructed up to a given time is not the greatest integer, that is, that there is an infinity of integers, without implying that there is an infinite class, in extension, which it is humanly possible for anyone to construct. To say that infinitely many integers can be constructed by means of the rule (o, ζ, $\zeta + 1$) is not to say that the rule generates a class, in extension, with an infinity of members. Wittgenstein remarked[1] that 'infinitely many' is not a number-word. 'It is possible to generate integers (or terms of π's expansion) endlessly' is not a statement which a human incapacity would falsify, but a statement about what signs the rule *allows* to be written. He said, 'What one calls an infinite possibility corresponds to what one might call an infinite permission; and this is not the permission to do something infinite.'[2] Generation of terms in accordance with a rule yields terms endlessly; it does not yield an endless extension. And where there is the possibility of generating terms endlessly, i.e., a *logical* as against a physical possibility, this is signalized by the presence *in a law* of such phrases as 'and so on *ad inf.*' Laws of construction indefinitely can be included in finitist mathematics, since there is no need to interpret them as laws for the construction of an endless *whole*. Thus 'the class of integers' and 'the expansion of π' will be unobjectionable if one takes them to refer to a law for constructing terms indefinitely.

---

[1] In the manuscript, *Grundlagen der Mathematik*, referred to above.
[2] *Ibid.*

5

INVENTION AND DISCOVERY

'It is the merest truism, evident at once to unsophisticated observation, that mathematics is a human invention.'[1] Quite evidently mathematics did not appear as such to G. H. Hardy, who wrote: 'I believe that mathematical reality lies outside us, and that our function is to discover or *observe* it, and that the theorems which we prove and which we describe grandiloquently as our "creations" are simply our notes of our observations'.[2] Proponents of the respective views that mathematics is invention and that mathematics is discovery would, I think, agree that both views cannot be true, and that certainly one must be false: the form of words in the two cases indicates that antithetical positions are being asserted. The difficulty is that no prospect of a decision between them presents itself. And this hopelessness of justifying either position suggests, not that there is some third compromise position which would satisfy both proponents, but that they misconceive the nature of the views they advocate and the point of the arguments they adduce for them. At least it suggests that a new investigation is in order, one which examines the nature of the rival theories and of the arguments for them rather than takes for granted that they are what they appear to be. Very likely Wittgenstein had something like this in mind when he wrote, '. . . what a mathematician is inclined to say about the objectivity and reality of mathematical facts, is . . . something for philosophical *treatment*'.[3]

In this essay I shall make application of Wittgenstein's general thesis that philosophical positions arise from misunderstandings concerning the use of words.[4] I shall maintain that we are misled by language when we accept either of the two rival views on the

[1] P. W. Bridgman, *The Logic of Modern Physics*, p. 60. (New York: The Macmillan Co., 1927)   [2] *A Mathematician's Apology*, pp. 63–4.
[3] *Philosophical Investigations*, p. 91 (Cambridge University Press, 1941).
[4] *Ibid.*, p. 43.

nature of mathematical investigation. And it will be most important to ascertain the precise nature of the views we are misled to
accept and what their semantic sources are. It is natural to assume
that if we are misled by language we are persuaded to accept
something false. But if two positions are each other's contradic-
tories then it cannot in both cases be *falsities* that we are misled
to accept. I shall take it that being misled into either of two rival
philosophical theses (whether or not they are each other's contra-
dictories) is to hold as true something which taken literally is
neither true nor false. If it can be shown precisely how language is
used to create the illusion that something true is being established
and the illusion that the counterview is false, then with the expo-
sure of the illusion both 'positions' reduce to pseudo-positions.
To expose an illusion in these cases is not to show a *theory* to be
illusory, i.e. false, but to show an assertion to be but the illusory
appearance of a theory. It is this which I wish to show in connection with the two apparently antithetical claims, 'Mathematics is a
human invention', 'Mathematics is a record of discoveries in its
special domain of objects'.

Wittgenstein has said that philosophy, as he does it, 'in the end
can only describe the actual use of language'.[1] And the actual use
of language when compared with its philosophical use sheds some
light on the latter. Language used in the actual doing of mathematics and also language correctly descriptive of various aspects of
doing mathematics lead very naturally to what appears to be a
theory when one *talks about* mathematics. And I want to say that
in the hands of the philosophical mathematician advantage is
taken of certain verbal analogies to gain acceptance of a manner of
speaking about mathematics which has the semblance of a theory.
This is what mustering support for a philosophical position comes
to. Argumentation apparently in support of a position is a means
of rationalizing the adoption or retention of a certain description
of mathematics. It is the source of a 'theory' but not the justification of a theory's truth. To make plausible this extraordinary claim
on my part I shall need to show the sources of the 'views' and of
the argumentation for them in the language used in the practice
of mathematics and in the language correctly describing it. It will
be useful first to record the different philosophical pronounce-

Philosophical Investigations p. 49

ments made on mathematics as discovery and as invention in order to have before us the 'talk about' mathematics of which we wish to trace the semantic genesis.

We begin with certain philosophical questions, to which these pronouncements are answers, and shall translate them into the concrete by directing them to various of the following examples: $2 + 2 = 4$, $2 - 4 = -2$, $x^3 + x^2 + x + 1 = 0$ has one real root and two imaginary roots, there are infinitely many primes. The questions, which, it will be noted, are not of the sort which need be answered in order to *do* mathematics, are as follows: What are these propositions *about*? Were the number -2 and the roots $+\sqrt{-1}$ invented, or only the symbolism for them? Can one invent, as opposed to discover, what necessarily exists? *Was* it *true* that $2 - 4 = -2$ and that $+\sqrt{-1}$ were roots of $x^3 + x^2 + x + 1 = 0$ before the domain of numbers was extended to negative and complex numbers? Is what we agree on as being a truth imposed upon us or decided by us?

To the first question, about the subject matter of mathematics, philosophers have given an answer which, judging by its persistence from antiquity, it is entirely natural to give, and for which the resources of our language provide a powerful bulwark. It is expressed in Theaetetus' answer in the *Sophist*[1] to the question of the Eleatic Stranger, 'And number is to be reckoned as among things which are?': 'Yes, surely number, if anything, has a real existence.' 'Uncreated and indestructible',[2] numbers for the arithmetician, 'the absolute square and the absolute diameter'[3] for the geometrician (who uses the visible forms only as an aid), lie open to the eye of the mind even more assuredly than the world of sense lies ready to inspection by the organs of the body. More than twenty centuries later the Platonic tradition appears again in Russell: '. . . the statement "two and two are four" deals exclusively with universals, and therefore may be known by anybody who is acquainted with the universals concerned and can perceive the relation between them which the statement asserts. It must be taken as a fact, discovered by reflecting upon our knowledge, that we have the power of sometimes perceiving such

---

[1] Sec. 238, Jowett translation.   [2] *Timaeus*, Sec. 52.
[3] *Republic*, Bk. VI, Sec. 510.

relations between univerals, and therefore of sometimes knowing general *a priori* propositions such as those of arithmetic and logic.'[1] It is obvious that on this account the mathematician is an observer, a discoverer—not an inventor. 'Invention' properly characterizes new symbolism, for example, expressions for negative numbers, irrationals, complex numbers, transfinite cardinals; but this symbolism is merely a convenient notation for what the mathematician perceives. Investigation in arithmetic and number theory is like an empirical investigation, but of a non-empirical reality. A field lies before our minds for exploration, and these branches of mathematics are but 'the natural history of the domain of numbers'.[2] As for truth, what could not conceivably be otherwise lies beyond our power to create or destroy. '. . . Mathematics is independent of us personally and of the world outside, and we can feel that our own discoveries and views do not affect the Truth itself but only the extent to which we or others see it. Some of us discover things in science, but we do not really create anything in science any more than Columbus created America.'[3] The remarkable agreement among mathematicians on the truth of a theorem results from the fact that the truth imposes itself upon any thinking person.

It scarcely need be said that this philosophical position has not gained unanimous assent. Indeed to some people it has seemed without any merit, while the counterposition has appeared to be compelling: '. . . we have overcome the notion that mathematical truths have an existence independent and apart from our own minds. It is even strange to us that such a notion could ever have existed.'[4] Within this position, which might be broadly characterized as 'conventionalistic', we find a quite different account of the subject matter of mathematics and of necessary truth. Where Hardy says $2 + 2 = 4$ is about numbers, Hilbert says it is about marks. Symbols are of course invented, and mathematicians who speak of the invention of numbers seem to equate this with the

[1] *The Problems of Philosophy*, 17th Impression, pp. 164–65.

[2] L. Wittgenstein, *Remarks on the Foundations of Mathematics*, p. 117.

[3] P. E. B. Jourdain, *The Nature of Mathematics* republished by James R, Newman in *The World of Mathematics* (London: Allen & Unwin, 1960). Vol. I, p. 71.

[4] Edward Kasner and James Newman, *Mathematics and the Imagination*, p. 359 (New York: Simon and Schuster, 1940).

invention of symbols. R. Courant refers to i as 'purely a symbol',[1] and asserts that 'extension of the number concept was made possible by the creation of new numbers in the form of abstract symbols like o, -2, and $\frac{3}{4}$'. 'By introducing new symbols'[2] the domain of numbers is said to have been extended. And the behaviour of those numbers is decreed rather than observed: '. . . rules for the addition, multiplication, and equality of our symbols are established by our own definition and are not imposed upon us by any prior necessity other than that of usefulness for the application we have in mind'.[3] 'It took a long time for mathematicians to realize that . . . the definitions governing negative integers and fractions cannot be "proved". They are *created* by us in order to attain freedom of operation while preserving the fundamental laws of arithmetic.'[4] 'We might whimsically decree some other rule for addition, such as $\dfrac{a}{b} + \dfrac{c}{d} = \dfrac{a+c}{b+d}$, which in particular would yield $\dfrac{1}{2} + \dfrac{1}{2} = \dfrac{2}{4}$, an absurd result from the point of view of measuring.'[5] Further, whether or not a generalization is extended to a new field, as when Kummer extended the theorem that a rational integer is uniquely factorable into primes to a new species of number, ideals, is a matter for mathematicians to *decide*. Precisely what the decision is may for some time remain unsettled. Descartes denied what Gauss later by implication asserted, that $x^3 + x^2 + x + 1 = 0$ has three roots. And this means that mathematicians are the arbiters of what is necessary and what is not. They are governed by quite various considerations, some having to do with the further conduct of their subject (Shall existence statements be accepted for which there is no constructive proof?), others with application, as indicated by Courant in the above quotation: for example, $\dfrac{a}{b} + \dfrac{c}{d} = \dfrac{ad + cb}{bd}$ is the accepted rule for determining the total amount of land owned by a legatee who has inherited 2/3 of one acre and 4/5 of another. It legislates that 'he owns exactly one acre in consequence

---

[1] R. Courant and H. Robbins, *What is Mathematics?*, p. 89 (Oxford University Press, 1941).
[2] *Ibid.*, p. 56. [3] *Ibid.*, p. 53. [4] *Ibid.*, p. 55. [5] *Ibid.*, p. 54.

of inheriting $2/3 + 4/5$ acres' shall express a contradiction. 'The mathematical proposition has the dignity of a rule'[1] (a rule concerning the use of language).

Looking on as a rule, $\dfrac{a}{b} + \dfrac{c}{d} = \dfrac{ad + cb}{bd}$ is arbitrary, something about which there is freedom of decision to accept or not. And yet it seems anything but arbitrary, a necessity arising from the nature of rational numbers which leaves us no freedom. It seems that there should be one correct description of this arithmetical identity, as a creation or as a discovery. How does it come about 'that mathematics appears to us now as the natural history of the domain of numbers, now again as a collection of rules'[2]? Can one decide which face it presents is the true one and which the false?

I wish to say that neither of the two philosophical positions which purport to be accounts of *the nature* of mathematics is what it appears to be. Neither shows the true face of mathematics. Nor is this to say that both are false, although if taken to be true-or-false descriptions, it is difficult to explain why the two considerations to follow are not accepted as showing both to be false: (1) Clearly $2 + 2 = 4$ is not about the symbols occurring in its expressions—the symbols are used, not mentioned; and this being the case it is not a rule about symbols. Nor can symbols and numbers be identified, as is obvious from the different uses in our language of 'the number 4' and 'the sign "4" '. E.g. one can say of the sign but not of the number that it is black. (2) But neither can the signs be taken to name abstract objects open to inspection by the eye of the mind, if one weighs the following fact: that mathematicians, rather than the mathematical facts, decided whether $x^3 + x^2 + x + 1 = 0$ had three roots. Had a different decision been made, a different proposition would have been necessary. Now on the 'discovery' view, since there *necessarily* are three roots it would be an illusion to suppose there was any freedom of decision in the matter of their number. Mathematicians had only to invent a notation for what lay ready to be found. Yet the fact that the symbol '$\sqrt{-1}$' was invented long before Descartes denied that the equation $x^3 + x^2 + x + 1 = 0$ had three roots, coupled with the fact that Descartes cannot be said to have made a mistake,

---

[1] *Remarks on the Foundations of Mathematics*, p. 47.   [2] *Ibid.*, p. 117.

makes such an account appear extremely unsuitable. The fact is that decisions have been made and followed. Even Hardy lapses into talk in keeping with this fact, for example, when he says 'There are technical reasons for not counting 1 as a prime'.[1]

If the 'creation' and 'discovery' views are understood as purporting to describe the subject matter of mathematics, i.e. to be true-or-false descriptions of it, considerations (1) and (2) above would refute both. In the face of these considerations and others like them, what needs to be explained is why through the centuries there have continued to be arguments in support of the conventionalistic and Platonistic positions. I wish now to examine the arguments brought forward for each position with a view to showing clearly the analogies from which they stem and the differences which they ignore. The arguments centre about two connected topics, the domain of mathematical investigation and the necessity of mathematical truth.

I shall begin with reasons for the view that in mathematics we investigate a special domain of objective fact, that this domain is constituted of abstract entities existing independently of our minds. It is worthwhile looking at one question which prompts such a claim: What are mathematical propositions *about*? It is indisputable that it is proper English to reply 'about numbers', 'about polygons', etc., though there is no very natural, nonphilosophical context in which such a question would be asked. One such natural context would be that in which one was asked to explain the meanings of the expressions 'mathematical proposition' and 'proposition of natural history' by someone who did not understand them. One could comply by indicating the subject matter to which they apply, distinguishing mathematical propositions as being about numbers, figures, series, etc., from propositions about the world of nature such as 'Elephants are a source of ivory' which is about elephants and ivory. Another such philosophically aseptic context would be that in which one referred to propositions about primes, conic sections, convergent series, etc., by giving the page numbers of articles in an encyclopaedia where such assertions are made. But when the philosopher of mathematics refers to propositions about numbers he uses his words to imply that these propositions are about entities con-

[1] *A Mathematician's Apology*, p. 33.

stituting a domain which he explores with a view to finding proofs that various truths hold of them. He can be represented as arguing as follows: (1) Just as the true statements, 'Ruthie was a clever circus elephant' and 'There are owls with tufted ears', are about a certain elephant and about certain owls, so '6 lies between 5 and 7' and 'There are factorable numbers of the form $2^{2^n} + 1$' are about numbers. Further, the latter being true, and their opposites being self-inconsistent, 6, and factorable numbers of the form $2^{2^n} + 1$, must exist. And if there exist factorable numbers of that form there must exist numbers of that form, and from this it follows that there must exist numbers. (2) If, as Euclid proved, there is an infinity of primes, then the numerals, which at any given time are finite in number, can be nothing more than names for what is there to be named. (3) The distinction between an empty and a non-empty domain as clearly holds for mathematical propositions as for empirical ones. If there were no numbers, and hence no non-empty sub-class of composite integers, would there be any difference between the proposition that all composite integers are uniquely factorable into primes, and the proposition that all square circles are square? Both would be true because the subject class was null, which flies in the face of the fact that mathematicians tested particular composite integers for factorability into primes before proving the generalization about all of them. (4) Finally, that the body of mathematics is constantly extended by the addition of new theorems derives from a possibility lying within itself. It is as though the possibility of proof is a mathematical fact.[1] What can be proved is strictly determined, as the impressive rigour of mathematical demonstration indicates. The conceptual connections established by proof exist of necessity, and what more natural explanation of their existence than that they are compelled by the properties of the mathematical objects? The roads to truth are already laid down in the world of mathematics by the nature of the entities in it, and with sufficient cleverness the mathematician can map out the road leading from one truth to another. To appropriate a phrase of M. Lazerowitz', he is a sort of cartographer of the supra-sensible—of what, according to Cayley, is 'a tract of beautiful country seen at first

[1] L . Wittgenstein, Lecture notes, 1939.

in the distance, but which will bear to be rambled through and studied in every detail of hillside and valley, stream, rock, wood and flower'.[1] The picture is in fact somewhat misleading, since the freedom to ramble is limited by the necessity of taking certain roads if one wishes to proceed from one truth to another. What roads are mapped are not subject to the will of the mathematician; only the choice among the possible roads is open. Courant's account of the identity $\dfrac{a}{b} + \dfrac{c}{d} = \dfrac{ad + bc}{bd}$ as 'not imposed upon us by any prior necessity' misdescribes a truth deriving from the essence of rational numbers. If this equality were *created* by definition, then its truth would be determined by a convention which had a date. But if, as this implies, its truth-value had a date, presumably there would have been a time when it was not a truth about rational numbers, and it is inconceivable that there should have been such a time. Its truth may have been discovered at a given time, but it did not come into existence with its discovery. It has no date of creation.

Puzzling questions concerning discovery of mathematical truth I shall leave aside in this paper except as they bear on the question concerning the domain in which discovery supposedly takes place. The Platonic account of that domain makes mathematics out to be 'a physics of mathematical entities'.[2] What now can be said for the claim that what are called discoveries had much better be called inventions,[2] that 'the mathematician is an inventor, not a discoverer'.[3] Some reasons to be adduced for it hinge upon features of necessary propositions which have led philosophers to say such things as that they are 'purely verbal',[4] 'purely about the use of the expressions they connect',[4] or alternatively, that their function is not to describe word usage but to 'prescribe how words are to be used',[5] that they are not really propositions, but 'rules which can be followed or disobeyed'.[5] Clearly symbolism is our invention and its use to some degree subject to our will. If $2 + 2 = 4$, for example, is a rule for the use of symbols, then the clear perception

---

[1] Quoted by Alfred Hooper, *Makers of Mathematics*, p. 382. (London: Faber & Faber, 1948).   [2] L. Wittgenstein, Lecture notes, 1939.
[3] L. Wittgenstein, *Remarks on the Foundations of Mathematics*, p. 47.
[4] John Wisdom, 'Mataphysics and Verification', *Mind*, vol. XLVII, p. 463, fn.
[5] A. J. Ayer, 'Truth by Convention', *Analysis*, vol. 4, nos. 2, 3, pp. 19–20.

of this fact precludes the notion that it is a truth having an existence independent of our minds. But as has been pointed out, $2 + 2 = 4$ uses but makes no mention of symbols. And when Wittgenstein says of a proof that it 'proves *first and foremost* that this formation of signs must result when I apply these rules to these formations of signs'[1]—a characterization worthy of a conventionalist—the obvious reply is that proof makes no mention of signs. However unacceptably they state their position, conventionalists nevertheless show an awareness of a connection between the necessity of a proposition and the usage of words, a connection whose importance Platonists totally ignore. This is, to put the matter paradoxically, that the necessity of a proposition rests on arbitrary facts about the words used to express it. What renders a proposition incorrigible is an accepted linguistic convention. To see that a proposition is necessary no special kind of seeing, appropriate to a special domain of objects, is required. In the simplest cases, e.g. 'A cube has six faces', 'Even numbers are divisible by 2', 'A pentagon has five angles', a sufficient means for convincing oneself of their truth is appeal to the dictionary—not appeal to facts of the mathematical world. Necessity rests on a fact of language, and language is our creation and our creature. The remarkable agreement among mathematicians on the necessity of a proposition is a direct correlate of their undeniable agreement in the use of language. If a precondition for their agreement in the use of language were inspection of objects whose properties logically determined their relations, then it would be more than remarkable that conventionalists, who deny apprehending any objects, should manage to convey a proof to Platonist mathematicians.

With this I conclude some of the main reasons which can be put forward for the two positions on the nature of mathematics. I have expounded them as having the aim their proponents intend: to establish the truth of one claim and the falsity of the counterclaim. Despite appearances to the contrary I think that truth or falsity is not at issue here, and that the arguments are not directed to establishing this. But it is obviously incumbent on me to state reasons for thinking so. I shall begin with the strongest case against my thesis—the dispute, couched in the language of truth

[1] L. Wittgenstein, *Remarks on the Foundations of Mathematics*, p. 80.

and falsity, between mathematical Platonists and their opponents over the existence of abstract objects. This is perhaps the most fundamental issue between them. The Platonist affirms the existence of abstract objects denoted by mathematical expressions whereas their opponents, no matter what positive claims they make, all by implication deny the existence of such objects. The claim of certain formalists that numbers are nothing more than numerals, and that it is numerals which $2 + 2 = 4$, for example, is about, if taken literally as a true-or-false-description, is so blatantly false that one can assume its point is in what it denies rather than in what it affirms: it is intended to preclude taking numbers to be objects for which numerals stand, and this is secured by identifying numbers with numerals. Undoubtedly part of the point of Hilbert's claim that '2' and '4' in the expression '$2 + 2 = 4$' are meaningless marks is to deny that there are objects which they *mean*. It is a way of countering the claim that since they have meaning there must be *something* which they mean.

Against claim and counterclaim, each ostensibly to the effect that a certain description of numbers is *true*, I call attention to two curious features of the dispute which argue against its being a truth-value dispute over whether numbers are abstract objects. One is that it should arise concerning a matter so simple and familiar as $2 + 2 = 4$, and the other, that there should be no method of settling it. If the disputants were on unfamiliar ground and could expect to establish their respective theories by finding some new fact which would clinch the matter, their arguments would appear in quite a different light. But in the presence of '$2 + 2 = 4$' there are no new facts to call on, nothing beyond what understanding the sentence yields. How is the discrepancy between the reports on what is found upon inspection to be removed? The Platonist may claim that by an 'organ of the mind' he apprehends ideal objects and truths about how they are related, but he cannot claim to possess an organ lacking to the conventionalist, who reports the apprehension of no such objects. This controversy will of course be recognized as a species of the longstanding controversy over the existence of universals, which also has for centuries remained unresolved despite the presence of all the facts relevant to settling it and the possession of all the requisite faculties on the part of the disputants. Such controversies have no parallel outside philosophy.

Further, to take the position that this controversy is over the truth of a theory commits one to an extraordinarily paradoxical belief about the disputants *vis à vis* each other, to see which provides a compelling reason for discarding the natural assumption that we have here a truth-value controversy. That there is a dispute of some sort cannot be doubted, but what must the disputants' attitude toward each other be if the truth or falsity of a theory is at issue? The conventionalist must suppose the Platonist to operate under the persistent illusion that he is apprehending objects which in fact do not exist at all, and that his 'discoveries', e.g. of complex numbers, represent the onset of fresh illusions. On the other hand, the Platonist must attribute to the conventionalist an inexplicable blindness to the objects of his acquaintance and an even more inexplicable confusion of these objects with symbols. Furthermore, the blindness of the conventionalist mathematician must be supposed to be of a most unusual sort. Whatever he may say about the meaningfulness of number symbols in the sentence '$2 + 2 = 4$', he cannot deny that they have meaning in 'I have two apples and four pears', which expresses an empirical proposition. And if he grasps their meanings in this sentence then he must be apprehending the abstract objects which are their meanings. The conventionalist who understands the words yet denies apprehending any such objects must be assumed by the Platonist to suffer from a blindness like that of the person who under hyponosis complies with the order to see a blank wherever the word 'the' appears on the page.[1] Can one believe that either of the disputants makes these suppositions about the other?

These considerations should certainly put in doubt if not preclude completely the interpretation of the disputed descriptions of numbers as antithetical factual claims about their nature. But pointing out curiosities of the dispute which shake our conception of it leaves it an enigma how arguments can be marshalled for something which only seems to be a theory, and it leaves us in the dark as to what each seeming theory in fact comes to. By way of explanation I want to show (1) that the arguments rest on mis-

[1] Example taken from John Wisdom.

leading analogies between the language of mathematics, both in the doing of mathematics and in talk about it, and the language of empirical fact; and (2) that the arguments do not demonstrate an analytic fact about numbers, but instead support a concealed revision of language whose aim is to justify the description of mathematics as discovery, or as creation. To show this it is required to show what, specifically, the linguistic analogies are and how being misled by them appears to dictate the divergent descriptions of numbers. We here reiterate the point that showing an analogy to be misleading does not show the description to be false, since, for one thing, the two formally contradictory sentences, 'Numbers are abstract objects', 'Numbers are not abstract objects', could not both express what is false.

The analogies which are the semantic sources of the illusion that theories are being propounded lie in several areas. In investigating these analogies I shall confine myself to one area, the talk about necessary existence. I begin with the first of the specific arguments given earlier for the Platonist position: that just as 'There are owls with tufted ears' is about owls, 'There are factorable numbers of the form $2^{2^n} + 1$' is about factorable numbers, and further, that since the opposite of this latter is self-inconsistent, factorable numbers of this form must exist, from which it follows that numbers must exist. Similarly, if 6 is an even number, it follows that 6 is a number, and from this that at least one number exists. The arguments here are analogical. The pattern of demonstration and the verbal forms of the constituent propositions are similar throughout to an argument establishing the existence, say, of owls. 'The clothing of our language', as Wittgenstein says, 'makes everything alike'.[1] It will be claimed that the only respect in which the argument differs from an argument establishing the existence of owls is that its conclusion is about objects which are ideal and that these exist necessarily—as if these were small differences. This claim makes clear the construction the Platonist places on 'There are numbers' and '6 is a number': that they are about ideal objects. If now we note the differences hidden under the verbal similarity of 'There are owls', 'There are numbers', 'There are ideal objects', we may be able to discern the

---

[1] *Philosophical Investigations*, p. 224.

semantic sources producing the illusion that 'Numbers are ideal objects' expresses a theory about the nature of numbers.

Leaving aside for the moment the fact that 'There are owls' is contingent and (according to the argument from the necessary existence of factorable numbers of the form $2^{2^n} + 1$) the inferred fact that 'There are numbers' is necessary, there is a more important difference between them. This is a difference which sets off 'There are numbers' from unquestionably necessary existential statements as well; and it is one which helps explain the fact that, apart from attempts such as Peano's to give the properties of natural numbers, there is no occasion to use such an expression as 'o is a number', nor even in the context of Peano's axioms to go on to infer as a necessary consequence that there are numbers. 'There are numbers' is unlike both 'There are owls' and 'There are even numbers between 3 and 9', despite the fact that '$(\exists x) . fx$' is the common form of all of them. An empirical process will determine whether there are owls, and something analogous to an empirical process will confirm that there are even numbers between 3 and 9. But there is no analogous process for confirming that there are numbers. The range of values of 'x is a number' does not include values which are numbers and values which are not, and in this respect it differs both from the function 'x is an owl' and 'x is an even number between 3 and 9'. To put the point otherwise, '$(\exists x) . x$ is a number' cannot be construed as asserting the existence of things in a domain of which it is sensible to say '$(\exists x) . x$ is not a number'. By contrast, '$(\exists x) . x$ is even $. 3 < x < 9$' has a sensible correlate '$(\exists x) . \sim(x$ is even $. 3 < x < 9)$'. The range of significance of the two functions 'x is even and lies between 3 and 9', 'it is not the case both that x is even and lies between 3 and 9' is the same. Admittedly certain values in their range of significance will yield a self-contradiction, e.g., '5 is even and lies between 3 and 9'. But in the case of 'x is a number' substitution does not yield something self-contradictory when it fails to yield something necessary. It is clear that any other substitute than number expressions for 'x' in 'x is a number' will yield, not a self-contradiction, but complete nonsense. For example, 'Mauve is a number' is not self-contradictory, but nonsensical in the way in which Russell's example, 'Quadruplicity drinks procrastination', is non-nonsensical. The range of significance of 'x is a number' is limited to its truth-range; it has no falsity-range. In this respect it differs from '*x* is an owl' and '*x* is an even number between 3 and 9', whose ranges of significance are constituted of both a truth-range and a falsity-range, that is, their possible values comprise two classes.

It is indeed curious that there should be functions which must have values—such functions as '*x* is an even number between 3 and 9'. It is perhaps more curious that there should be a function, '*x* is a number', none of whose values results in a self-contradiction, whose range of significance is confined to its true values. This feature of '*x* is a number', which distinguishes it from '*x* is even and lies between 3 and 9', is paralleled by still another curious feature which sets it off from other functions. This appears on examination of what it comes to to deny that this function has values. Consider the consequence of supposing it to be true that $\sim(\exists x) . x$ is a number, i.e. of supposing that the sentence 'There are no numbers' rather than the sentence 'There are numbers' expresses a necessity. In this case the word 'number' would have no use in the language, and the paradoxical consequence is that there would be no way of expressing the fact that there are no numbers. The resources of language would be inadequate, for the same sort of reason that a language in which there were no numerals and no word 'number' could not frame as a meaningful sentence 'There are no numbers'. The fact that we can frame this sentence implies that the word 'number' has a use, but the assumption that the sentence expresses a necessity implies that the word has no use. From the assumption it would follow that it was no more sensible to say 'There are no numbers' than 'There are no runcibles'. Comparison with the sentences 'There are no centaurs' and 'There are no primes between 13 and 17' is instructive. The fact that the first expresses a contingent truth implies two things, that the word 'centaur' has a use in the language and that as a matter of empirical fact it does not apply to anything. The fact that the second expresses a necessity implies that the phrase 'prime and between 13 and 17' has no use. But its difference from the sentence 'There are no numbers' is that the phrase which has no use has constituents which do have a use, and our language can express the fact that the combination has no use. Were it the case that the single word 'number' had no use the words 'There are no numbers' could not express anything.

This peculiarity bears on the argument, in support of Platonism, to the effect that if there were no numbers then all universal propositions about numbers would be vacuously true, in which case the theorem 'All composite integers are uniquely factorable into primes' would be no different from 'All odd numbers of the form $2n$ are odd'. It will be recalled that the theorem was suggested by the result of testing particular numbers for factorability, and that this process precludes its being true vacuously. If what I have said about 'There are numbers' is correct, there would be no intelligible way of expressing the hypothesis of the above argument for Platonism, and the argument would become a piece of literal nonsense. It must be admitted that the peculiarities of the function 'x is a number' and of the apparent generalization '$\sim(\exists x).x$ is a number' raise the question whether '$(\exists x).x$ is a number' can be taken to express a necessity. Its status is very unclear. It will be useful to examine what it comes to for a more usual sentence to express a necessity, in the hope of shedding some light on the following questions: what 'Numbers exist' must express *if* it expresses a necessity, why this sentence plays no role in normal mathematical pursuits, whether necessary propositions of number theory can be said to be about numbers, and finally, what the dispute between Platonist and non-Platonist comes to.

Wittgenstein said that arithmetic propositions say nothing about numbers and geometric propositions nothing about cubes.[1] He could have said a similar thing about the subject of any necessary proposition, e.g. 'Bachelors are unmarried male adults'. Why would he wish to say this statement is not about bachelors when in some sense it obviously is? The reason is that to speak as if it were is to assimilate it to an empirical generalization, e.g. 'Whales are a source of ambergris', and thereby to obscure the radical difference between them. The difference is this: the fact that a sentence expresses a necessity, unlike the fact that the sentence about whales expresses a contingent truth, gives us only verbal information. If this is the case then it cannot at the same time be held to give information about something the subject term stands for. In support of the claimed difference from which this consequence is drawn I cite the following. To know that the sentence 'Even numbers are of the form $2n$' expresses a necessary truth,

[1] Lectures, Cambridge University, 1933-34.

and to know this in virtue of knowing the meanings of the involved terms, is to know the following empirical verbal fact, which I shall call the verbal correlate of the sentence: that 'being of the form $2n$' applies to what 'even' applies to, or alternatively, that 'even but not of the form $2n$' has no use. This is not to say that the sentence 'Even numbers are of the form $2n$' means the same thing as the sentence about the phrase 'even but not of the form $2n$'. But it illuminates the position of a necessary proposition *vis à vis* an empirical non-verbal proposition on the one hand and an empirical verbal proposition on the other, to see that understanding the sentence expressing a necessity involves nothing more than knowing that its verbal correlate expresses a true empirical proposition about usage.[1] The fact that a sentence s expresses a necessary proposition is equivalent to the fact that its empirical verbal correlate s' expresses a truth about usage. What makes the non-verbal sentence 'Even numbers are of the form $2n$' express a necessity is the fact that the sentence ' "Even but not of the form $2n$" has no use' expresses an empirical truth. In other words, it is not a fact about even numbers which makes the sentence 'Even numbers are of the form $2n$' express what is true, but a fact about the usage of words occurring in it. It becomes apparent why Wittgenstein said that an arithmetical proposition asserts nothing about numbers: To understand the sentence expressing it is to know a fact about words, not about anything the words stand for. This is all that knowing necessary facts about numbers comes to; it is not knowing fact about rarefied objects.

With this account of what it is to understand sentences which express necessary propositions, we can now examine the sentences '6 is a number' and 'There are numbers', assuming that they do express necessities. On this assumption their empirical verbal correlates are, respectively, ' "6" is a number-word' and ' "Number" has a use'. Granting that the Platonist's argument establishes the necessity of the propositions expressed by the two non-verbal sentences, then what guarantees that these sentences express necessities are entirely trivial facts about the use of the word '6' and of the word 'number'. It is not surprising that mathematicians have no occasion to prove or use such propositions. But the fact

[1] For the detail of this description of sentences expressing necessary propositions, *see* M. Lazerowitz, *The Structure of Metaphysics*, pp. 265–71.

that they are trivial leaves in question what the dispute between Platonists and non-Platonists is about. The apparent dispute is over whether there are numbers, but it of course cannot be over whether the word 'numbers' and specific number-words have a use. It must be over what both take to be a consequence of 'There are numbers', namely, that there are abstract objects. I think we may assume that the Platonist supposes himself to be asserting the existence of a category of objects, and that 'Numbers are objects' expresses a necessary truth about numbers. The fact that Platonists are not moved from their position by any evidence brought forward by non-Platonists, such as that inspection reveals to them no objects, would indicate that this is the interpretation we must place on this sentence. Further, the Platonist would maintain that 'There are objects' follows from 'There are numbers', and since the latter is necessary the former also must be necessary.

We have now reached the core of the dispute, whether 'Numbers are objects' does or does not express a necessity. And this dispute is usually conceived of, not as being over what this sentence expresses, but as being over whether what it expresses is true, or false. It is accepted that 'Numbers are objects' expresses a view, whose truth is in question; and this is the assumption I wish to challenge. A comparison of 'Numerals are signs' with 'Numbers are objects' will be instructive. That the first expresses a necessity is guaranteed by the convention for the use of the words 'numeral' and 'sign'. But there is no convention for the use of the word 'number' and 'object' which stipulates that 'object' applies to whatever 'number' applies to, or alternatively, that 'number but not an object' expresses an inconsistency. In order for the sentence 'Numbers are objects' to express a necessity, it is required that an empirical fact about usage be expressed by the sentence ' "Object" applies to whatever "number" applies to'. But no such fact of usage exists. This is not to say that there is a *contrary* fact of usage, such as the one which falsifies the claim that 'Numbers are scratches on paper' expresses a necessity. Rather there is no convention at all, despite the Platonist, who seems to deny this by implication. But the consequence of the fact that there is no convention which assures its expressing a necessity and no counter-convention which precludes its doing so is this: that the sentence itself, 'Numbers are objects', does not express either a truth or a falsity.

What I wish to say is that the Platonist who urges that numbers are objects disguises, perhaps to himself as well as others, the nature of his claim. His dispute with the non-platonist is carried on in the language of assertion, i.e. of truth and falsity; it is ostensibly over whether 'Numbers are objects' is *true*. No mention is made of the word 'number' or of any other verbal matter. But if he claims necessary truth for his assertion he commits himself (in the language in which he states himself, here the English language) to the verbal claim that the sentence 'Numbers are objects' expresses a necessity, i.e. that it expresses an entailment between *being a number* and *being an object*. And whether it does so is readily decidable by appeal to established usage, as readily as whether 'Red things are coloured' expresses a necessity. No chain of entailments need be gone through to see whether the end result is necessary. What is required here is quite unlike what would be required to determine whether 'There are no odd perfect numbers' is necessary. It is clear that, usage being what it is, it is false that 'Numbers are objects' expresses a necessity. We might then suppose that the Platonist, who apparently commits himself to this false verbal claim, must be saying something false in holding numbers to be objects. But since he knows usage and would know his assertion to be false, I prefer to take it that he is doing something else in making his assertion and arguing for it. He states, as if it were a fact of logic, that 'There are numbers' implies 'There are objects', and he argues this on the ground that arithmetical statements must be about something. As an alternative to supposing that he thereby commits himself to holding that a convention exists which guarantees the necessity of 'Numbers are objects', I suggest that he is urging, in a concealed way (since he mentions no matter of usage), that a convention be accepted. If accepted it would *create* an entailment where none now exists. And the factual idiom in which he frames his argument is primarily a persuasive device for effecting this. When in recent years Parisian artists disputed over whether grey is a colour one cannot suppose that they did not know the established usage of the word 'grey' to name a colour. One can only construe their arguments as reasons either for retaining established usage or for altering it. In the case of the dispute over whether numbers are objects, the fact that no convention or counter-convention already exists makes it easy to view the dispute as arising from the difficulty of deciding what the essential features of numbers are. But in fact what makes it easy is unfixed usage.

Why the Platonist should wish to settle the essential features of numbers as he does, where 'settling the essential features' is a disguised way of fixing usage, I cannot explain. What is interesting is that his disguise, effected by the non-verbal idiom in which he discourses, results in the illusion that 'Numbers are objects' expresses something true or false, depending on what numbers in fact are. I have already indicated some semantic sources of this illusion, in the question 'What is mathematics *about*?' and in the failure to attend to the verbal correlates of necessary propositions. There are other semantic sources which I should like to mention. One is the preoccupation with the noun use of number-words, e.g. in '6 > 5', 'There is an even prime', 'the series of numbers', etc. As a concomitant of this preoccupation the adjectival use of number-words in such empirical contexts as 'There are three apples on the table' is ignored. Here the numeral '3' is applied to a collection of objects, and can and does apply to many other collections. But unlike the term 'apple', which is a general name, applying to each of a number of things, '3' is a special name for *one* number. '3' is not the general name of a number of things each of which is three; there is but one number three. And what is more natural than to go on from 'There is but one number 3' to 'There is but one object that "3" names', as one can rightly go on from 'There is but one Ghengis Khan' to 'There is but one person whom "Ghengis Khan" names'? The difference is supposedly summed up in the claim that '3' stands for an ideal object. Of this claim Wittgenstein says: '[It] is evidently supposed to assert something about the meaning, and so about the use, of ["3"]. And it means of course that this use is in a certain respect similar to that of a sign that has an object, and that it does not stand for any object. But it is interesting what the expression "ideal object" makes of this fact'.[1] I think we may take it that what this expression does is successfully to conceal a fact of grammar. For 'ideal object' is taken as a description of what there is, as though 'ideal' and 'real' were adjectives functioning like 'red' and 'green' to distinguish amongst objects. 'There is an ideal object which "3"

[1] *Remarks on the Foundations of Mathematics*, p. 136.

stands for' and 'There is no object which "3" stands for', the one in a disguised way and the other openly, express our recognition of the fact that '3' has not the naming function which 'Ghengis Khan' has. But there is a metaphysical world of difference between the two forms of words, if I may be forgiven a small levity. Ideal objects, unlike imaginary objects and unlike no objects at all, require a habitat and enjoy a form of being—albeit less robust than the existence possessed by real objects. The import of the word 'ideal', i.e. *not real*, is forgotten. The picture of an enormous extension created by such phrases as 'the infinity of primes', an extension whose members are named by the numerals as one reaches them by counting, is another result of neglecting, whether intentionally or not, the import of words. Euclid's proof that there is an infinity of primes assures us that the technique of calculating primes 'lacks the institution of an end'.[1] To know that the concluding sentence of the proof expresses a necessity is merely to know that 'greatest prime' has no use in the language of mathematics. There is nothing further to know.

Now if necessary arithmetical propositions are neither about numbers nor about symbols, certain of our original questions disappear, viz. Were the number -2 and the roots $+\sqrt{-1}$ invented when the domain of numbers was extended to negative and complex numbers? Or was the possibility of an extension discovered? How can one invent objects which necessarily exist? Yet if the roots of $x^2 = -1$ exist necessarily, how account for the historical fact that it was a matter of decision whether there are roots? It is obvious that the language of both invention and discovery suggests a common point of agreement, that mathematical propositions are about objects, the disagreement being over whether they are invented or discovered. A similar point of agreement is evident in the dispute between Platonists and conventionalists over whether mathematical propositions are about ideal objects or marks, namely, that they must be about something. Conventionalists are not content with denying that inspection reveals objects corresponding to numerals: on the assumption that necessary propositions must be about something, what is visible to all, the symbols occurring in their expression, is all that remains for them to be about. The semantic sources of the dis-

---

[1] *Remarks on the Foundations of Mathematics,* p. 60.

agreement thus lie in part in their agreement. I have tried to show that neither the agreement nor the disagreement is about the truth-values of putative views. If they were, then there is no explaining why the existence of objects, whether discovered or invented, should be in dispute by people who have every means at their disposal for coming to a decision and nevertheless continue to dispute.

6

ON ENTAILMENT AND LOGICAL
NECESSITY*

Given that a proposition 'p' is necessary, does 'p' entail that 'p'
is necessary? That is, does a necessary proposition, e.g. 'A bachelor
is unmarried', entail its own necessity? A whole cluster of problems, both about necessity and about entailment, attaches to this
question. One such problem, with which I shall have occasion to
deal in this paper, is: Is entailment such that a necessary proposition can be entailed by a contingent one?

It has been maintained that matters of this kind cannot be
settled unless the terms in question, here 'necessary' and 'entails',
figure in some formalized language. R. M. Martin, for example,
has maintained this concerning the term 'analytic in L'[1]: L must
be some formalized language. However, as Benson Mates points
out,[2] we have an explication of 'analytic' in so far as L and the
natural language approximate to each other. Were a *new* symbol
'analytic in L' being defined, no light would be shed on 'analytic'.
If we explicate a familiar concept in the way Carnap requires, viz.
giving the corresponding exact concept by means of 'explicit rules
for its use, for example, by a definition which incorporates it into
a well-constructed system of . . . scientific concepts',[3] we must
recognize one fact: that we rig our definition so as to make it conform to prior notions about the meaning of the term as it is used
in ordinary, or at least non-formalized, language. Recognition of
this fact is implicit in Mates' remarks that 'There is probably a
fair amount of agreement about some of the requirements of an
adequate definition of "analytic". Presumably it should lead to a
usage which would not differ greatly from standard or preferred
usage; in other words, it should not yield paradoxical results.'[4]

---

* Reprinted from *Proceedings of the Aristotelian Society*, Vol. LVI, 1956.
[1] 'On "Analytic" ', *Philosophical Studies*, vol. III, No. 3, pp. 43-4.
[2] 'Analytic Sentences', *Philosophical Review*, vol. 60, p. 533.
[3] *Logical Foundations of Probability*, p. 3 (University of Chicago Press 1950).
[4] *Op. cit.*, p. 529.

There could, of course, be no paradoxical results unless certain features of the non-systemic use of these terms were already fixed. Nor should we know which proffered explications of them were acceptable. Further, uncertainties about these notions is what makes possible continued uncertainties about the formalized language, for example, C. I. Lewis' uncertainty about the truth or falsity[1] in his calculus S_4 of the postulate '$\sim \Diamond \sim p. \prec. \sim \Diamond \sim \Diamond \sim p$'. This uncertainty will, of course, infect the theorems derived by means of it, one of which is '$\sim \Diamond \sim p. \prec .p \prec \sim \Diamond \sim p$', the analogue in S_4 of the principle in question in this paper: 'If "p" is necessary, then "p" entails that "p" is necessary.'

In this paper I shall deal with questions about the terms 'necessity' and 'entailment' which are pre-systemic, questions which if settled would guide the framing of definitions in a formalized language, but which, since unsettled, give rise to the kind of query Lewis makes about a principle in his formalized language. And I shall do what appears to me particularly important here, examine the nature of the questions and of the attempts at settling them. The questions whether a necessary proposition entails its own necessity, and whether it can be entailed by a contingent proposition, appear to call for answers whose correctness is determined by the meanings usage has given to 'entails' and 'necessary'. They appear to be decidable in the way we decide whether 'being a cube' entails 'having twelve edges', i.e. by determining what follows from the meanings of the terms involved. Arguments given for one answer or the other purport to show that the answer arrived at is correct. Yet these arguments, as will appear in what follows, have a curious character of inconclusiveness. This fact suggests that the questions before us may be misleadingly set —that is not a question as to what a necessary proposition *does* entail or whether entailment *is* such that a necessary proposition can be entailed by a contingent one. Instead, it may be that these questions have no decisive answer dictated by the usage of the terms, and that an argument apparently demonstrating a given answer is a reason for creating an answer where none as yet exists —that it shows, not what follows from the meaning of the terms in their ordinary use, but what, in the recast use of the terms, we

---

[1] C. I. Lewis and C. H. Langford, *Symbolic Logic*, p. 502.

should say follows. The argument thus assigns meanings rather than analyses them. This is the general thesis to be maintained in this paper, that the questions raised about necessary propositions involve terms whose use is such as not to permit a decisive answer, and that arguments purporting to establish one answer or the other in fact provide justification for coining usage—for making, in effect, a linguistic innovation. It is difficult to disentangle arguments which delineate the consequences of meanings from those which create them, and arguments seldom have the appearance of doing the latter. I might comment that this kind of situation with regard to the term 'analytic', together with the existence of cases to which usage leaves it undetermined whether the term applies, seems to me responsible for the claim of W. V. Quine[1] and Morton White[2] that no tenable distinction between analytic and factual propositions can be drawn.

I leave these general considerations now to deal with the question, Given that 'p' is necessary, does 'p' entail that 'p' is necessary? I shall present the question as being of the kind suggested by the way in which it is framed, as having a correct answer which argument shows to be correct. In particular, I wish to focus attention on an argument for a negative answer to it, given by Dr C. Lewy in his paper 'Entailment and Necessary Propositions'.[3] Treatment of this question will necessitate considering the additional question whether a necessary proposition can be entailed by a contingent one. I begin with a slightly modified version of the question he posed: Does (B) entail (N)? where (N) and (B) are, respectively:

It is necessary that all brothers are male
All brothers are male.

Lewy considers it undoubted that (N), to the effect that it is necessary that (B), entails (B). The question is whether (B), which we all recognize as necessary, entails its own necessity.

First, how is the question, Does (B) entail (N)?, to be understood? Lewy makes it clear that he is not using 'entail' to mean 'strictly imply', where ' "p" strictly implies "q" ' means 'it is

[1] 'Two Dogmas of Empiricism', *The Philosophical Review*, vol. 60, pp. 20–43.
[2] 'The Analytic and Synthetic: An Untenable Dualism', in *John Dewey: Philosopher of Science and Freedom*, pp. 316–31.
[3] *Philosophical Analysis*, edited by Max Black, pp. 195–211 (Cornell University Press, 1950).

logically impossible that p and not-q'. It will be recalled that Lewis supposed 'that the relation of strict implication expresses precisely that relation which holds when valid deduction is possible',[1] that the system of strict implication explicated those properties of the relation which holds between 'p' and 'q' when 'q' is deducible from 'p'. If the question whether (B) entails (N) were the question whether (B) strictly implies (N), then all that would be required to show that (B) entails (N) would be to show that (N) itself is necessary, i.e. if it is a necessary proposition that it is necessary for all brothers to be male, then any proposition whatever, and therefore, of course (B), will strictly imply it. There are well-known serious objections to Lewis' identification of entailment and strict implication which I need not canvass here. Suffice it to say that if the identification held we should have to say that 'It is necessary that all brothers are male' follows from the contradiction $\sim (B)$, 'There is a brother who is not male'. I might remark in passing that this consideration against identifying entailment and strict implication differs from an argument designed to show, say, that a square and a triangle are not identical. Were we to identify the latter two, a contradiction would be derivable, whereas the identification of strict implication and entailment results in an unwelcome extension of our use of 'entails'. And the point of the argument against it is to show that it has this result.

Now what is involved in our use of 'entails'? This question usually is put in the form, Under what conditions does an entailment hold? To return to our specific example, What are the necessary and sufficient conditions to be satisfied by (N) and (B) if (B) is to entail (N)? First of all, it is necessary, though not sufficient, that (B) strictly implies (N). Inasmuch as Lewy takes the position that 'It is necessary that all brothers are male' is itself necessary, its denial being self-inconsistent, we may take it that he supposes (B) does strictly imply (N) and thereby satisfies one necessary condition for (B)'s entailing (N). Now according to Lewy, two further conditions must be satisfied in order for (B) to entail (N), and these are the conditions distinguishing strict implication between any propositions P and Q from entailment. Lewy's argument is that (B) is not so related to (N) as to satisfy these conditions. For P to entail Q it is necessary '(1) that the

[1] *Op. cit.*, p. 247.

propositional function "*R* counts in favour of *P*" should strictly imply "*R* counts in favour of *Q*", and (2) that the propositional function "*R* counts against *Q*" should strictly imply the propositional function "*R* counts against *P*".[1] These conditions, though necessary for the truth of '*P* entails *Q*', are not sufficient. But they have the merit that any natural interpretation of 'counts in favour of' necessitates our denying an entailment holds between propositions which are materially, i.e. in respect of *content*, irrelevant to each other but which are such that if *Q* is necessary it is strictly implied by *P*, whether *P* be necessary, impossible or contingent. That is, if in order for *P* to entail *Q*, what counts in favour of *P* must count in favour of *Q*, then we have a condition eliminating the possibility of reconstructing the paradoxes of strict implication. For example, granting that 'It is necessary that all brothers are male' is itself necessary, it will be strictly implied by 'Some brothers are not male', 'All daughters are female', and 'There have been ten meetings of the Society'. But any evidence which would count in favour of any of these would certainly not be said to count in favour of 'It is necessary that all brothers are male', for such evidence is either non-existent or entirely irrelevant to it.

This I think sets out the preliminaries to Lewy's argument that 'All brothers are male' does not entail 'It is necessary that all brothers are male'. It is this argument that I want to consider in detail. Lewy describes a state of affairs which he supposes we all should take to 'count in favour of' 'All brothers are male' but which would not count in favour of 'That all brothers are male is necessary'. The state of affairs is as follows: that all siblings are males, i.e. a woman whose first child is female can have no other children, and if her first child is male all subsequent children are male—so that all siblings are male. This hypothetical matter of fact, says Lewy, would count in favour of 'All brothers are male'. For it would be correct to say, 'If all siblings are male, then all brothers are male'. But he thinks it provides no reason for 'The proposition that all brothers are male is necessary'. According to him we should not say, 'If all siblings are male then it follows that it is necessary for all brothers to be male'. The point of the example is that evidence which counts in favour of (*B*) will not count in favour of (*N*), whence (*B*) does not entail (*N*).

[1] *Op. cit.*, pp. 195–96.

What we now must ask is: What does 'counting in favour of' come to? Can one analyze the notion of entailment by reference to it? Evidently it must mean 'being evidence for'. And the curious thing about Lewy's argument is that the evidence adduced in favour of (B) but claimed to be irrelevant to (N) is a plain matter of fact. And unless a sense can be attached to 'evidence for' or 'counting in favour of' such that a matter of fact can properly be called evidence for 'All brothers are male', Lewy's argument will fail. And I think it does fail. We all see that no fact can be evidence for a proposition which is true regardless of fact. Part of what is meant by saying that a proposition is necessary is that matter of fact is no ground for its truth.[1] As Wittgenstein said of tautologies, '[They have] no truth-conditions, for [they are] unconditionally true.'[2] The truth table for '$p \lor \sim p$' tempts one to describe this function as true under all conditions, but one could more properly describe it as showing that its so-called truth-conditions are not conditions at all[3]—that the only reason for holding it to be true under all conditions is the vacuous one that there are none. For '$p \lor \sim p$' is true no matter what. That is to say that the truth or falsity of 'p' is not *evidence for* '$p \lor \sim p$'. We should not argue for the truth of '$p \lor \sim p$' by saying, ' "p" is true, and this justifies concluding that "$p \lor \sim p$" is true', that is, we do not establish the truth of '$p \lor \sim p$' by deducing it from a matter of fact. Considerations of this kind are undoubtedly what made F. P. Ramsey characterize such functions as 'degenerate'.

I think the case is the same with saying 'All siblings are male' counts in favour of 'All brothers are male'. An hypothetical accident of nature is being said to support a necessary truth. No doubt this is said because of the formal analogy which holds between an argument which can be constructed with 'All brothers are male' appearing as the conclusion and what one might call a 'genuine argument'. For example, compare:

---

[1] In an article by A. Pap which has come into my hands since this paper was written this point is used in a criticism of Lewy's argument. See 'Strict Implication, Entailment, and Modal Iteration', *The Philosophical Review*, vol. 64, pp. 606–07.

[2] *Tractatus Logico-Philosophicus*, 4.461 (Routledge & Kegan Paul, 1961).

[3] This point has been argued at length by M. Lazerowitz in 'Tautologies and the Matrix Method', *Mind*, vol. XLVI, No. 182.

All blue-eyed people sunburn	All siblings are male.
All people with fair complexions have blue eyes.	All brothers are siblings.
∴ All people with fair complexions sunburn.	∴ All brothers are male.

But despite being of the same verbal pattern, there is a radical formal difference, namely, that one premiss, 'All brothers are siblings', being necessary, can be dropped from the syllogism, whence the argument reduces to:

All siblings are male
∴ All brothers are male.

Obviously to drop either premiss of the first syllogism would be to invalidate it, whereas the reduced argument about siblings simply appears as an instance of the entailment ' "All siblings are f" entails "All brothers are f".' But now again this instance differs from such an instance as:

All siblings are dishonest
∴ All brothers are dishonest.

For since 'All brothers are male' is a necessary proposition, the empirical premiss 'All siblings are male' plays no role in establishing the conclusion. 'All brothers are male' carries its own justification *a priori*, and is true regardless of what entails it. Obviously 'All brothers are dishonest' has its justification in the premiss which entails it; to use Lewy's language, it is true because there is something which counts in favour of it. But we cannot say 'All brothers are male' is true *because* there is something which counts in favour of it. No fact counts in favour of it since a necessary proposition has no empirical justification. The oddity of saying 'All siblings are male' does count in favour of it shows up clearly if we modify the argument to read:

In Brazil all siblings are male
∴ In Brazil all brothers are male.

Placing a spatial condition on 'All siblings are dishonest' would produce no oddity in the conclusion then inferable: 'In Brazil all brothers are dishonest'. But there is some sort of absurdity in

94

prefacing 'All brothers are male' with 'in Brazil'. The preface suggests a limitation on the generality of what follows it, whereas no limitation is conceivable. And it is merely misleading to say that since it is true in all possible worlds it must be true in Brazil; for to be true for all *possible* worlds is to be necessarily true, true in such a way that no state of affairs would, if it existed, make it false. A proposition which is true in this sense conveys no information about any actual world. Hence, if we wish to say it is true of an actual world we should nevertheless have to say it says nothing about that world. So to speak, it is true of the world only by 'grammatical courtesy'; it is a descriptively empty truth.

Now to speak as if it were not, is to classify (B) 'All brothers are male' with (S) 'All siblings are male'. And as M. Lazerowitz pointed out to me, we also classify them together in speaking as if (B) and (S) could have the same kind of evidence count in their favour. If (S) can count in favour of (B), as for example 'All siblings are dishonest' counts in favour of 'All brothers are dishonest', then (S) and (B) themselves apparently can rest on the same kind of evidence. This is to make a *stretched* use of the word 'evidence'. That it *is* stretched shows up when one considers how a person who has given as a reason for 'All brothers are male' that 'All siblings are male' would react. If he understood us to be passing logically to a necessary proposition when we said '*Therefore, all brothers are male*', he would say that our 'therefore' was a fake, since no empirical reason is relevant. And if he did take this empirical reason as evidence in support of the conclusion it would be doubtful whether he had understood that the sentence, by means of which we expressed the conclusion, actually expressed something necessary.

It is the use of the crucial phrase 'counts in favour of' which stands in need of justification. For only if considerations can be adduced which would persuade one to accept the stretched use Lewy makes of it need one proceed to his conclusion that (B) does not entail (N). In the light of Lewy's comments on strict implication, 'All siblings are male' cannot be said to count in favour of 'All brothers are male' *merely* because it strictly implies it. For then 'The clock stands at ten to three' also would count in favour of it. I think it is clear that 'All siblings are male' would not count in favour of it unless it entailed it. But of course this explanation is not open to Lewy since he is in the process of analyzing '*P* entails *Q*'.

But now it must be admitted that Lewy's argument for saying that 'All brothers are male' does not entail 'It is necessary that all brothers are male' could be strengthened in such a way as to avoid the objection I have presented. Suppose no attempt is made to explain '*P* entails *Q*', and instead, one takes it as an unanalyzed notion occurring in contexts, like syllogistic inference and proofs of mathematical theorems, with which we are all acquainted. One could revise his argument, or state an analogue of it, which might carry conviction where his own has failed. Suppose we agreed that 'All siblings are male' *entails* 'All brothers are male' and that it does *not* entail 'It is necessary that all brothers are male'. On this basis we can construct an argument having the following structure:

$(S) =$ All siblings are male. (S) entails (B).

$(B) =$ All brothers are male.   If (B) entails (N) then (S) entails (N).

$(N) =$ It is necessary that   But (S) does not entail (N). all brothers are male. $\therefore (B)$ does not entail (N).

Now if one is to hold, as I am inclined to, that there is mutual entailment between (B) and (N), and in general, that if '*p*' is necessary then ' "*p*" is necessary' follows from '*p*', this argument must be met. Two alternative means of meeting the argument present themselves, and perhaps neither is satisfactory. Or perhaps it is incorrect to say that (B) entails (N). Either this, or there is no good reason for making it accepted usage to say this. Nevertheless, I should like to present for consideration the following possible means of meeting the argument whose conclusion is that (B) does not entail (N):

(1) that (S) does not entail (B);

(2) that (B) entails (N) quite independently of whether (S) entails (B), but assuming (S) does entail (B), (B) nevertheless entails (N) despite the consequence Lewy rejects, that (S) entails (N).

As for the first alternative, I doubt that this means of meeting the argument would carry any weight with most logicians. I was at first inclined to deny that any necessary proposition is ever entailed by a contingent one, just as I denied, or at any rate refused to assent to saying, that it could have a contingent proposition as supporting evidence. But, as a general claim about the relation of contingent and necessary propositions, this seemingly won't do. For one is brought up short by the logical relation existing between 'p' and '$p \, v \sim p$'. One scarcely wishes to deny that this relation is one of entailment. And yet one is not entirely comfortable in asserting that it is. Some reason for this feeling will be detailed shortly.

Recent literature testifies abundantly to the general uneasiness about entailment and related notions. In a recent paper Quine comments: '. . . there are philosophers who have, through use and custom, grown to feel . . . at home with the notion of entailment which so pervades G. E. Moore's philosophical analyses. There are philosophers of ordinary language who have grown so inured to the philosophical terms "entails" and "inconsistent" as to look upon them, perhaps, as ordinary language. But the reader without such benefits of use and custom is apt to feel . . . [an] insecurity over these notions . . .'[1] I contend that the term 'entails' is familiar enough to count as part of the educated person's ordinary vocabulary, where it means merely the converse of the familiar 'follows from'. The insecurity about it lies instead in the fact that it can occur in an unusual setting, e.g. in ' "p" entails "q" ' where 'p' is contingent and 'q' necessary. How in a given case are we to answer the question, 'Does "p" entail "q"?' If the question is whether two contingent propositions, or two necessary propositions, are connected by entailment, the answer can be arrived at decisively by the usual procedures. Any uncertainty about the answer derives from an uncertainty about what steps to take to settle it. But quite a different uncertainty attaches to the question when 'p' is contingent and 'q' necessary. This question arises in no very natural context (not within mathematics and not in the course of reasoning about matters of fact). For this reason we find ourselves in an uncharted sea. We expect concepts of logic to be so determinate that questions framed in terms of them can always be answered. But this expectation in fact meets with disappointment. And this, I think, is not because we cannot find the answer but

[1] 'Mr Strawson on Logical Theory', *Mind*, Vol. LXVII, no. 248, p. 434.

because we are at liberty to decide the answer. We try to decide on the one involving the least sacrifice. And because the sacrifice would be great were we to place a restriction on entailment so that it could not hold between a contingent proposition and a necessary one (in particular, between 'p' and '$p \ v \sim p$') I should hesitate to meet Lewy's argument by denying that 'All siblings are male' entails 'All brothers are male'. For the relation between these two propositions seems to be the same as that between 'p' and '$p \ v \sim p$', between '$p.q$' and '$p \ v \sim p \ v \ q$', etc.

But I should point out that though we define entailment in such a way that we can say that 'p' entails '$p \ v \sim p$', certain abnormalities emerge in doing so, abnormalities which require that a restriction be placed on the notion 'logically inconsistent with'. Suppose we were to define 'P entails Q' to mean that P is logically inconsistent with the contradictory of Q. Evidently between 'p' and '$\sim(p \ v \sim p)$', and between 'All siblings are male' and 'Some brothers are not male', there is a logical inconsistency. But we need to place a special restriction on 'logically inconsistent with' if we are to avoid the paradoxical consequence of having to say that, e.g. 'The clock stands at ten to three' entails 'All brothers are male' and that 'Some cats are not feline' entails 'Jones is ill'. This restriction is that the logical inconsistency must be due to the *conjunction* of the antecedent and the negation of the consequent, that it does not result merely from a single member of the conjunction. There being no inconsistency between 'The clock stands at ten to three' and the negation of 'All brothers are male', since these propositions are entirely irrelevant to each other, the restriction would preclude a paradoxical entailment. But it still leaves ground for discomfort over admitting an entailment between 'All siblings are male' and 'All brothers are male'; though there is an inconsistency between the first and the negation of the second, this case has in common with the paradoxical case that a logical inconsistency exists even though the contingent proposition is dropped from the conjunction. This abnormality is also present in the entailment of '$p \ v \sim p$' by 'p'. 'p' vanishes into the inconsistency '$\sim(p \ v \sim p)$', and the inconsistency between 'p' and '$\sim(p \ v \sim p)$' merely duplicates the inconsistency already present in '$\sim(p \ v \sim p)$'.

I come now to a further means of meeting the argument against holding that (B) entails (N): this is simply to argue for the entailment quite independently of any relation of the propositions (B) and (N) to (S). (But I shall argue that if it is supposed that (S) entails (B) then (S) equally entails (N), something which Lewy denies as so obviously incorrect that it requires no discussion.) Two considerations that might be adduced against a mutual entailment between (B) and (N), I should like to dispose of at once. The fact that (N), ' "All brothers are male" is necessary', is *about* (B), 'All brothers are male', is not sufficient, as Lewy points out,[1] to show that they do not mutually entail one another, since ' "*p*" is true', though about '*p*', entails and is entailed by '*p*'. Nor can it be argued that (B) and (N) do not mutually entail each other on the ground that (B) is necessary and (N) not. P. F. Strawson has said that ' "*p*" is necessary' is a contingent proposition,[2] but admits in saying this that he is recommending the adoption of a convention so as to avoid the paradoxes of strict implication.[3] It appears to me that if one says that (N) is necessary one is not, even in a concealed way, urging the adoption of a convention, a different one from Strawson's, for the use of the term 'necessary', but rather is saying something in conformity with a convention. It is an accepted criterion for the proper application of 'necessary' to a proposition that the truth of the proposition can be established without appeal to empirical eivdence. (N), as well as (B) ,conforms to this criterion, as Lewy points out.[4] One sees that 'It is necessary that all brothers are male' is true in exactly the same way that one sees the truth of (B), namely, by inspection of the proposition alone, independently of empirical inquiry. In similar manner one sees that 'It is not necessary that all brothers are male' is self-contradictory.

Thus, necessity is, to use Moore's term, an 'internal property', a property which a proposition such as 'All brothers are male' 'cannot fail to have'. Has one, then, in saying (N), said anything over and above what one has said in saying (B)? If (B) is necessary, has one not uttered a redundancy in saying that it is? Since the truth of (B) can be ascertained non-empirically, i.e. by examina-

---

[1] *Op. cit.*, pp. 200–1.
[2] 'Necessary Propositions and Entailment-Statements', *Mind*, vol. LVII, No. 226, p. 184.
[3] *Ibid.*, p. 186.   [4] *Op. cit.*, pp. 198–99.

tion of it and of nothing else, in knowing (*B*)'s truth one knows (*N*), whence the phrase 'the necessary proposition, "All brothers are male" ' means no more than 'the proposition, "All brothers are male".' The former phrase is redundant in the same way 'unmarried bachelor' is redundant. But from this fact it follows that (*B*) entails (*N*).

The same conclusion may be argued as follows: Consider the consequence of denying that (*B*) entails (*N*). '(*B*) does not entail (*N*)' says it is possible both that all brothers are male and that it should not be necessary that they are. That is, it is possible for it to be true that all brothers are male and at the same time possible that some are not male. Now is this a contradiction? If it is, and further, if the contradiction exists *between* the members of the conjunction, then it would seem we must admit that (*B*) entails (*N*). I think such a contradiction does exist. Consider what anyone who utters the sentence 'All brothers are male' understands by it. It is clear that he would not be understanding it if he believed that it did not express a necessary proposition, nor would he be understanding it if he did not know whether it expressed one. Understanding this sentence involves knowing that it expresses a necessary proposition. He will, in other words, know that it is impossible for there to be a brother who is not male. And between this and 'It is possible that some brothers are not male' there is clearly an inconsistency.

It may be objected that only of such simple sentences as 'All brothers are male' can one say that understanding them involves knowing that they express necessary propositions, and that the argument just given holds only for such cases. We should have to say of Fermat's sentence, for example, that we do not understand it since we do not know whether the proposition it expresses is necessarily true or necessarily false. And it is clearly proper English to say that a mathematician who works with it understands it even though he does not know the truth-value of the proposition it expresses. To deal with this objection adequately would require discussion of matters rather far removed from the topic of this paper, but a few comments might be made briefly to indicate how the objection is to be met. First, it is clear that the objection is an exact parallel of a correct objection which could be made to any claim that we do not understand empirical sentences when we do not know the truth-value of the propositions they stand for. Knowing the truth-value of such propositions is not at all requisite for the understanding of the sentences we use to assert them. It is being argued that the case is the same with sentences which express *a priori* propositions, either necessarily true or necessarily false. The objection presupposes that demonstrative proof or disproof, analogously to empirical confirmation or refutation, merely shows which modal value the proposition expressed by the given sentence has, and that our understanding of the sentence is at all times the same.

But does the analogy hold? Can it be said that understanding an *a priori* sentence is the same whether it occurs prior to or subsequent to its appearing as the final sentence in the statement of a demonstration? That we understand Fermat's sentence from the beginning cannot be denied. But it seems to me that understanding it comes to no more than knowing the syntax of the sentence, knowing the constituent words, and having a very rough idea as to which deductive manipulations are relevant. By contrast, understanding Fermat's sentence S at the conclusion of a proof of which S or $\sim S$ is the final statement, consists in apprehending the proposition S expresses: if a necessarily true one, then one which cannot be an impossibility (have the modal value: impossible), and if an impossible one, then one which cannot be a necessity. What the proof of a non-evident *a priori* statement does is to give us this sort of understanding; it leads us to the proposition which S denotes. Understanding a sentence at the end of a proof is thus something different from understanding it in the beginning. In the case of an empirical sentence we understand it both prior to and subsequent to confirmation or refutation. But in the case of an *a priori* sentence which concludes the statement of a demonstration, what the demonstration does is to gain for us something we did not have in the beginning, knowledge of *the* proposition the sentence in question expresses, i.e. a different understanding of the sentence than we had before the proof—when we entertained *no proposition* as the meaning of the sentence. Something like this account was, I think, intended by Wittgenstein when he said the meaning of a mathematical statement is given by its proof. Of course the proposition expressed by an *a priori* sentence can be known in some cases merely by knowing the meanings of the constituent words.

Such is the case with 'All brothers are male'. Here anyone who did not know the proposition it expresses would not be said to understand the sentence in any sense.

To return now to my claim that 'All brothers are male' entails its own necessity. If it is supposed that 'All siblings are male' entails 'All brothers are male', there is, by implication, an inconsistency in denying that 'All siblings are male' entails 'It is necessary that all brothers are male'. For I take it to be a necessary feature of entailment that it is transitive. It would run counter to an actual feature of the use of 'entails' to say that (S) entails (B) and (B) entails (N) but that (S) does not entail (N). That (S) entails (N) is not a consequence about which I feel comfortable; but I prefer accepting it to denying either that (S) entails (B) or that (B) entails (N).

In conclusion I should say something about the conflicting positions set out here concerning the relations of (B), (N) and (S). I have indicated that Lewy's conclusion that (B) does not entail (N) rests on his having made an unorthodox, extended use of 'counts in favour of' which I see no good reason to accept. His argument only appears to prove that (B) does not entail (N); actually it assumes acceptance of a linguistic innovation which has this consequence. As for '(S) entails (N)', the unpalatable consequence of the admission that (S) entails (B), which I am inclined to make, here again there is nothing in the established usage of 'entails' and 'necessary' either to disqualify or to warrant, with certainty, an argument of which '(S) entails (N)' is the result. For there is nothing in established usage to warrant or exclude '(S) entails (B)' on which it rests. '(S) entails (B)' seems more palatable than '(S) entails (N)' because it is terminologically more like the admitted cases of entailment which do not involve a mixture of contingent propositions and explicitly modal propositions. But that an entailment should be said to hold between a contingent proposition and any modal proposition, whether explicitly modal or not, is again better described as something we choose to accept than something which language dictates that we accept. I have called your attention to the sacrifice involved in refusing to accept it, viz. that 'p' could no longer be said to entail '$p \vee \sim p$'. But the abnormalities involved have also been pointed out.

To return to our original problem then, there is warrant in usage for asserting that (*B*) entails (*N*), but any argument for the counter-assertion in which '(*S*) entails (*B*)' figures is to that extent not justified by usage.

7

WITTGENSTEIN ON UNIVERSALS*

'Consider the geography of a country for which we have no map or else a map in tiny bits. The difficulty about this is the difficulty with philosophy: there is no synoptic view. Here the country we talk about is language and the geography grammar. We can walk about the country quite well but when forced to make a map we go wrong.'

In this analogy, which gives the gist of Wittgenstein's introduction in his lectures of Michaelmas term 1933[1] to problems connected with understanding, thinking, meaning, lies the hint of an important and original conception of what the philosopher's task should be. To 'command a clear view of the use of our words' so as to 'see connexions'[2] was the way Wittgenstein expressed this task some years later. But the *point* of such activity in connection with traditional philosophical problems is what differentiates it from the investigation other philosophers have made of language. Bertrand Russell, for example, set himself the problem of determining 'whether anything, and if so, what, can be inferred from the structure of language as to the structure of the world'.[3] And G. E. Moore attempted to show the falsity of views running counter to common sense, e.g. 'Space is unreal', 'Time is unreal', 'Causation is self-contradictory', by 'translating them into the concrete', that is, by considering the views in terms of concrete applications of space-denoting words, time-denoting words, etc. The philosophical investigations of the later Wittgenstein were neither aimed at obtaining information about the world nor at refuting the positions of philosophers who claimed to have succeeded in this. According to him philosophical 'solutions' arise

*Reprinted from *Metaphysics: Readings and Reappraisals*, edited by W. E. Kennick and Morris Lazerowitz, (Prentice Hall, Inc. 1966.)
[1] Preceding the dictation of the *Blue Book* (abbreviation *BB*). My notes.
[2] *Philosophical Investigations*, p. 49. References to this work to be abbreviated as *PI*.
[3] *Inquiry into Meaning and Truth*, p. 429 (London: Allen & Unwin, 1940).

as the result of an initial linguistic muddle: 'A philosophical problem has the form: "I don't know my way about".'[1] We lack the map which clearly sets out the grammar of the language we use, and get into difficulties which are quite unlike ordinary difficulties. We can neglect philosophic difficulties, says Wittgenstein, in a way we can't neglect those of the engineer because philosophers' difficulties, unlike the others, are due to misunderstandings[2]: 'misunderstandings concerning the use of words, caused, among other things, by certain analogies between the forms of expression in different regions of language'.[3] We can become obsessed by a certain language form, and if we can remove the obsession we can dissolve the difficulty—make it disappear as would an illness with proper treatment.[4] The task then is to recognize the linguistic obsessions, for like other obsessions they are not recognized as such. Philosophical questions sound as if they were questions about fact of which we do not yet know enough, rather than questions about language, and accordingly are approached as one would a scientific problem.[5]

Now in virtue of Wittgenstein's conception of philosophical puzzles as arising from the philosopher's use of language, it is to be expected that the word 'meaning' would play a prominent rôle in his investigations. It is not, he insists,[6] that it is of more importance to talk about meaning than to talk of chairs or time—there are many problems in philosophy not concerned with the meaning of 'meaning'. But a cluster of inherited problems are associated with the term 'meaning', several of central importance in the history of philosophy. Here I wish to present Wittgenstein's treatment of the metaphysical position that there are universals— abstract objects which are the meanings of general words. Parmenides said that one cannot think of what is not, that thought must have an object. The Platonist counter to this claim is that thinking must indeed be about something but that what does not exist can be thought of *via* a universal: to think that something of a given kind, ϕ, does not exist is to believe with regard to an

---

[1] *PI*, p. 49.
[2] Discussion in the intervals between dictation of the *Blue Book*, 1933–34. Notes taken by Margaret Masterman and Alice Ambrose. Hereafter to be referred to as the *Yellow Book*. Abbreviation, *YB*.
[3] *PI*, p. 43.
[4] *Ibid.*, p. 91.
[5] Lectures, 1934–34. My notes.
[6] *Ibid.*, 1932–33. My notes.

ESSAYS IN ANALYSIS

apprehended object, ϕ-ness, that it has no instances. Similarly, to think of what does exist is to think of a thing or things which exemplify what is common to everything called by the same name. 'Wherever a number of individuals have a common name,' says Plato, 'we assume them to have also a corresponding idea or form....'[1] '... the things to which the term "many" is applied ... may be brought under a single idea, which is called the essence of each. ... The many, as we say, are seen but not known, and the ideas are known but not seen.'[2] 'These, unlike objects of sense, have no separate organ, but ... the mind, by a power of her own, contemplates the univerals in all things.'[3] The picture created by these excerpts of what understanding a general word consists in is that of a refined object being apprehended by an inner vision. This object is the word's meaning, something in virtue of which the word is applied to a number of things. Hearing or uttering a general word has as its accompaniment a mental process of laying hold of the element common to things the word designates. This common element, like an essential ingredient, makes them what they are. '... nothing makes a thing beautiful but the presence and participation of beauty . . . by beauty all beautiful things become beautiful.'[4] *What* it is could theoretically be specified by a complete analysis, for its boundaries are exact. Any uncertainty over whether a thing possesses a property ϕ is due to our imperfect grasp of the perfectly definite essence, for a thing must have either ϕ or non- ϕ.

This, now, is the view from whose spell Wittgenstein sets out to free us, an enchantment 'which forms of expression exert upon us'.[5] For the germ of the verbal malady finding expression in every philosophical view lies in the language of everyday use.[6] Not that our language is not perfectly adequate to its job. No reform of language on the part of a philosopher is necessary.[7] In fact, says Wittgenstein, we are going to find out that everything is all right except what the philosophers say. What the bedmaker says is all

[1] *Republic*, Book X, sec. 596. Jowett translation.
[2] *Ibid.*, Book VI, sec. 507.   [3] *Theaetetus*, sec. 185.
[4] *Phaedo*, sec. 100.
[5] *Blue Book*, p. 27. Abbreviation, *BB* (Oxford: Basil Blackwell, 1958)
[6] Note also G. E. Moore's complaint that 'language should have grown up just as if it were expressly designed to mislead philosophers'. *Philosophical Studies*, p. 217.   [7] *PI*, p. 51; BB, p. 28.

right, but what they say is all wrong.[1] This is because in doing philosophy they are inclined to view our language as much simpler than it is.[2] (Cf. St Augustine's description of learning Latin by learning the names of things.) Similar structures in language—verbally analogous forms—can mislead, for example, the noun form of 'understanding' and 'walking', and of 'the meaning of a word' and 'the man sitting next me'. 'The cases in which particularly we wish to say that someone is misled by a form of expression', says Wittgenstein, 'are those in which we would say: "he wouldn't talk as he does if he were aware of the difference in the grammar of such-and-such words".'[3] Several misinterpretations of what Wittgenstein does when he takes up the Platonic view, or, for that matter, any philosophical position, should be noted at once, in advance of fuller discussion. These misinterpretations are understandable, for there is no doubt that his language often encourages them. One misinterpretation is to suppose he is holding that we are misled by a form of expression into pronouncing a *false* view. Another is to think that because his investigations often are empirical, they are directed to *denying* what some philosophers assert to be true.

I turn now to an account of his procedure in dealing with various of the claims comprised in the Platonic view on universals, presenting first the kinds of investigations he engages in and then the interpretation, consonant with his own statements, which is properly to be placed on them. The following, all of which look to be empirical directives, are some of the lines he invited his pupils to pursue: (1) Look at what understanding a general word comes to, (2) Try thinking of the meaning of a word without thinking of the word, (3) Look and see whether you find something common to all the things having a common name, (4) Look at how 'understanding' is used, at how 'meaning' is used.

(1) Is understanding a word or sentence a mental accompaniment of a sign, and is the difference between understanding and not understanding an expression constituted by the presence in the one case and the absence in the other of meanings in addition to the verbal expressions? Wittgenstein's answer is No. 'When I

---

[1] *YB.*   [2] Lectures, 1933–34.
[3] *BB*, p. 28.

think in language, there aren't "meanings" going through my mind in addition to the verbal expressions.'[1] Nor does one always discover a mental event or process happening concomitantly with a heard or spoken word which is understood. If the two were concomitants then presumably the one could be found in divorce from the other like the melody and words of a song. Yet thinking 'seems to be an accompaniment of speech. A process, which may accompany something else, or can go on by itself'.[1]

To see that thinking the meanings is not an activity independent of or in addition to the activity of using an expression, nor the meanings independent of symbols, Wittgenstein suggests (2) our 'mak[ing] the following experiment: Say and mean a sentence, e.g.: "It will probably rain tomorrow". Now think the same thought again, mean what you just meant, but without saying anything . . . '[2] One can of course speak without thinking.

'Speaking a sentence without thinking consists in switching on speech and switching off certain accompaniments of speech. Now ask yourself: Does thinking the sentence without speaking it consist of turning over the switch (switching on what we previously switched off and vice versa); that is, does thinking the sentence without speaking it now simply consist in keeping on what accompanied the words but leaving out the words? Try to think the thought of a sentence without the sentence and see whether this is what happens.'[3]

It certainly seems to be correct to describe the proposed investigation here as an experiment conducted for the purpose of justifying an empirical statement about understanding. It looks as though a point of psychology has been raised, to be settled by introspection, and that Wittgenstein has simply denied a factual claim about 'the eye of the mind' and its objects. It is important therefore to take note of Wittgenstein's remark in this connection: 'This, of course, doesn't mean that we have shown that peculiar acts of consciousness do not accompany the expression of our thoughts! Only we no longer say that they *must* accompany them.'[4] There may be nothing at all going on in the mind; '. . . the

[1] *PI*, p. 107. [2] *BB*, p. 42.
[3] *BB*, p. 43. [4] *BB*, p. 42.

experience of thinking *may* just be the experience of saying'.[1]
What I shall try to make clear is the philosophical point of citing
facts which will remove the temptation to say that understanding
a word, or having a general idea, *must* be a mental event. A hint is
given by Wittgenstein in the following comments:[2]

'. . . philosophy arises out of prejudices—prejudices in favour of
one form of description. Every philosophical problem contains one
particular word or its equivalent, the word "must" or "cannot".
When you ask yourself what happens in your mind when you hear
or use a sentence in which the word "plant" occurs, you immediately tend to say that there must be an image before your mind,
either an image of a particular plant or if not this, then a Galtonian
composite photograph. But on examination you find there is often
no image. When you discover this you tend to say that you must
have something like it: "If it is not an image it must be something
more subtle." There must be some idea, else what do we mean
when we say a man understands the word "plant"? Understanding
must be some process in his mind. This "must" is a sign of a
philosophical problem.'

(3) Parallel comments apply to his injunction to look and see
whether there is anything common to all the things having a
common name. To revert to our consideration of understanding a
word, it comes natural to suppose that the phrase 'having a general
idea' stands for one kind of phenomenon (else why use the same
phrase for each of the cases we call 'having a general idea'?), and
that *what* is grasped in the act of having a general idea is the element common to all entities subsumed under it. Socrates' search
for the definition of virtue, knowledge, etc. was avowedly a search
for such a common element, an essence. Wittgenstein comments
that 'the idea of a general concept being a common property of its
particular instances . . . is comparable to the idea that *properties*
are *ingredients* of the things which have the properties, e.g. that
beauty is an ingredient of all beautiful things as alcohol is of beer
and wine.'[2] People who try to find something common to all
applications of the word 'good' maintain: 'There is one word,
therefore there must be one thing'.[3]

The kind of fact Wittgenstein wants to point out in this connec-

[1] *BB*, p. 43.   [2] Lectures, 1934–35.   [3] *BB*, p. 17.

tion he illustrates in several places[1] by using the example of games: 'We are inclined to think there must be something in common to all games, say, and that this common property is the justification for applying the general term "game" to the various games; whereas games form a *family* the members of which have family likenesses',[1] for example, build, gait, temperament, mannerisms. Instead of one common feature, one finds overlapping similarities. These form a series in which adjacent members resemble each other and things at later points in the series may have no similarity to those at earlier points. Socrates fails in his search for what is common to all instances of knowledge because there is no one property possessed by *every* thing to which the term 'knowledge' applies. We use the term 'knowledge' in all sorts of ways.[2]

It might be supposed that Wittgenstein was simply denying the truth of the Platonic claim that there is something common to all things having a common name. My exposition thus far leaves it open whether he intended to conclude with a counter *position* such as Locke intended by his challenge: 'For I demand, what are the alterations [which] may or may not be in a horse or lead, without making either of them to be of another species? . . . [we] will never be able to know when anything precisely ceases to be of the species of a horse or lead.'[3] Locke, like Wittgenstein, is saying that were there a common property ϕ which if lacking to a thing made it cease to be what it is, it would be possible to know, as it gradually transformed into something else, *exactly* the point where this happened. But we know that when a change proceeds by imperceptible gradations, this is not possible. The difference between Wittgenstein and Locke is in the *point* of calling attention to such a fact. Actually it is a way, on Wittgenstein's part, of calling attention to our use of language. He explicitly denies that he is attempting to ascertain what the facts are that are described by language. '. . . our considerations could not be scientific ones . . . Philosophical problems . . . are, of course, not empirical problems; they are solved, rather, by looking into the workings of our language. . . .'[4] 'The work of the philosopher,' he says, 'consists in

---

[1] *BB*, p. 17; *PI*, pp. 31–32.   [2] Lectures, 1934–35.
[3] *Essay Concerning Human Understanding*, Bk. III, Ch. iii, sec. 13.
[4] *PI*, p. 47.

assembling reminders for a particular purpose.'[1] The question is, reminders of what? and for what purpose?

The answer, as it bears on the questions, expressed in the factual idiom, 'What is the meaning of a word?', 'Is understanding a general word the mental activity of apprehending an abstract object?', exhibits what his conception of a philosophical problem and its solution is, and the therapy by which the *dis*solution of a problem may be effected. This brings us to his injunction (4), Look at how 'understanding' and 'meaning' are used in the language. The question this injunction naturally raises is whether Wittgenstein is not, after all, proposing an investigation of matter of fact—of linguistic fact as against the non-linguistic facts philosophers believe themselves to be dealing with. Linguists and grammarians have this kind of interest. What is the difference between Wittgenstein's and the linguist's study of grammar? Wittgenstein denies that he is interested in the natural history of human beings.[2] He is no more interested in recording linguistic conventions than in investigating psychology[3]—he neither wishes to give a definition of the word 'understanding' nor a psychological description of what usually goes on in understanding. What then is his concern with the 'grammar' of a word? If he states what is correctly substitutable for a word,[2] does this not duplicate the work of the lexicographer? Wittgenstein admits that what he as a philosopher does under the heading of 'grammar' often departs from what is generally called 'grammar'.[4] For example, ordinary grammar does not preclude substantives which in their occurrence in sentences appear to have a use to denote objects when in fact they do not: the word 'sake' is such a spurious substantive. Nor does ordinary grammar tell us that the use of 'time' in 'Time flows' cannot be explained by ostensive definition (in the usual sense of pointing to a *thing*) as can the use of 'water' in 'water flows'.[5] It is part of the 'grammar' of 'time', 'or', 'perhaps', 'one' that they do not have a definition of this kind. Now such facts we all know as well as he. I cannot teach you any new fact, he says, but I can help you to recognize certain facts which otherwise you would not recognize.[6] Sometimes I have to describe the actual use of a word

[1] *PI*, p. 50.
[2] Lectures, 1934–35.
[3] *Ibid.*, 1933–34.
[4] *Ibid.*, 1932–33.
[5] *Ibid.*, 1932–33.
[6] *YB*.

if you have forgotten it,[1] and sometimes to construct new uses of a word which differ from any actual use. And what is the point of this? The answer distinguishes Wittgenstein's and the linguist's interests, and more important, makes clear a new conception of what traditional philosophical problems and solutions are, and the means Wittgenstein conceives as the only one relevant to dealing with them.

Wittgenstein states he is interested in language only insofar as it produces certain puzzles we want to get rid of. He only describes the actual use of a word in order to remove certain troubles.[1] The questions to which Platonic, and other, answers have been given, 'What is the meaning of a word?', 'What is understanding a word?', seem merely to be transferred to a verbal plane when one puts them in the form 'What is the meaning of "meaning"?', 'What does "understanding" mean?' However significant this step may appear, it seems quite another matter to adopt the procedure Wittgenstein recommends, of replacing 'meaning of a word' by 'use of a word', and correspondingly, 'understanding a word' by 'knowing the use of (being able to use) a word'. He seems to move even farther from the question when instead of examining 'meaning of a word' he examines 'explanation of the meaning of a word'. In the *Blue Book*,[2] he argues the relevance of the latter procedure as follows: Suppose you were asked to explain what 'length' means, or to explain 'to know'. It helps us in answering these questions to consider what we call 'measuring a length' and what we call 'getting to know'. Similarly with the phrase 'explanation of meaning': 'For, surely, to understand the meaning of "meaning" you ought also to understand the meaning of "explanation of meaning". Roughly, "Let's ask what the explanation of meaning is, for whatever that explains will be the meaning".'[3] These questions concern the 'grammar' of the words 'length', 'to know', 'meaning'. The phrases in which they occur provide the contexts in which it makes sense to use these words; the fact that 'to explain a length' and 'to explain a meaning' are not parallel usages and that 'to measure a meaning' has no use at all shows up the differences between 'length' and 'meaning'.

Wittgenstein says: All I can give you is a method; I cannot teach

[1] Lectures, 1934–35. [2] Pp. 1, 24.
[3] *BB*, p. 1.

you any new truths.[1] The method is, in part, a therapy for curing one of the fascination of certain linguistic moulds in which one's thinking is habitually channelized. The virtue of replacing 'meaning of a word' and 'understanding a word' by 'use of a word' and 'being able to use a word' is that the latter do not suggest pictures which block our seeing the use of these expressions in their 'original home',[2] i.e. in a non-philosophical setting. When the philosopher says, 'Understanding a general word, like having a pain, is a private inner process', 'Thought must have an object, as surely as must the senses', he has succumbed to the enchantment of a spurious picture. And although he does not express his position as an account of a word ('understanding', 'meaning'), he has fixed his own boundary around its use and supposes himself to have delineated the essence of what the word applies to. This implies a certain blindness to other criteria for the use of a word. Wittgenstein reminds him of these criteria, so as to destroy the pre-eminence of the preferred criterion. Of understanding he says[3]:

'The characteristics of words like "understanding" is that they are used alternately for (a) something happening in a person's mind as a conscious event and (b) a disposition. Actually, very often words in sentences are accompanied by something or other, images and whatnot. (It is this which gives rise to the notion of a general idea.) When you say "I said so-and-so while thinking of something else", we take it that two activities are going on at the same time, saying and thinking. But does it follow that understanding, thinking, etc. are activities accompanying speaking? Is there something in our minds like a set of bells, so that when a word is heard one chimes, and when a sentence is heard several chime one after the other? (Cf. William James, who took understanding to consist in impressions made by every word.) Now it may be the case that whenever anyone hears a word a peculiar mental event occurs. I do not wish to deny this. Perhaps when a word is heard something like a bell sounds. But is this what we mean by "understanding a word"?'[4]

The fact that we use the phrase 'understands a word' in cases

[1] Lectures, 1934–35. [2] *PI*, p. 48. [3] Lectures, 1934–35 (Oxford: Basil Blackwell, 1958). [4] See also *PI*, p. 107, and the *Brown Book*, p. 157.

where no one kind of mental event occurs and even when none at all occurs shows that the presence of a mental event cannot be the criterion for its use. (This is the linguistic point of what looked to be a psychological investigation of what goes on in our minds when we are said to understand an expression.) Yet the model for describing the use of 'understanding a word' which attracts philosophers is 'experiencing a mental image'. Understanding and imagining are assimilated to each other by treating each as having a content, the one a meaning and the other an image, both being determinants under the determinable 'mental'. But 'meaning' and 'image' are not related as 'red' and 'blue'.[1] One can have a parade of images, but in making the ordinary use of words one does not have a parade of their meanings.[1] Of course it cannot be doubted that there *is* a similarity between the expressions 'grasping a meaning' and 'having an image'. Their similarity, however, is only skin-deep, no deeper than school grammar. But like beauty it is capable of casting a spell over our minds. Preoccupation with the similarity prevents one's recognizing that an important criterion for anyone's understanding a word is his being able to use it. We do use 'understanding a word' for this disposition; whether or not a conscious inner process takes place, 'understanding a word' will not be correctly applied if the ability to use the word is lacking. And the ability to use the word is the only test for determining that its meaning has been grasped. This is what justifies Wittgenstein's replacing the verbal noun 'understanding' by 'being able to use'. Further, the replacement has the advantage that 'being able to use' does not stand for an activity. It makes us aware of the difference between the functioning of the word 'understanding' and that of 'walking' and 'having an image'. 'The scrutiny of the grammar of a word weakens the position of certain fixed standards of our expression which . . . prevent us from seeing the facts with unbiassed eyes. Our investigation trie[s] to remove the bias, which forces us to think that the facts *must* conform to certain pictures embedded in our language.'[2]

The Platonic picture of the mind's grasp of general notions as a vision of 'the colourless, formless, intangible essence'[3] incorporates two pictures which arise from our obsessions with one

---

[1] *PI*, p. 176.   [2] *BB*, p. 43.
[3] *Phaedrus*, sec. 247.

linguistic model. One is to take 'understanding' as the name of an activity ('the mind, by a power of her own, contemplates the universals in all things'), the other is to take 'meaning of a word' as the name of an object. I have already indicated how Wittgenstein loosens the hold of the first obsession. I now turn to the other. That 'meaning of a word' is a noun form is already a potential trap. Consider any general word: '. . . you think of [its] meaning as a thing of the same kind as the word, though also different from the word. Here the word, there the meaning.'[1] If a philosopher asks 'What is meaning?', we feel we ought to be able to point to something. 'We are up against one of the great sources of philosophical bewilderment: we try to find a substance for a substantive.'[2] Now it is quite true that many substantives do have a naming function, e.g. proper names, like 'John', names of specific colours, like 'cerise', general names, like 'chair' (though amongst these there are important differences). But not all words stand for things that can be pointed to, any more than what money buys can always be pointed to, e.g. permission to sit in a theatre, a title, one's life.[3] This is to say that it is part of their grammar that they cannot be explained by pointing to something. 'Meaning' is such a word. Yet there is a great propensity upon hearing the substantive 'meaning' to think of it as naming an ethereal entity. We speak of meanings as abstract objects, in contrast to the concrete things of sense, and the difference is treated as analogous to that between the solid and the gaseous, rather than between a chair and the permission to sit in a chair.[3]

The temptation to do this is especially evident in connection with number words. 'What is the number 3?' prompts us to look for an object which it names, for since '3' is not the general name of a number of things each of which is three, nothing seems more natural than to take it to be the special name of a single object. Arithmetic becomes 'the natural history of the domain of numbers'.[4] Disputes then arise as to what kind of objects numbers are. Numerals are one candidate, but since, for one thing, the infinity of numbers and the finitude of the set of actual numerals precludes their identification, the argument is that inasmuch as there *must* be something numerals stand for, the objects denoted are ideal.

[1] *PI*, p. 49.   [2] *BB*, p. 1.   [3] Lectures, 1932-33.
[4] *Remarks on the Foundations of Mathematics*, p. 117. Abbreviation, *RFM*.

Wittgenstein says: ' "The symbol '*a*' stands for an ideal object"
is evidently supposed to assert something about the meaning, and
so about the use, of "*a*". And it means of course that this use is
in a certain respect similar to that of a sign that has an object, and
that it does not stand for any object. But it is interesting what the
expression "ideal object" makes of this fact.'¹ What the expression
does is to suggest that 'ideal' and 'real' are adjectives functioning
like 'red' and 'blue' to distinguish amongst objects. It is a step in
the right direction to note that no object corresponds to 'the
number 3' in the sense that there is one corresponding to 'Smith',
but it is not enough.

'There are several traps we constantly fall into, because we are
inclined to look at language as something much simpler than it is.
(1) One primitive feature is that we look for an object when we see
a sign of the language. (2) We think of anything we mention as
falling under one genus only. (3) We compare the qualities of a
thing with the ingredients of a mixture. . . . This is difficult to
avoid because it is embodied in our language. The genus, as being
something in common, is treated as if this common element were
an ingredient. . . . There is a great difficulty in philosophy because
all words look so much alike. The dictionary, in which they are
united, is like a box of tools which do look alike but which have
enormously different uses.² The use of words differs in the way
beauty differs from a chair. They are entirely incomparable. . . .
When we talk of words and their meanings we tend to compare
these with money and the things bought rather than with money
and its use.'³

There is a certain spell exercised by the phrase 'meaning of a
word', which results in such notions as that there must be a single,
perfectly definite property meant by each noun and adjective, that
this object is the meaning of the word, and is named by it analogously to the way an individual is named by a proper name. To
break this spell Wittgenstein urges speaking, not of the meaning of
words, but of the use of words. For in ordinary, non-philosophical
contexts, 'meaning of a word' can be replaced without loss by 'use
of a word', e.g. in 'knowing the meaning of a word', 'explaining
the meaning', etc. One advantage of this replacement is that 'use'
carries with it no suggestion of an object corresponding to a word.

¹ *RFM*, p. 136.   ² See also *PI*, p. 6.   ³ Lectures, 1933–34.

Wittgenstein's analogy of language with a box of tools aptly illustrates the point of the replacement: one is not tempted to speak of the use, say, of a hammer, as something independent of a tool and as itself an object. How misleading it is to construe every noun as standing for an object shows up if we contrast 'meaning of a word' with cases where no one could contest that it is proper to say a noun has an object corresponding to it: when we can give an ostensive definition, i.e. point to an object in order to explain a word's meaning. It is never the case that we explain or give a word's meaning by pointing to a meaning. Explaining its meaning consists in explaining its use, and though in some cases this may be done by pointing to things the word applies to, if the meaning were merely a different kind of object than its denotata it should make sense to ask that it too be pointed out. The retort that, being abstract, it cannot be pointed out but can only be seen by the eye of the mind simply sidesteps the question why the meaning of a word can be given by describing its use, in some cases without ostensive definition and in all cases without providing a procedure for becoming acquainted with a universal. If it is maintained that both ostensive and verbal definition *are* such procedures, we have reached the kind of stalemate characteristic in philosophy where a matter under dispute is 'treated perfectly hopelessly, as if it were a scientific problem about which we had to find out something new'.[1] It is one of Wittgenstein's most original insights that an examination of the *philosopher's* use of language, in relation to the uses in non-philosophical contexts of the words figuring in a problem, will show what a philosophical position is.

It is obvious that Wittgenstein has a reason for urging our attending to the uses of words, and a reason for equating 'for a *large* class of cases'[2] 'meaning of a word' and 'use of a word'.[3] I shall try now to show the bearing of his procedure on the dissolution of the position that a shadow world of universals stands between names and the things named. For some connection needs to be made between a view not explicitly about any verbal matter and the thesis that it is the result of a linguistic muddle. As a first step, we should discover the linguistic point of certain investigations Wittgenstein engages in which seem not to be linguistic. Although he recognizes that the phrases 'meaning of a word' and

[1] Lectures, 1934-35.   [2] *PI*, p. 20.   [3] See also *RFM*, p. 40.

'use of a word' are not precisely intersubstitutable,[1] the fact that he nevertheless treats them as such has a direct bearing on what he has to say about the meaning of the word 'meaning', namely, that it is not related to 'meaning' as an object to its name. We can understand his directive to try thinking of the meaning of a word without thinking of the word as a graphic way of inviting us to look at the use of the substantive 'meaning'. For the result of the 'experiment' is to find that this substantive is without a substance, that it does not have a naming function. In our language, some words are *general* names of objects, such as 'chair', 'man', 'planet', and some are *special* names (i.e. proper names) of objects, such as 'John', 'Saturn'. 'Meaning' is neither a general name like 'chair' nor a proper name like 'John'. It does not have a name use, although its use in sentences is name-like.

When in philosophy we ask such questions as 'What is time?', 'What is number?', 'What is beauty?', evidently what we want is an analysis of the meanings of the words 'time', 'number', 'beauty'. It is taken for granted that there is *a* meaning which an analysis will explicate, that there are features which must be had in common by things covered by the term, and that a complete analysis will attain a completely exact delineation of essence. Wittgenstein's challenge, 'Look and see whether you find anything common to the things having a common name', and his assertion that there need not be anything common to all things for which a word is used, but only a number of overlapping resemblances, do not on the surface place him in a different light from other philosophers, say the nominalists. But if we heed his injunction to look at the use of words the linguistic point of his assertion becomes clear: that general words may have a number of related uses which gradually merge into one another, so that it is a mistake to try to find a boundary to the use when none has been drawn in our language. When he says there is no one thing common to all things said to be good, no single strand running the length of the rope, he is making the linguistic point that 'good' is used in a variety of related ways. The Platonist says there *must* be something common to things called by a common name, and he tries to state the boundaries of the concept by an exact definition. But 'Can you

[1] When one understands a word 'in a flash' the whole use does not come before one's mind. (*PI*, pp. 54, 80).

give a boundary? No. You can *draw* one; for none has so far been drawn.'[1] '. . . the boundary will never entirely coincide with the actual usage, as this usage has no sharp boundary.'[2] Inexactness is commonly taken as a defect, either in our grasp of a perfectly definite concept, or in our language: 'Frege compares a concept to an area and says that an area with vague boundaries cannot be called an area at all.'[3] But this is 'like saying that the light of my reading lamp is no real light at all because it has no sharp boundary'.[4] The fact that a word has a family of uses does not trouble us when we use it, for example, when we use 'beautiful' to describe things so different as a face, a sonata, and a mathematical proof. When we need a more restricted use we redefine (cf. the physicist's redefinition of 'work').

The philosopher who is puzzled about the nature of goodness and seeks for its essence is asking that a boundary be drawn. What he puts forward as a theory shows the boundary which he wishes to draw. But it is not apparent that 'an assertion which the metaphysician makes expresses discontentment with our grammar . . . he is not aware that he is objecting to a convention'.[5] When a philosopher says 'Thought must have an object' he has already made his boundary-decision, but it looks to be a decision about fact rather than about language. In the 'disputes between Idealists, Solipsists and Realists . . . the one party attack the normal form of expression as if they were attacking a statement; the others defend it, as if they were stating facts recognized by every reasonable human being'.[6] Suppose one said, 'Everyone is really going to Paris; true, some don't get there, but all their movements are preliminary'.[7] The form of idiom here is factual; but the use of the statement is to exclude from language, from descriptive use, 'He is going no farther than the market'. (Like 'All lines in a plane meet, parallel lines as well, but they meet at infinity'.) The words 'really', 'must', 'cannot' are the signals that a philosopher 'wish[es] for a notation which stresses a difference more strongly, makes it more obvious, than ordinary language does, or one which . . . uses more closely similar forms of expression than our ordinary language'.[8] By means of these words he expresses his refusal to depart from a notation to which he is attracted, or his decision to

[1] *PI*, p. 33.   [2] *BB*, p. 19.   [3] *PI*, p. 34.   [4] *BB*, p. 27.
[5] *BB*, p. 57.   [6] *PI*, p. 122.   [7] Lectures, 1932–33.   [8] *BB*, p. 59.

reject another which repels him. But he appears not to be doing this at all. Nor is it what he supposes himself to be doing. He has the illusion pervasive throughout philosophy, that a philosophical problem concerns a fact of the world instead of a matter of expression.[1]

The object of my bringing out the linguistic point of trying to think a meaning without thinking of a symbol and of looking to see whether anything common is to be found among things having the same name, is to destroy a wrong notion of what Wittgenstein is doing. This is the notion, which has considerable currency, that he is simply denying the truth of the assertions 'Understanding a word is a mental accompaniment of the word', 'Meanings are definitely circumscribed objects'. Wittgenstein's own words make clear what his intentions are: 'What we deny is that the picture of an inner process gives us the correct idea of the use of the word. . . . We say that this picture with its ramifications stands in the way of our seeing the use of the word as it is. . . . Why should I deny that there is a mental process? . . . If I do speak of a fiction, then it is of a *grammatical* fiction.'[2] Wittgenstein is not concerned to question matter of fact and is not to be construed as contesting the claimed truth-value of any philosophical position, although he can be interpreted as concerned to remove the temptation to adopt one and defend it. Whenever we encounter a view in philosophy 'the thing to do . . . is always to look how the words in question *are actually used in the* language'.[3] For this will weaken the obsessive hold of certain language forms, usually extremely simple forms taken as models in accordance with which everything is construed.[4] Another means to this end is the invention of artificially simple languages—'language-games'—set up as 'objects of comparison'[5] with our ordinary language whose words have a greater variety of uses. In these we may see the models to which we assimilate ordinary language, for the grammatical obsessions consist just in taking our language to be simpler than it is.

Although Wittgenstein did not explicitly develop the bearing of these general comments on the Platonic theory of universals, I shall try now to indicate briefly their application in a way consonant with what he has said on the subject. What specifically is

[1] YB.   [2] PI, pp. 102-3.   [3] BB, p. 56.
[4] Lectures, 1934-35.   [5] PI, p. 50.

the picture of language 'which [holds] us captive'[1] when we picture thought as directed to the 'invisible, intangible essences'? It is the picture of a very simple language in which all words are names—labels for things. 'Meaning', 'chair, and' 'John' have a superficial grammatical similarity: all are substantives. The philosopher who is impressed by their common grammatical form may be tempted to ignore their extraordinarily different uses and redraw the boundaries of the word 'meaning' so as to stress the similarity. To treat it as a name is to recategorize it under a stretched use of 'name'. The appeal of viewing every general word as a proper name is the Platonic 'grammatical obsession'. Ordinary language encourages it, for 'the clothing of our language makes everything alike'[2]. But the Platonist who asserts that there must be common properties of things to account for the application of a single name does not recognize the presence of an obsession:

'The philosopher is the man who has to cure himself of many sicknesses of the understanding before he can arrive at the notions of the sound human understanding.'[3]

---

[1] *PI*, p. 48.   [2] *Ibid.*, p. 224.   [3] *RFM*, p. 157.

8

UNKNOWABLES AND LOGICAL ATOMISM

I begin with a quotation from *The Problems of Philosophy*: '. . . If we take any common object of the sort that is supposed to be known by the senses, what the senses immediately tell us is not the truth about the object as it is apart from us, but only the truth about . . .' how it appears. 'What we directly see and feel is merely "appearance" which we believe to be a sign of some "reality" behind. But . . . have we any means of knowing whether there is any reality at all? And if so, have we any means of finding out what it is like?'[1] These questions, raised by Russell and in effect by Descartes much earlier, set the problems to which logical atomism, the doctrine to be discussed here, was proposed by Russell as a solution. The questions themselves only arise when one reflects on the changing appearances any object can present from different points of view and the similarity of recurring appearances at different times. The one consideration raises the question as to what the real nature of the object is, the other the question as to what accounts for the observed similarity. It is natural to suppose that when we perceive a table, something unlike any of its various appearances is, together with our sense-organs, the cause of our sensations, and that the table continues to exist when it is not being perceived and is the cause of the similarity among the appearances from time to time. Now clearly the cause of our sensations is not given with the effects. Both the existence and nature of this cause are, to quote Russell, 'an inference from what is immediately known'.[2] Further, it is an inference which cannot be checked independently of observation, nor can it be checked by observation. For what fresh observations yield are new data of sense, not a correlation between the original data and their cause. No observation discloses a correlation since only one term of the correlation

[1] Pp. 23–24. [2] *Ibid.*, pp. 16–17.

ever falls within experience. To check the data of sense with their cause would be to compare a term in experience with a term which by hypothesis lies beyond it. The cause of our perceptual experience is an unknowable, like Kant's noumenal object, whose nature as effectively eludes us as do the features of the perpetrator of the perfect crime.

This situation is unsatisfactory, and not only because it cannot be verified either that things exist or what their nature is. With regard to the nature of physical objects, description as well as discovery seem equally impossible. Things would be constituted of their aspects and the x of which they are the aspects. And this x is an ontological surd, a component which not only eludes detection but which is incapable of being described. It is one thing to be unable to discover an entity; it is quite another to be unable to describe what it is one is looking for. The possibility suggests itself that no such unknowable component of a thing exists and that this fact will show up on a logical analysis. Russell accordingly sets himself the task of taking a cosmological inventory, with the aim of showing which elements are indispensable building blocks of the world. Will a metaphysical entity, i.e. the kind of entity that is not empirically given and which is an infinitely elusive object of inference, be part of the ultimate furniture? And by what principles is one to be guided in reaching the cosmological ultimates? These are the questions to which the doctrine of logical atomism gives answers. Its programme is two-fold: to make an inventory on a cosmic scale of the primary elements from which ordinary phenomena can be reconstituted, and to devise a technique for deciding what to list in one's ledger. The programme was carried out in the lectures entitled 'The Philosophy of Logical Atomism'.[1] Guided by the methodological principle not to multiply entities unnecessarily—the principle of Occam's Razor—Russell arrived at ultimates simples of such a nature as could be known empirically with absolute certainty. No inferred metaphysical unknowables entered his ledger. Further, such inferred entities as are unavoidable are of a kind with those known without inference, and 'common objects of the sort that is supposed to be known by the senses' have their complete description, without remainder, by reference to these knowables.

[1] *The Monist*, 1918, 1919–20.

Now we know how Descartes arrived at his own existence by the method of systematic doubt. Let us examine Russell's use of Occam's Razor to arrive at ultimate simples out of which the world is built. The question he set himself was this: 'What is the smallest number of simple undefined things at the start, and the smallest number of undemonstrated premises, out of which you can define the things that need to be defined and prove the things that need to be proved?'[1] Now one of the notions that needs to be defined is the notion of a thing. He is asking what is the most economical and at the same time adequate set of materials for doing this. Suppose that when logical analysis is applied to the concept *thing* it is not found that a thing is divisible into two sorts of components, one of which lies outside the scope of knowledge. Suppose also that all the uses served by the unknowable component which it is so natural to assume are equally served by entities that are empirically verifiable. Then Occam's principle enjoins us to dispense with that supposed unknowable component —to dispense with what is dispensable. Substratum, in the language of the last war, is expendable.

Russell makes a point of disclaiming the denial that substratum exists, asserting only that he has no need of this hypothesis. Actually, by examining the history of the idea of substratum and its cognates, matter and substance, we can find adequate ground for denying that the term 'substratum' stands for any conception whatever. If so, we must *a fortiori* deny that logical analysis applied to the concept *thing* can reveal the concept of an underlying substance which is the bearer of attributes and the invariant subject of change. Aristotle would maintain that it could. The existence of a thing, he said, implies more than the existence of attributes. For since attributes depend for their existence on being instantiated, something besides them must exist. There must be a common subject of attribution, something which is the possessor of attributes and distinct from them. This he called matter. Suppose now we make the analytical experiment of stripping away its attributes. We encounter a blank. Matter, Aristotle said, is unknowable in itself. Apart from its attributes it is inconceivable. But it must be admitted that *with* its attributes it is also inconceivable. For the bearer of attributes, something in addition to

[1] *The Monist*, 1919–20, p. 366.

them and distinct from them, is as Locke said 'an I know not what'. The term 'matter' stands for no conception at all. It is *logically* precluded that an *x* which underlies appearances be found, because it is inconceivable that such an *x* exist.

What then remain as the indispensable constituents of things once analysis has yielded no unknowable component? Only the sense-given appearances, now no longer the appearances of a subject distinct from them. A thing is merely the sum of the appearances, systematically connected by certain similarities and exhibiting a continuity in their changes. What makes one say one is seeing the same thing on successive occasions, for example, a desk, is not that one observes an identical substance which presents appearances. The empirical reason for saying the same desk is before one is simply that the appearances are organized in a certain way. This, says Russell, 'is all that is *certainly* there in the way of unity. Anything that may be over and above that, I shall recognize as something I cannot know. What I can know is that there are certain series of appearances linked together, and the series of those appearances I shall define as being a desk.'[1] 'More generally, a "thing" will be defined as a series of aspects . . . collected together by the same motives which led us to regard it as one thing. . . . To say that a certain aspect is an aspect *of* a certain thing will merely mean that it is one of those which, taken serially, *are* the thing.'[2] Thus a thing is nothing more than a class of appearances. And appearances are the kind of things of which one is immediately conscious in sense experience—'patches of colour, sounds, tastes, smells, etc. with their spatio-temporal arrangements'.[3] Evanescent as they are, these are the ultimate elements to which, on analysis, things reduce, and out of which things are constructed. The constructs Russell calls fictions, to distinguish them from the ultimate elements, which he calls logical atoms. The atoms, but not the constructs from them, would be listed in his inventory of the world. One is reminded of Kronecker's claim about the numbers: God made the integers, mankind the rest. Rational, real, and complex numbers are artifacts,

---

[1] *The Monist*, 1919–20, pp. 369–70.
[2] *Our Knowledge of the External World as a Field for Scientific Method in Philosophy*, p. 106 (London: Allen & Unwin Ltd., 1926).
[3] *Mysticism and Logic*, p. 145. (London: Allen & Unwin, 1917).

but integers, the building blocks indispensable to their construction, are not.

It should be observed that the use of Occam's razor to arrive at the position described here has two aspects, one to reduce common objects of sense to logical atoms without substratum remainder, and the other to explain how this reduction is capable of preserving the properties we usually attribute to these objects. The reductionist programme which rids us of an inferred metaphysical entity I have now described. To complete the account of what is usually called the phenomenalist position it remains to explain how the programme attempts to preserve for physical objects certain realist features: namely, that these systems of aspects, including each of their constituent aspects, should be public objects for all observers and that they be capable of existing unperceived.

That this is a problem would appear to be the case from the little that has been said so far about the nature of the atoms of which physical objects are constructs. Physical objects have been defined as classes of appearances. But appearances are appearances to some mind, and it is not clear how they could exist at times when they were not objects of awareness to anyone, nor how, therefore, there could be a single persistent object instead of many transitory objects. Further, at no time are more than a few appearances present to a perceiver, and if a thing were the class of such appearances it would shrink to a fragment of what we consider to be a thing. As for appearances to other observers, it is a mystery how these and ours would on Russell's account thus far be appearances of a single object, for there would evidently be no one public object. How we should manage to correlate our private experiences so as to converge on what we call one and the same restaurant appears inexplicable. All this is to say that if the aspects exist only at the moment of being aspects then we are left with precisely those difficulties Berkeley's position would have without benefit of God. Russell was aware of these difficulties, and possibly aware, granting the assumption that God exists, of the following difficulty inherent in Berkeley's account: A stable world of permanent physical objects exists in virtue of each object's being an infinity complex system of ideas apprehended continuously by God. In relation to us the world is public, open to apprehension by all observers, each of whom perceives certain members of the class of ideas entertained by God. But in relation to God, the world is his cosmic dream and would come to an end if he left off dreaming. The serious difficulty which this view encounters is that ideas in anyone's mind are private to that mind and cannot be apprehended by another mind. And the privacy is a necessity of logic: it is logically impossible that numerically the same idea be had by two minds. So the world with which Berkeley's view leaves us is not the objective non-intermittent world he thought it assured.

The difficulties of subjectivism cannot be patched up by the hypothesis of God's existence, and this hypothesis certainly would not in any case be open to Russell if he were to abide by Occam's principle and admit into his account of reality only such entities as are either known without inference or are of a kind with those which are so known. The only recourse is to deny that the appearances or aspects which are present to us in sense-experience are subjective. 'Sense-data at the times when they are data are', he says, 'all that we directly and primitively know of the external world; hence in epistemology the fact that they are *data* is all-important. But the fact that they are all that we directly know gives, of course, no presumption that they are all that there is.'[1] Understanding by the term 'sense-data' 'the things which are immediately known in sensation: such things as colours, sounds, smells, hardnesses, roughnesses, and so on',[2] which we can rightfully suppose are among the atomic building blocks, what else is there? Besides these, he says, there probably is 'a mass of objects more or less like them' from which the particular objects which are data to a mind are 'a rather haphazard selection'.[3] Of course we cannot point to a particular datum and say of it '*This* lies outside my present experience'. But he thinks entities lying outside our present experience may legitimately be inferred provided the inference is guided by the principle that they 'should . . . be similar to those whose existence is given, rather than, like the Kantian *Ding an sich*, something wholly remote'.[4] Accordingly an inferred unknowable substance is displaced by a class of inferred objects which are knowable in the way sensed appearances are.

Russell grants that 'it may be thought monstrous to maintain

[1] *Mysticism and Logic*, p. 148.   [2] *The Problems of Philosophy*, p. 17.
[3] *Mysticism and Logic*, p. 148.   [4] *Ibid.*, p. 157.

that a thing can present any appearances at all in a place where no sense organs and nervous structure exist through which it could appear', but says, 'I do not myself feel the monstrosity'.[1] His reason is that as soon as the necessary distinction is made, within a sense experience, between the object of which one is aware and the awareness of it, the main obstacle against supposing such objects can exist beyond the moment of awareness is removed. If as Berkeley maintained 'the object and the sensation are the same, and cannot therefore be abstracted from each other',[2] then it would be logically impossible that the ultimate constituents of things exist independently of a mind. But sensation, Russell asserts, is the fact of the subject's being aware of an object, and the confusion between seeing and what is seen 'only needs to be pointed out in order to be obviated'.[3] Accordingly he makes a distinction, possibly taken over from Moore's earlier 'Refutation of Idealism', between sensibilia and sense-data, the former being 'those objects which have the same . . . status as sense-data, without necessarily being data to any mind . . . the relation of a *sensibile* to a sense-datum is like that of a man to a husband: a man becomes a husband by entering into the relation of marriage, and similarly a *sensibile* becomes a sense-datum by entering into the relation of acquaintance'.[4] 'What the mind adds to *sensibilia* . . . is *merely* awareness.'[5] Clearly the awareness is mental, but there is no reason to suppose its object is. Physical objects thus become constructs from sensibilia, not from sense-data, and logical atoms are freed of the stigma of subjectivity. They are know*ables*, that is, things whose presence and nature can be known, but are not such that they *must* be known in order to exist.

It is clear that by this distinction Russell hopes to escape the difficulties which Berkeley's omniscient perceiver served to circumvent. The world of physical objects can exist unperceived by us, not because God is perceiving it, but because the ultimate constituents of things can exist when not experienced by anyone. No physical object will shrink into the few data experienced, for the unperceived aspects are equally real. A physical object can sensibly be said to hide another from view, whereas of a datum

---

[1] *Mysticism and Logic* p. 158.
[2] *Principles of Human Knowledge, Part First, sec. 5*
[3] *Mysticism and Logic*, p. 131.   [4] *Ibid.*, pp. 148–49.   [5] *Ibid.*, p. 150.

which is by definition given, we cannot sensibly suppose a datum behind it—a given which is not given. Russell's account of physical things as consisting of sensibilia most of which are not sensed thus preserves a property usually attributed to things, that they have parts we do not perceive. But *everything* that is not perceived is comprised in the sensibilia which *could* be perceived. No unknowable remains. The logical atoms are not all known, but they are know*able*. In this respect Russell's phenomenalist view of things as clusters of atoms and the similarly worded Greek view are radically different. By implication, on Democritus' view a thing consists of a vast number of unknowables in which properties inhere. According to Russell, a thing is composed of a vast number of knowables. Democritus said that 'by convention sweet is sweet, by convention bitter is bitter, by convention colour is colour. But in reality there are only atoms and the void'. Russell turns the tables and declares it is the atoms of modern physics which exist by convention—these are but constructs—and in reality there are the experienceable attributes instantiated in sensibilia.

The difference between the account of a thing as a class of sensibilia and as a substratum of which our data are the effects dictates a corresponding difference in the account to be given of our knowledge of things. In fact, part of the motivation for a different account of things was that factual assertions about things should be verifiable. The inferences, made in empirical science, to the existence and properties of things can, theoretically, be checked. The phenomenalist account is in accord with this, whereas if a thing consists of a theoretically unknowable component no conceivable check would bring us closer to knowledge. Actually, the difference between the accounts of our knowledge on the phenomenalist and substratum descriptions of things is not as great as, on the surface, it appears. First of all, it is clear that since there are as many sensibilia constituting a thing as there are possible points of view, a thing will be an infinite system of sensibilia. Second, what is known in perception without inference is on Russell's view relatively little. Any knowledge of a thing would be knowledge of more than could be given in any perception and would hence be inferential. Knowledge of things, as Russell says, is knowledge by description, i.e. of 'the thing of which my present datum is a member'. On the phenomenalist view knowledge would be reached after an infinite number of verifications, although not even this could secure knowledge of substratum. To know the cause of our sense-data is theoretically impossible. But so also, I should say, is knowledge which lies at the end of an infinite series of sense-tests. To exhaust an infinite series I should say is logically impossible, not merely, as Russell once held, 'medically impossible'.[1] If so, the programme of substituting constructions for inferred entities does not get us closer to the goal of knowledge of an external world.

With regard to the exposition I have given of Russell's theory of logical constructions it should be noted that I have proceeded upon one of two utterly different accounts given by him of those primary elements of the world which enter into the constitution of things. These elements, which he called simples, bear very different descriptions in the lectures on logical atomism in 1918–19, from which I have drawn here, and in the paper on logical atomism six years later.[2] The term 'simple' as applied to these objects has two quite different senses: (1) it refers to entities which remain after an Occamite analysis, as the reductionist residue indispensable to the construction of things; (2) it refers to objects which are not decomposable into further parts, the terminal points theoretically arrived at by division. The first are sensibilia, the kind of things that are given in sense, in memory, and in imagination. To these we stand in the relation of acquaintance, that direct relation to objects when our awareness of them involves no process of inference. The second are indivisibles, 'something not experienced . . . but known only inferentially as the limit of analysis'.[3] In accordance with these divergent accounts the reductionist programme took two different paths. The first is the path of 'reducibility to acquaintance'. The second is that of reducibility to simples which according to Russell are not discoverable in experience. This second path is suggested by a combination of Leibniz' thesis that what is composite must be composed of simples, and Melissos' claim that body is not a true unity. A single substance cannot be body, for body has extension as its attribute, which involves

[1] 'The Limits of Empiricism', *Proceedings of the Aristotelian Society*, Vol. XXXVI p. 143.
[2] 'Logical Atomism', *Contemporary British Philosophy*, First Series (Muirhead Library of Philosophy) (London: Allen & Unwin, 1924).
[3] *Ibid.*, p. 375.

plurality.[1] Body is a class, an assemblage of elements rather than an element. As Russell put it, classes are not part of the ultimate furniture of the world. What is ultimate must be an indivisible, on the order of a Leibnizian monad. Presumably these would be ultimate in the sense in which sensibilia are not, for the latter are extended. The difficulty is, as Hume pointed out concerning the self, that they cannot be found. The unextended constituents of the extended complex elude discovery. This seems a far cry from the reductionist programme dictated by the maxim of Occam's Razor, and I take it to be the less representative of Russell's two doctrines.

What else remains when the work of Occam's principle is complete I shall now detail, so far as the inconsistencies of Russell's pronouncements over the years permit. Up through the lectures on logical atomism in 1918–19, among simples were listed not only the immediate objects of sense presentation but data grasped by 'a different kind of act of mind'.[2] These are universals, the entities denoted by predicates and relation-words. With regard to these Russell has been like a broken field runner who swerves and goes back on his tracks; only in the early years did he unequivocally assert universals to be part of the ultimate furniture of the world. In those years we can say that the reductionist programme which eliminated substratum, for the reason that it eluded both the senses and the intellect, left as an irreducible remainder elements grasped by either, namely, sensibilia and universals. With both sorts of element, he at that time held, we are acquainted, acquaintance in the one case consisting of sense awareness, in the other of conception, the non-sensory awareness of abstract entities. So the world taken as a totality consists of logical atoms from two areas, the sensible and the supra-sensible. To the latter belong *precedence*, and *redness*, and *similarity*. This is to say that to some distinctions between parts of speech, for example, between demonstratives like 'this' and 'that', and predicates or relation-words, there correspond objective distinctions. At least one of each distinct kind of entity figures in all of the simplest facts, what Russell calls 'atomic facts'. An inventory of the world will include all such facts, the simplest being those consisting of a sensibile's possessing a quality and of two sensibilia

---

[1] *Human Knowledge*, p. 201.   [2] *The Monist*, 1919–20, p. 34.

standing in a relation. Any fact is a complex and what symbolizes it will stand in a different relation to it than do the symbols for the simple elements. Atomic sentences express propositions which if true *assert* atomic facts, whereas words for particular objects of sense awareness *name* them. No sentence *names* a fact, nor does a *description* such as 'the object of attention' name a sensibile. A name, that is, a 'logically proper' name, of which the best example is 'this', applies to only one entity and can be used only at the moment of acquaintance, not in the sensibile's absence. But how are predicates and relation-terms related to what they mean? Russell's unclarity on this point is an index to his ambivalence about the status of universals. The word 'red', he says in the lectures on atomism, is understood only through acquaintance, but it does not *name* an object of acquaintance, else what it named could be a subject of attribution. And only a particular sensibile can be that. To understand the word 'red' is to understand a sentence of the form 'x is red'.[1] The proper symbol for the attribute *red* is not the single word 'red' but the expression 'x is red', 'where the structure of the symbol shows the position which the word . . . must have if it is to be significant. Similarly the relation "precedes" must not be represented by this one word, but by the symbol "x precedes y", showing the way in which the symbol can occur significantly'.[2]

Already in the claim that 'attributes and relations, though they may not be susceptible of analysis, differ from substances by the fact that . . . there can be no significant symbol which symbolizes them in isolation,'[3] we have the beginnings of a reductionist programme as applied to universals. Symbols not definable in isolation from a context, what he called 'incomplete symbols', are symbols for logical constructions, not for simples. As early as 1921 he wrote: 'A universal never appears before the mind as a single object in the sort of way in which something perceived appears. I *think* a logical argument could be produced to show that universals are part of the structure of the world, but they are an inferred part, not a part of our data.'[4] In the same book he said, 'whether there is a universal called "whiteness", . . . is a question . . . which

[1] *The Monist*, p. 34.   [2] *Contemporary British Philosophy*, p. 376.
[3] *Ibid.*, pp. 375–6.
[4] *The Analysis of Mind*, p. 228 (London: Allen & Unwin, 1921)

I believe to be strictly insoluble'.[1] And he goes on immediately to say: 'For our purposes, we may take the word "white" as denoting a certain set of similar particulars. . . .'[2] Between such words, which denote qualities, and general nouns such as 'man', there is he says no very great difference, the latter meaning 'a whole class of such collections of particulars'[3] as have the English names 'Jones', 'Robinson', etc. And classes, as we know, are not regarded as part of the ultimate furniture of the world. The assimilation of adjectives with general nouns is a reductionist move. Adjectives like nouns will stand for constructs: an attribute reduces to a set of concrete particulars united by similarity, the particulars being among the ultimate simples, but not the attributes. General words we have, but no element of reality denoted by them. Here is the nominalist counter to the Platonism of the earlier years. Further, Occam's Razor when applied to universals has the consequence that no part of reality lies beyond the reach of the senses. In this respect Russell's reductionism is a most important precursor of the more radical doctrine of logical positivism. Russell's agnosticism as to the existence of substratum and univerals was to give way to Ayer's denial that the assertion of their existence made any sense. The use made of Occam's Razor was in the one case ontological, in the other semantic. I might remark as an addendum that between the early non-reductionist account of universals and the later reductionist account is a still later intermediate position. It is expressed tentatively in the words: 'I conclude . . . though with hesitation, that there are universals, and not merely general words. Similarity, at least, will have to be admitted; and in that case it seems hardly worthwhile to adopt elaborate devices for the exclusion of other universals.'[4]

I turn now to the linguistic correlate of the search for ultimate constituents. Although I have given the doctrine of logical atomism a setting in questions concerning the nature of things and our knowledge of them, partly as an expository device and partly because I suspect these were the questions motivating Russell's study of language, nevertheless the question he explicitly set himself made language rather than material fact his starting point. Both in the early lectures on atomism and as late as 1940 there was

---

[1] *The Analysis of Mind*, p. 196   [2] *Ibid.*   [3] *Ibid.*, p. 194.
[4] *Inquiry into Meaning and Truth*, p. 436 (New York: W.W. Norton).

one persistent question: 'whether anything, and if so, what, can be inferred from the structure of language as to the structure of the world'.[1] In Russell's opinion ordinary language was far from an ideal vehicle for any such inferences. For one thing, there is nothing in traditional logic, framed for ordinary language, which would prevent my making the self-contradictory statement that what I am now saying is false. For another, its structure mis-leadingly suggest that fact has the same structure and that the ultimate constituents of fact might even be such things as the present King of France and the ghost of the murdered man. Note the similarity of grammatical form between 'This is red' and 'The present King of France is bald'. Further, ordinary language is imperfect because its words are often ambiguous and are more or less infected with vagueness, in the sense that 'it is not always clear whether they apply to a given object or not'.[2] Had language 'been invented by scientifically trained observers for purposes of philosophy and logic'[3] these defects would not exist. We might have 'a grammatically correct account of the universe'[4] if only an ideal logical language could be constructed.

Whether or not Russell supposed a programme for reforming ordinary language could be carried out, he made two contributions towards its reform, the theory of logical types and the theory of definite descriptions, and for the rest described what a logically perfect language would be like. About the two reforms I shall say little since these are compatible with other metaphysical doctrines than logical atomism. I want now to turn attention to the linguistic correlate of the search for simples and the elimination of unknow-ables from the description of the nature of things constructed from simples. A successful search would be reflected in a successful construction of an ideal language. His description of this language is as follows: 'In a logically perfect language the words in a pro-position would correspond one by one with the components of the corresponding fact, with the exception of such words as "or", "not", "if", "then", which have a different function. In a logically perfect language, there will be one word and no more for every simple object, and everything that is not simple will be expressed by a

---

[1] *Inquiry into Meaning and Truth*, p. 429.
[2] *Contemporary British Philosophy*, p. 376.
[3] *The Analysis of Mind*, p. 193.　　　　　　　　　[4] *Philosophy*, p. 257.

combination of words, by a combination derived, of course, from the words for the simple things that enter in, one word for each simple component.'[1] Such a language would be possible to God but hardly for us. At any given moment *all* the simples would be present to him, and each would have its symbolic tag. Aristotle's description of nature as a good housekeeper comes to mind. In the world apprehended by God every simple would be labelled. Further, to continue with Russell's description, 'A language of that sort . . . will show at a glance the logical structure of the facts asserted or denied. The language which is set forth in *Principia Mathematica* is intended to be a language of that sort. It is a language which has only syntax and no vocabulary whatsoever. . . . It aims at being that sort of a language that, if you add a vocabulary, would be a logically perfect language.'[2] With respect to vocabulary, in distinction to syntax, the following description from his *Introduction to Mathematical Philosophy* indicates its difference from ordinary language: In '. . . a complete symbolic language, with a definition for everything definable, and an undefined symbol for everything indefinable, the undefined symbols . . . would represent symbolically what I mean by "the ultimate furniture of the world"'.[3] That is, between the final terms in the analysis of a compound and the indefinable terms of language there would be a one-to-one correspondence. He goes on to say, what we already know from my previous exposition concerning the primary elements, that 'no symbols . . . for . . . classes would be included in this apparatus of undefined symbols . . . all the particular things there are in the world would have to have names which would be included among undefined symbols'.[4] Here is the modern echo of an ancient Greek doctrine. Socrates said in the *Cratylus* that we come to terminological ultimates when we 'come to the names which are elements of all other names and sentences. . . . If we take a word which is incapable of further resolution, then we shall be right in saying that we have at last reached a primary element. . . .' Or to put the matter in terms of the converse process of logical construction of things from their constituents, the following from the *Theaetetus* is in essentials the same description: 'Just as what consists of these primary elements

[1] *The Monist* 1918, p. 520.   [2] *Ibid.*, p. 520.
[3] P. 182.   [4] *Ibid.*

is itself complex, so the names of the elements become descriptive language by being compounded together. For the essence of speech is the composition of names.'

Now the elimination of an unknowable component from the analysis of a thing's nature is paralleled in the fact that no name in a logically perfect language could designate it. For a logically proper name can only name an object of acquaintance. That we are led to suppose there is such a component Russell credits to the hold exercised over our minds by the subject-predicate form of ordinary language. When we attribute a quality to a perceived physical object, the subject-predicate form of our judgment suggests that the quality inheres in a substance which causes our data of sense. And when put to it to explain what this substance is, the best we can do is to give the description 'the thing which is the cause of my present data', or 'the thing which supports qualities'. These descriptive phrases, by contrast with the descriptive phrase 'the class of sensibilia of which my present datum is a member', Russell maintains cannot really be understood. His criterion for understanding any sentence, i.e. for grasping the proposition it expresses, is as follows: 'in every proposition we can apprehend . . . all the constituents are really entities with which we have immediate acquaintance. . . .'[1] Let us call this the principle of reducibility to acquaintance. It follows that any sentence having a phrase of the form 'the so-and-so' as grammatical subject will not be understood unless 'the so-and-so' is a symbol for a construct out of objects of acquaintance. Such sentences, for example, as 'The cat owned by my neighbour is ginger-coloured', if understood, must translate into a sentence involving only symbols for simples. From these the descriptive phrase would have disappeared, and since no descriptive phrase is a *name* in Russell's sense (else it could not be used sensibly in the absence of what it denotes), no part of the translation-sentence will be replaceable by the phrase.

Now this account couples the doctrine of logical atomism and the epistemological principle of reducibility to acquaintance with a doctrine concerning the translation of sentences of the form 'the so-and-so has f'. The latter, which Ramsey called 'that paradigm of philosophy', is the theory of definite descriptions. It is very likely

[1] 'On Denoting', *Mind*, vol. XIV (1905), p. 492.

what Wittgenstein had in mind when he said 'Russell's merit is to have shown that the apparent logical form of the proposition may not be its real form'.[1] The apparent logical form of 'The cat owned by my neighbour is ginger-coloured' is subject-predicate. But the sentence for this proposition translates into: 'There is one and only one thing which is a cat owned by my neighbour and which is ginger-coloured.' In the translation-sentence there is no single expression which is a simple abbreviation for the descriptive phrase 'the cat owned by my neighbour', and this phrase has disappeared in the translation. Were the description a *name* of an object it would not break up in this fashion. And since it is not a name, although in some grammatical respects it functions like a name, there is no need to assume among the ultimate building blocks of reality fictitious persons or things. That is, we need not interpret 'The Queen of Faerie is capricious' as truly or falsely attributing a property to a fictitious entity, in order to assure that the proposition expressed has a subject. In fact the translation shows that it is not logically of the subject-predicate form at all, and we are taken in by its grammar if we suppose it is.

To hold that phrases of the form 'the so-and-so' are symbols which disappear on translation of the sentence in which they occur seems very different from holding the following: that all sentences involving any expression for a logical construct from sensibilia are translatable into sentences in which the sensibilia are named. This is to hold that ordinary English proper names, descriptive phrases, general nouns such as 'cat' or 'neighbour' will all disappear in translation, the translation containing only symbols from the logically perfect language. The difficulty is to produce even one example of such a translation-sentence. For one thing, no words in our ordinary language are logically proper names. Even the words 'this' and 'that' do not qualify, since the ideal language has no more than one name for every simple. For another thing, a logically proper name would have meaning only to the speaker, and only at the time of utterance, since what is named is an object of his acquaintance, and the same sensibile cannot be an object of acquaintance to two minds. Associated with two points of view are two distinct sensibilia, and sensibilia are too evanescent to be apprehended consecutively by two minds from the same point of

[1] *Tractatus Logico-Philosophicus*, 4.0331.

view. Russell admits that 'A logically perfect language, if it could be constructed . . . as regards its vocabulary, would be very largely private to one speaker. That is to say, all the names that it would use would be private to that speaker and could not enter into the language of another speaker'.[1] One might maintain that it is a mere practical drawback that it could not be used for purposes of communication. But it is a *logical* drawback that a sentence such as 'The cat owned by my neighbour is ginger-coloured', which is publicly understood, should translate into a set of sentences none of which is publicly understood. No single sentence publicly understood could be equivalent to a class of sentences not publicly understood, and not capable of intra-personal communication. On Russell's principle of reducibility to acquaintance the sentence 'The cat owned by my neighbour is ginger-coloured' has no public meaning (a meaning which is a construct of public objects, i.e. objects not reducible to sets of private objects); nor can it consist of private meanings. It is therefore itself without meaning. This consequence would seem to constitute a *reductio ad absurdum* of Russell's principle. For it is undeniable that such a sentence as 'The cat owned by my neighbour is ginger-coloured' does have a meaning and that by uttering it I convey information to someone.

It is just possible that the preclusion of intra-personal communication by the view that things are reducible to sensibilia is in part responsible for another and quite different attempt at reduction, made in the *Inquiry into Meaning and Truth*. Here a thing is described as a bundle of qualities, each quality being absolutely specific. The physical-object statement 'This is red' is given the translation 'Redness is here', where 'redness' functions as a name, not a predicate. What Russell formerly called names, viz., words for particulars, now become dispensable, and words for universals take over their function. I should suppose that universals, unlike sensibilia which according to Russell probably do not have exactly the same nature when unperceived as when perceived, might be objects whose names would have the same meaning for all users. But this point is left unclear, and it is doubtful whether it was even hoped that the new language reflecting this sort of reduction of things would be any the less private. For there is

[1] *The Monist*, 1918, p. 520.

apparently no escape from words for what Russell calls 'egocentric particulars', in this case the word 'here'. One motivation for such a reduction Russell does make explicit. He says: 'One is tempted to regard "This is red" as a subject-predicate proposition; but if one does so, one finds that "this" becomes a substance, an unknowable something in which properties inhere, but which, nevertheless, is not identical with the sum of its properties.'[1] I think it is clear that this same difficulty breaks out whether 'this' is used in the presence of a physical object or in the presence solely of one's sense datum. One can ask in the latter case too, as Wittgenstein pointed out, what the x is which has the quality red. I should suppose that an ideal language which got round this difficulty would dispense with the subject-predicate form of speech in all of its hiding places in language. The ideal of the logically perfect language would be the same: that some of its sentences, those which are atomic, should have a structure identical with the structure of facts. That is, the way its elements are combined would be the same as the way the simple objects in facts are combined. To quote: '. . . in a logically correct symbolism . . . the complexity of the symbol corresponds very closely with the complexity of the fact symbolized by it'.[2] The structure of fact, as Wittgenstein asserted in the *Tractatus*, cannot be expressed even by the ideal language, for structure is not another constituent in fact, but the way the constituents are put together. There are symbols for the content of a proposition but not for the structure which the contents have. According to most of what Russell has written about the logically perfect language, however, even what is expressed by the symbols for content could not be expressed by them to anyone except the user: some among the symbols for content would be names of particulars, which 'do not enter into the language of another speaker'. It is hard to see how the fact that it is 'a grammatically correct language' offsets this disadvantage, for sounds used without the possibility of communicating anything can scarcely be said to constitute a language. Paradoxically, the very privacy of the ideal 'language' is supposedly an advantage over ordinary language.

A reason for this supposed advantage may appear on examining

---

[1] *Inquiry into Meaning and Truth*, p. 120.
[2] *The Monist*, 1919–20, p. 519.

what is often taken to be an inadequacy of ordinary language. It is often said that no current language is capable of expressing the ineffable in experience, that what we experience 'words cannot describe'. The specificity of experience always escapes embodiment in general terms. But note that the ideal language has words for the absolutely specific, and by the principle of reducibility to acquaintance general names are understood by the user because they stand for constructs from the absolutely specific. At least the language in which we talk *to ourselves* will express everything. It will be completely adequate, for nothing inexpressible will remain over. Here is the supposed advantage of privacy. In ordinary language Russell says 'there is no direct way of designating one of the ultimate brief existents that go to make up the collections we call things or persons'.[1] For ordinary language is intra-personal and I cannot, therefore, convey by it the absolutely specific character of my object of acquaintance to anyone else.

But how can this inability to convey the specific be construed as an inadequacy in ordinary language? If it betokens a defect then it is a defect which it is *logically* impossible that any language used for communication should make good. For the required remedy would be that in understanding what the speaker says, the hearer should have the speaker's experience. But it hardly appears to be a complaint against language that it fails to do what is logically impossible. Only if language falls short of what it could conceivably achieve is it to be found wanting. The complaint has the air of referring to what cannot be done by means of language, whereas in fact it refers to nothing of the sort. It is a pseudo-complaint, formulated in the language of a real complaint. What, now, is to be described as the special merit of a private language? It is difficult to find any merit whatever. For understanding this language, if a true proposition is expressed, would consist in the immediate presence to one of the fact symbolized. The constituents of the true atomic proposition would be identical with the constituents of the fact. Such a language, since it could only be understood by oneself, would be otiose; to use it would merely be to label what is known without the label. And the label would not serve for future reference, since the evanescent particulars can be named but once. Talking to oneself, however odd in ordinary

[1] *The Analysis of Mind*, p. 193.

language, would be a completely pointless oddity in this language. To turn Wittgenstein's comment round, Whereof one *can* speak, one may as well be silent.

9

LINGUISTIC APPROACHES TO
PHILOSOPHICAL PROBLEMS*[1]

Views about the nature of philosophical theories answer to one of two rough descriptions, one orthodox and seemingly having the best claim to truth, the other heterodox and seemingly false. In this paper I shall set out the considerations both for and against accepting various forms of the heterodox position; but I shall argue without reservation against the orthodox position. The latter commonly describes philosophy as a pursuit of truth, where 'pursuit of truth' is interpreted in conformity with common usage as the attempt to acquire knowledge about our world. The contrasting position comprises a series of views held by philosophers whose primary concern appears to be the language in which purported truths are expressed. This concern reflects a conception of philosophy, a conception often not explicit and sometimes even disclaimed, namely, that a philosophical theory has its sources in linguistic facts rather than in facts about our world, and that despite appearances it gives us information only about language. A theory about causation, for example, tells us something about the word 'cause' rather than about causation as a feature of our world.

This rough description of the position of linguistic philosophers makes it appear to ignore a distinction we all know, between the use and mention of a word. It is clear, for example, that philosophical views about causation do not translate into any statements about the word 'cause'. But of course this fact is already known to philosophers whose approach is linguistic. To maintain their thesis it is therefore incumbent upon them to specify in what way philo-

* Reprinted from *The Journal of Philosophy*, Vol. XLIX, No. 9, April 24, 1952.
[1] Read at a Symposium on Linguistic Conceptions of Philosophy, Smith College, May 20, 1951.

sophical theories yield only verbal information and, first of all, to show that such theories are not what they seem. This latter thesis I want now to defend.

Descartes remarked that 'Philosophy teaches us to speak with an appearance of truth on all things, and causes us to be admired by the less learned . . . '.[1] But this appearance of truth is much more an appearance than he ever supposed. Philosophical views quite clearly have an empirical air, i.e. they appear to state matters of fact. To take some sample illustrations: a physical object is a bundle of properties, perception of physical objects involves an inference to something beyond one's experience, man's mind is necessarily given to antinomies, one cannot know one is not dreaming, it is impossible to know other people exist, motion is impossible, etc.

I want to hold that despite appearances these are *not* factual statements about physical objects, perception, the human mind, one's knowledge; first, because investigations which come to these conclusions are clearly not empirical. I do not propose here to discuss in a positive way the kind of evidence the philosopher adduces for a theory; here I can only say the evidence is not empirical. And I back this claim by pointing out that he has no laboratory, no experiments figure in his demonstrations or refutations, he cannot claim to closer observation of phenomena than other folk. Empirical conclusions cannot be expected to derive from non-empirical evidence. Second, they are not empirical because philosophic disputants come to opposite conclusions although the same facts are available to them and no possible further fact can decide betwixt them; i.e. their dispute cannot, even theoretically, be settled by recourse to any sort of matter of fact. Examples of such disputes are: the long-standing controversy over whether universals exist (consider Russell's, Carnap's, and Quine's changing positions), Locke and Berkeley's dispute over the existence of abstract ideas, disputes over the existence of sense data and over the extent of our knowledge. Third, some (possibly all) philosophical theories cannot be empirical because they imply the logical impossibility of what is patently and undeniably possible. For example, it appears to be a consequence of some of

[1] *Discourse on the Method of Rightly Conducting the Reason and Seeking for Truth in the Sciences*, Pt. I.

Bradley's views that it is self-contradictory (not merely false) that we should all be here now, or somewhere else before, or that we should have walked here, or that I should be sitting next to B.

There are two points to be made about views which have this sort of consequence, (1) that a philosopher need make no appeal to fact to show the incorrectness of such views, and (2) that whatever implies that something is logically impossible cannot itself be empirical. (1) It is an adequate objection to such a philosophical view that it has as a consequence the impossibility of what is clearly possible. (I am taking the position that if we know anything at all we know, for example, that sitting next to B is entirely possible. This is a minimum claim to knowledge. It requires only the understanding of the sentence asserting it.) Citing the relevant *possibility* constitutes a sufficient objection to such a view; if a philosopher cites a fact he has merely cited something logically stronger than is necessary. It is the mere possibility, not the fact, that he requires. The possibility of there being a right act the total consequences of which do not contain as great a balance of pleasure over pain as any act the agent could do is enough to refute the theory that every right act must have consequences containing such a balance. That the possibility is remote or fantastic does not prevent it from being a test case. In other words, the theory is tested by a mere logical possibility. And what is merely possible cannot serve to refute a statement of fact. This is support for my claim that philosophical investigation of a theory is not empirical and hence that the theory itself is not empirical. (2) An additional reason for asserting the theory to be non-empirical is that whatever implies that something is logically impossible cannot itself be factual. No factual statement has as a consequence a logical impossibility.

The three considerations cited against holding philosophical views to be empirical are obviously different in character. The first two call attention to matters of fact about philosophical investigations and philosophical disputes, while the last one rests on the logical points (1) that only a non-empirical statement can be tested by citing a possibility, and (2) that whatever implies that something is logically impossible cannot itself be factual. All entail the consequence that a philosophical investigation does not consist in the attempt to ascertain the truth-value of a theory.

Without pretending to have met various reasons that might be advanced for the thesis that a philosophical theory does assert something factual, I am now going to proceed as though enough had been said to dispose of this thesis, in order to take up another view, which at least in appearance contests the claim that philosophical theories inform us only about the use of words. Philosophers holding this view do make a careful examination of the language used to express a theory, but they consider this linguistic task merely as a preliminary necessity for ascertaining truth. This view is the most plausible alternative both to the view that philosophical theories are factual truths or falsities and to the view that their function is to convey facts about words. It is the most plausible, first, because it is consistent with the fact that philosophical investigations are not empirical and that philosophical disputes are not settled by appeal to fact, and second, because it has the support of the undeniable fact that philosophical theories are expressed in what may be called the ontological as opposed to the linguistic idiom.[1] According to this alternative view philosophical statements are analyses of puzzling concepts; and philosophical reasoning, at least a good deal of it, is directed to defending or attacking the correctness of an analysis. Philosophical questions and answers, and philosophical disputes, all have on this view a non-linguistic description. A philosophical question is a request for the analysis of a concept, i.e. for a statement of what concepts constitute (are logically entailed by) the given concept. The analysis will be correct if the statement of it is a logically necessary truth. Vagueness of concepts is the explanation of philosophical disputes.

Now the history of philosophy is full of what appear to be attempts to arrive at necessary truths. The following are illustrations: (1) Body is extended. This was set out by Descartes as an indubitable truth, indubitable because ascertainable by reason alone. Being a physical body necessarily implies being extended in space. (2) Socrates' attempts in the *Republic* and other dialogues to find the 'essence' of justice, courage, virtue, etc. are also good illustrations of attempted analyses, as is evidenced by his procedure of dismissing any feature not characterizing all possible instances of the concept in question. (3) Zeno's argument that motion is impossible was directed to showing the concept of motion to have

[1] I have taken the phrase 'ontological idiom' from Prof. M. Lazerowitz.

contradictory consequences. At least this is the natural description of his argument that the hypothesis that a body moves from A to B is self-contradictory. (4) Bradley's argument for the impossibility of relations, namely, that in order for two things to be related there would have to be an infinity of relations between them, also clearly derives from an investigation of the notion of a relation. (5) Hume's claim that a cause is nothing more than an invariable sequence appears likewise to be an analytic account of causation.

Now the activity illustrated in these examples is according to some philosophers not to be described as in any way requiring the examination of language, except as language is a crutch to our apprehension of concepts. Some go so far as to lodge a general complaint against language, not only because it is so often abused but because it is a barrier rather than a window to our ideas. Berkeley, for example, enjoins each of us to 'use his utmost endeavours to obtain a clear view of the ideas he would consider, separating from them all that dress and incumbrance of words which so much contribute to blind the judgment and divide the attention. . . . We need only draw the curtain of words to behold the fairest tree of knowledge, whose fruit is excellent and within the reach of our hand.'[1] For himself, since ideas so little profit from their quite fortuitous association with words, he says that 'whatever ideas I consider, I shall endeavour to take them bare and naked into my view; keeping out of my thoughts, so far as I am able, those names which long and constant use hath so strictly united with them. . . . So long as I confine my thoughts to my own ideas, divested of words, I do not see how I can easily be mistaken. The objects I consider, I clearly and adequately know. . . . To discern the agreements or disagreements there are between my ideas, to see what ideas are included in my compound idea and what not, there is nothing more requisite than an attentive perception of what passes in my own understanding.'[2] This evidently is what C. H. Langford in our time calls considering a statement, 'not verbally, but in terms of genuine ideas'.[3]

If any philosopher takes the position that a concern with ideas is positively hampered by attention to words, and that ideas are the

[1] *The Principles of Human Knowledge*, Introduction, sec. 24.
[2] *Ibid.*, sections 21, 22.
[3] C. I. Lewis and C. H. Langford, *Symbolic Logic*, p. 475.

philosopher's proper concern, he clearly will be far from admitting that philosophical views are in any way about words or that examination of language is anything more than an unfortunate necessity. It is my contention that complaints which philosophers have made against language are pseudo-complaints—pseudo because they express dissatisfaction with the fact that language does not come up to a standard which it is self-contradictory that it should come up to. But I have argued this point elsewhere[1] and so shall not discuss it here. If it is correct, then philosophers are robbed of an important reason for holding that analysis should be of concepts but not of language, and that attention to language is a second-best to inspection of ideas. I suspect it is nonsense to speak, as Berkeley did, of taking ideas 'bare and naked' into one's view, divested of their linguistic encumbrances. But disregarding this point, what I want to propose (though with some reservation) is that an analyst, even though he claims linguistic study is merely a tool in the analysis of concepts, is in fact engaging in *one* linguistic approach to philosophical problems.

I define a linguistic approach to philosophy as one arising from the view that what a philosopher does when he produces or tries to refute a philosophical theory is to inform one about language. Whether or not the so-called analytic approach in philosophy can be classified as a linguistic approach I admit is uncertain. But we may take it as evidence that it can be if the analysis of a concept which a philosophical theory is claimed to state turns out to be a linguistic analysis. This evidence is provided by G. E. Moore's statement in Cambridge lectures that the analysis of a notion is identical with the definition of a word, in a strictly limited sense. Roughly, 'analytic definition' covers what that sense is. An analytic definition is intended to clarify a concept by making explicit those concepts implicitly contained in it. This it will succeed in doing only if the words occurring in the expression of the analysans stand for 'such ideas as common use has annexed them to', to quote Locke. That is, if the analysans is expressed by means of words not having a usage in the language or by means of old words used in a new way, the analysis will not clarify a concept. A

---

[1] 'The Problem of Linguistic Inadequacy', *Philosophical Analysis, A Collection of Essays*, edited by Max Black (Cornell University Press, 1950), pp. 15–37. See ch. 10

successful analysis then will secure the same end as a correct definition: state how a word or phrase is conventionally used. However, from his Cambridge lectures there is reason to suppose that Moore, who would I think agree that some philosophical theories state analyses, would deny that they state something about the correct or established use of language, and for reasons over and above the fact that they are not *about* words.

Whether or not Moore would deny this thesis about what analysis does I am not concerned here to decide. I am concerned to evaluate it since it is an emphatically linguistic view in which the increasing attention to language naturally eventuates. According to this view the appearance which a philosophical theory has of being about empirical fact, or of being about the implications of concepts, merely conceals an attempt to express correct usage. Philosophical theories are to be examined neither for their necessary truth nor for their correspondence with those non-linguistic facts which make up our spatio-temporal world, but for their linguistic correctness—that is, for their correspondence with the linguistic facts that words are customarily used in such-and-such a way. I am not sure that anyone has ever held this view about philosophical theories. However, though one might not explicitly hold it, one might do philosophy as though one did. Moore and Norman Malcolm have often proceeded in such a way as to suggest this, for example, when they criticize a theory for misuse of words. Recall Moore's criticisms of views, say on the nature of material objects, for going counter to ordinary English, and Malcolm's recent criticisms of Moore's use of 'know' in the claim 'I know material objects exist' and of Russell's use of 'perception' in his claim that perception involves an inference. This type of criticism at least suggests that a philosopher was interpreted as attempting, but failing, to give a proper account of conventional usage.

The attempt to answer one or other of the questions, 'Does this analysis state a necessary truth?' 'Does this account of the use of the word correctly describe its established, conventional use?', characterizes the tasks, respectively, of the two positions I have thus far called linguistic. Either position differs markedly from one further linguistic approach to philosophical problems, stated explicitly by Morris Lazerowitz, and by John Wisdom in some of his papers, according to which philosophers are neither analyzing concepts nor stating correct usage in giving a view, but are doing something else equally linguistic, namely, revising language. This approach stems from the view that philosophical theories are not, as they appear to be, answers to questions, but are proposals to alter language: that they do not in fact attempt to clarify a concept or to explain a current usage, but instead, in a concealed way, propose that a word's use shall be modified for philosophical purposes. Practitioners of this persuasion conduct what might be called meta-philosophical investigations—that is, they do not aim at establishing or refuting a theory, i.e. at answering a philosophical question, but instead show what linguistic features a philosopher is emphasizing in order to persuade other philosophers of the need of a linguistic change. They try to show what a philosophical theory comes to; and they arrive in the end at the Wittgenstein position that once one sees what a question comes to the craving for an answer disappears.

We have now three views about the nature of philosophical theories, one that they state analyses of concepts, another that they state what is the established usage of words, and another that they conceal a proposal for linguistic change. In order to make clear the differences between the first two and the last I shall try to set out what, ideally, their proponents would say about Berkeley's defence of his theory about physical objects. Berkeley grants that the expression 'What we eat, drink, and are clothed with are ideas' departs from the familiar use of language. But he asserts he is not disputing 'about the propriety, but the truth of the expression'.[1] 'If . . . you agree with me that we eat and drink and are clad with the immediate objects of sense, which cannot exist unperceived . . . I shall readily grant it is more proper or conformable to custom that they should be called *things* rather than *ideas*.'[1] In other words, he seems to say that 'We are clothed with material things' is proper enough language, that is, that what we are clothed with *is* the sort of thing to which 'material things' is applied, but that it fails to express what is true; while 'We are clothed with ideas' offends against linguistic proprieties but does say what is true. He recommends our compromising between these two facts by employing 'those inaccurate modes of speech which use has made

[1] *Principles of Human Knowledge*, Part First, sec. 38.

inevitable',[1] but with full awareness of their inaccuracy. For purposes of philosophizing 'We are clothed with fine raiment' will be understood to mean 'We are clothed with raiment-ideas'. Thus we shall 'think with the learned, and speak with the vulgar'.[2] In this way he insists that 'the common use of language will receive no manner of alteration . . . from the admission of our tenets',[2] and that 'in the tenets we have laid down there is nothing inconsistent with the right use and significancy of language, and that discourse, . . . so far as it is intelligible, remains undisturbed'.[3]

About these claims there are two things to say: (1) Quite clearly, as English is at present, 'We are clothed with ideas' is not a proper interpretation of 'We are clothed with material things'. There is no rule of synonymy which makes it correct to replace 'material thing' by 'class of ideas'. (2) Berkeley preserves the *status quo* of ordinary English at the cost of constructing a philosophical language to which his arbitrary rule of translation, 'material thing' = 'class of ideas', provides no bridge. For 'We are clothed with ideas', which he says is true, cannot translate into 'We are clothed with material things', because that is, according to Berkeley, false, or, by turns, nonsense.

About these facts proponents of the three linguistic theories about philosophy would take, respectively, the following positions: the first two that Berkeley is misusing language; the third that he is suggesting an alteration, for academic purposes, of philosophic discourse, and that it is a misinterpretation of his intention to suppose he is stating the accepted meaning of the phrase 'material thing'. Only in philosophical usage is his meaning to obtain, which is to say that the phrase 'material thing' will come to have no function in philosophical discourse since 'class of ideas' will displace it.

The sharp difference between these positions shows up when each is considered with reference to the question 'Why is it so often asserted that Berkeley's position on material objects, though not substantiated, is unrefuted?' Accepting the view that Berkeley is either analyzing the nature of material objects or defining the phrase 'material object', the charge that he is misusing language

---

[1] *Principles of Human Knowledge*, sec. 52.
[2] *Ibid.*, sec. 51. [3] *Ibid.*, sec. 83.

would imply that his analysis, or definition, is *in*correct. But as the quotations make clear, Berkeley was perfectly aware, even admits, that his account uses 'ideas' in a way not in accord with ordinary linguistic proprieties. Yet he insists on his account nevertheless. If the aim of a philosophical theory is to give a correct analysis or a correct account of established usage, then the theory should be refuted so soon as it is shown that it fails to do this. And it would then be inexplicable why his theory is thought to remain unrefuted.

The third linguistic view, on the other hand, is constructed to explain just this phenomenon. If Berkeley's theory is an attempt to alter language for purposes of *philosophic* (as against ordinary) discourse, then it is understandable why pointing out a linguistic impropriety in no way persuades him to relinquish his view. Berkeley's reasoning for this view also has its explanation: if his view conceals an attempt to persuade one to accept a modification of language—conceals because of its being expressed in the indicative and its using but not mentioning words—then his reasoning will be construed not as showing its correctness but as urging the virtue of a proposed re-definition and the demerits of present usage. The first two linguistic approaches would thus take Berkeley's theory as an attempt to give a correct answer to one or other of the questions, 'What is the analysis of the concept "physical object"?', 'What is the proper use of the words "physical object"?'; the last takes it as not attempting a true answer to any question whatever. It therefore directs its efforts, not to refuting Berkeley but to showing what his view comes to, i.e. what linguistic features he emphasizes in order to persuade one of the need for a linguistic alteration.

Although a number of philosophers have, in working with a particular philosophical theory, done the kind of meta-philosophical analysis I have just described, i.e. shown what specific linguistic modification is being recommended, they have not always proceeded in this fashion and consequently have not subscribed to the above general account of the nature of philosophical theories. Norman Malcolm, for example, describes the sceptic as recommending the discontinuance of the application of the word 'certain' to empirical statements, but in some of his writings he seems not to take this kind of view. Max Black describes the critics of induction as proposing a change of terminology, viz. of 'practically know' for 'know for certain', holding that their criticism arises because they prefer to construe 'know' in a limiting sense, that is, as meaning 'deductively certain'.[1] Nevertheless, Black denies he is analyzing the dispute between defenders and critics of induction as being about how inductive inference ought to be described. Similarly, Moore denies, in his comment on a paper of mine, that the sceptic is proposing how the word 'know' ought to be used, and in a comment on a paper by Morris Lazerowitz, that he is proposing anything about the use of the word 'unreal'.[2]

I should like now to canvass briefly the objections to the view that a philosophical theory proposes a linguistic change. In *Language and Philosophy* Max Black, in referring to Moore, cites the fact that 'the man who might be supposed to know best whether he is making a recommendation strenuously resists the suggestion'.[3] This it seems to me is not a convincing reason. Normally it would be, but when one considers the scandalous fact that after more than 2000 years philosophers are still so unclear about what philosophy is as not to be puzzled by the fact that no single theory remains undisputed, I think we can grant Moore nothing further than that he certainly *thinks* he is not making linguistic recommendations. What one thinks one is doing and what one is in fact doing may be quite different things. Hume certainly thought he was urging us to establish empirically, by introspection, that there could not be a simple idea without a correspondent impression; and yet he had already stated that 'by *ideas* I mean the faint images of [impressions]'.[4] It should be pointed out that to hold that traditional philosophers are making linguistic proposals is not the same as to say they are making *conscious* linguistic proposals. Any person holding the proposal theory would certainly say that philosophers are unaware of the fact that they are revising language, and that what they do with language deludes them as well as others. Freud's well-known study on the psychopathology of

[1] Max Black, *Language and Philosophy* (Cornell University Press, 1949), pp. 75–78 (Cornell University Press, 1949)
[2] *The Philosophy of G. E. Moore*, The Library of Living Philosophers, Vol. IV, pp. 673–75, edited by P. A. Schilpp (Laselle, Ill. Open Court Publishing Co.)
[3] Max Black, *Language and Philosophy*, p. 79.
[4] *A Treatise of Human Nature*, Bk. I, Pt. I, sec.I.

everyday life is sufficient evidence for the possibility of this being the case.

But there is one much more crucial criticism, directed against every linguistic theory about the nature of philosophy, which must be weighed. This criticism rests on the obvious fact that philosophical views are not ostensibly about the use of words at all. Philosophical statements use but do not mention words. They are expressed as though they were about matters of fact or, alternatively, about relations between concepts. Some philosophers appear to claim they are about both, for example, rationalists who hold the task of metaphysics to be discovery of the necessary features of *reality*. I should like to hold that just as the form of expression of philosophical theories misleads some philosophers into saying they are about our world, so the form misleads critics of linguistic approaches into supposing they do not convey merely verbal information.

What then about the view that they state the relation between concepts, and further, that their function is in no way to convey any facts about words? It seems to me that the likeness of an analysis, that is, a necessary proposition, to an empirical one, and its unlikeness to such a proposition as 'The word "triangle" means three-sided figure', deceive one about the linguistic information it provides, information about the application of a word. It would be too great a task here for me to show in detail that necessary propositions yield only verbal information, but I shall try to sketch some reasons for holding this. However, it must be admitted to begin with that it is simply incorrect to say a necessary proposition is directly about words. 'Material bodies are extended' will not translate into any statement mentioning the phrase 'material bodies'. Nevertheless it is a fact that in understanding a sentence for a necessary proposition and knowing that what it expresses is necessarily true, what one knows is a *verbal* fact. In understanding the sentence 'Material bodies are extended' and knowing that it expresses a necessary truth one knows the phrase 'unextended material body' has no application.

Nevertheless, you might say, in understanding the sentence 'There are no white crows' and knowing that it expresses something true one likewise knows that 'white crows' has no application. This is correct, but putting the matter in this way obscures an important difference, which it is essential to be clear about: viz. that, in knowing that the one sentence expresses something contingently true, one knows the verbal fact that 'white crows' has in our language a descriptive use and the non-verbal fact that it applies to nothing; while, in knowing that the other expresses something necessarily true, one knows that 'unextended material bodies' has no descriptive use and one need know no non-verbal fact to know that what the sentence expresses is true. Knowing the verbal fact is sufficient for knowing a truth-value; there is no further fact to know. And this I take as grounds for holding that what a necessary proposition conveys is merely verbal information. One can understand the expression for a contingent proposition but lack knowledge as to whether what it describes exists or not. But in knowing that 'unextended material bodies' describes nothing conceivable, no such knowledge can be lacking. For nothing is described; if it were, then 'Material bodies are extended' could theoretically be false—when what is described by 'unextended material bodies' exists. The sentence 'It is impossible for unextended material bodies to exist', into which 'Material bodies are extended' translates, suggests that an imaginable state of affairs, namely, a state of affairs expressed by 'Unextended material bodies exist', is impossible. But when we understand the sentence 'It is impossible . . .' we know the linguistic fact that 'unextended material bodies' has no descriptive use, not that it describes what is counter to natural law. Thus, although our necessary proposition does not assert any linguistic fact it does indirectly give us information about usage. And further, it gives us no more than this, since when we understand an expression not to have a use we cannot go on to say we either know or can come to know a non-linguistic fact. For we cannot know that what is described by a phrase which does not describe either could or could not, or does not, exist.

This linguistic aspect of necessary propositions is what justifies the linguist in philosophy in maintaining the relevance of attending to the verbal information concealed by the form of expression. Both the philosopher who interprets a theory as attempting either a correct analysis or a correct account of usage and the philosopher who interprets it as proposing a revision of language are attending to just this concealed information. The latter arrives at his position via the thesis that a philosophical theory is being proposed for acceptance, in philosophical discourse, as a logical necessity, for example, that 'Physical objects are classes of ideas' shall be understood by philosophers to express a necessary truth. And thus what is proposed on the verbal level is that 'unperceived physical object' shall not have a use. On all of these views about philosophical theories then, the focus is on the verbal fact which the theories conceal.

Something should be said about one remaining view which is usually construed as linguistic, namely, the positivistic view that metaphysical statements are nonsense. This view is arrived at by the use of a criterion for determining the meaningfulness of indicative sentences, the so-called principle of verifiability in sense experience. This criterion has a number of different formulations, but each of them seems open to conclusive objections. One formulation is as follows: a declarative sentence which does not express an *a priori* proposition is meaningful if and only if the proposition it expresses can be confirmed or refuted in sense experience. So formulated the criterion implies a contradiction, for it implies that a sentence open to testing by the criterion expresses a proposition and at the same time might fail to express one, since the criterion may show the sentence to be literally meaningless. For there must be a proposition in order for the criterion to have a non-vacuous application, and if the proposition fails to meet the test the criterion implies that no proposition was expressed.[1] This objection can be avoided by saying that a declarative sentence which does not express an *a priori* proposition is meaningful if and only if it expresses a proposition verifiable (or refutable) in sense experience. But this formulation avoids the contradiction only by begging the question: it is artificially tailored to exclude as meaningless any sentence failing to express a proposition open to *sense* testing. Metaphysical sentences are eliminated from intelligible discourse by linguistic fiat—by an arbitrary decision to apply 'senseless' to them.[2] Despite these

---

[1] For an attempt to meet this criticism, which was made in M. Lazerowitz' 'The Principle of Verifiability', *Mind*, Vol. XLVI, pp. 372–78, see A. J. Ayer's Introduction to the second edition of *Language, Truth and Logic* (1948) (London: Victor Gollancz, 1948)

[2] This criticism together with others are elaborated in M. Lazerowitz' *The Structure of Metaphysics*, pp. 49–57.

difficulties, it must in fairness be said that the positivist critique of philosophical language has the merit of making perspicuous the unique position occupied by the sentences of metaphysics. It has underlined the need for a correct understanding of the differences between these and commonsense, scientific, and mathematical statements.

10

THE PROBLEM OF LINGUISTIC
INADEQUACY*

'In how far is it possible to express the processes of mathematical thinking by means of symbolic languages?'[1] Such a question gives vent to a pervasive distrust, not merely of our mother tongue, but even of artificially constructed languages, which are the best we have as models of clarity. The question 'Is any language adequate?' expresses openly the doubt that one often detects in semiconcealment and that quite frequently is answered boldly in the negative. Whitehead, for example, says, 'It is merely credulous to accept verbal phrases as adequate statements of propositions'.[2] 'No verbal statement is the adequate expression of a proposition.'[3] Further, 'language, in its ordinary usages, penetrates but a short distance into the principles of metaphysics'.[4] 'Philosophers can never hope finally to formulate . . . metaphysical first principles. Weakness of insight and deficiencies of language stand in the way inexorably.'[5]

These statements condemn language as being seriously defective and as failing to do what it is intended to do. They give rise to the idea that language is like a tailored suit that does not fit. If the comparison is justified, then the duty of philosophers who have led the cry against language is clear: to silence the criticisms by making alterations of such a sort that language will expose what it is designed to express. In this paper I want to maintain that such criticisms are quite unlike ordinary ones, that they are pseudo complaints, which masquerade as genuine. The curious thing about them is that they remain even after each specific vocabulary limitation, each specific clumsy expression, is remedied. Non-

---

* Reprinted from *Philosophical Analysis, A Collection of Essays*, edited by Max Black (Cornell University Press, 1950).
[1] See P. Bernays' review of E. Beth's *Inleidung tot de wijsbegeerte der wiskunde*, *Jour. Symbolic Logic*, VIII (1944), p. 145.   [2] *Process and Reality* (1929), p. 17 (Cambridge University Press, 1929). [3] *Ibid.*, p. 20. [4] *Ibid.*, p. 254. [5] *Ibid.*, p. 6.

philosophical people on the whole, seem to be satisfied with language; and when they are not they know how to remove their dissatisfaction—as when they become aware of important phenomena for which there are no words or when no words at hand are just the right ones. By contrast, philosophers who find fault with language are *chronically* dissatisfied; and, what is to be noticed, their attempts at linguistic reform always fail of realization. Philosophers appear to have discernment where ordinary sensibilities are blunt. They appear to be genuinely attempting to correct language in accordance with their discernment, and their attempts at reform create the impression that reform is possible. These impressions are, as I shall argue, illusory. For what is in theory corrigible should not always fail of correction. What, then, is the cause of their failure? Why should their complaints be chronic? I think the answer is that these complaints are *theoretically* impossible to silence.

Now, language, particularly ordinary language, has been the object of an extensive catalogue of criticisms, some of them genuine and, as just claimed, some of them not. It is important to distinguish these two sorts of criticism, since outwardly, because of their verbal form, they appear to be the same. I shall call genuine those complaints against language which settle upon deficiencies for which there is at least in theory a remedy, a remedy which removes the dissatisfaction decisively. All of us are acquainted with shortcomings in language which have been satisfactorily corrected. For example, ambiguity. Double meanings are quite usually capable of elimination with the exercise of care. Further explanation removes misunderstanding. Inconsistency is another such fault in language, the theory of types serving as a satisfactory means of eliminating inconsistencies the source of which was at one time unknown. Still others are specific vocabulary inadequacies, vagueness, inexactness of expression.

In the case of each of these latter three features, the remedies are familiar: when we find our vocabulary too restricted to make useful discriminations, we introduce new classifications. At one time the term 'insane' was adequate for the purposes of describing the mentally unbalanced. When differing types of mental unbalance were observed, convenience dictated the introduction of new terminology—'schizophrenia', 'paranoia', etc.—and with its introduction the cause of dissatisfaction was removed. The same type of remedy suffices in the simple situation in which some new phenomenon is discovered for which a name is needed. Again, we all know what kind of thing satisfies us when we are 'groping for the proper words' and feel that the way in which we have expressed ourselves is inexact, does not say precisely what we mean, or describe exactly how we feel. The right words exist in the language and we struggle to make a point clearer or to describe a feeling more carefully by a new choice of words. Again, when we feel that language is vague, as when we find ourselves arguing at odds about religion or democracy, we remedy the situation, and thereupon carry on or dismiss the argument, by agreeing on a definition of terms. This agreement will represent a decision to fix on some feature or features not yet fixed by convention. When terms are vague, the vagueness is not a result of any lack of information about facts. *All* evidence relevant to deciding the application of a term, e.g. 'vegetable', is at hand, and the indecision remains. That is, it is not logically possible, by reference to the fixed criteria and the presented facts, to decide either that a term or its opposite is applicable. For this reason the only means of decision will be an arbitrary one. The fruit vendor who argued against his prosecution for selling tomatoes on a Sunday, on the ground that anything containing its own seed is a fruit, was asking that he be acquitted of the charge of selling vegetables by an arbitrary decision to fix on 'containing its seeds' as the defining feature of fruit. Any dissatisfaction felt with a decision is then not with language but with how the decision has affected one's fortunes.

Of course dissatisfaction with a decision that is not determined by rules but for which new rules are invented, i.e. which is made arbitrarily, may be turned back upon language. When this happens the fact that there exists a twilight zone of cases which we cannot classify as either ϕ or non-ϕ is cited as evidence of linguistic inadequacy. It is argued that if the only ways open to us of resolving vagueness are either to add new criteria for the application of a word, or to add new words in place of the old, then language is at fault—and not only ordinary language but artificially constructed languages. Questions which cannot be answered because of vagueness are somewhat of a commonplace in ordinary English; for example, 'Is this a plant or an animal?' 'Is he in his right mind or not?' 'Did he break his promise or not?' But their existence does not indicate shortcomings of ordinary English from which a language of less rambling growth is free. Within the language of mathematics, which by comparison with English is carefully constructed, we come upon similar questions. For example, 'Is an existential argument employing noneffective processes to be classified as a proof or not?' Even in a logistic system, where a point is made of stating exactly what constitutes a correct proof, the question whether the use of noneffective processes declasses an argument can arise. The suspicion grows that no matter how carefully a language system is set out, the problem of vagueness will inevitably crop up. Further, supposing, with Whitehead that 'one source of vagueness is deficiency of language',[1] the deficiency is of a kind which defies remedy. Penumbral cases spring up afresh with every attempt at elimination. No sooner is a classification effected by the introduction of a third category 'perhaps ϕ' in addition to the categories ' ϕ' and 'non-ϕ' than a new indecision, Hydra-like, arises over the application of ' ϕ', 'non-ϕ' and 'perhaps ϕ'. Inasmuch as there are *always* real or imaginary cases which we are unable to classify, there appears to be some justification for the complaint that language is chronically incapable of making sharp distinctions.

Nevertheless, I wish to hold that this is a pseudo-complaint and fundamentally different from those complaints which are silenced by such practical remedies as the introduction of new terminology ('neutrons', 'quanta'), a better choice of words for the expression of an idea, or an arbitrary decision to resolve vagueness. There is a series of complaints like this one, 'metaphysical' complaints of the kind commonly made by philosophers, which continue to arise despite the remedies that remove the specific dissatisfactions felt at the time, and which remain no matter what philosophic attempts at reform are made. It is with such complaints, which I shall argue are completely nongenuine because they are raised against situations hopelessly, i.e. theoretically, beyond remedy, that we shall concern ourselves.

A number of these grievances are connected with the claim that our vocabulary is too limited to express what we wish to express, that there are gaps in language comparable to those left between

---

[1] *Essays in Science and Philosophy* (1947), p. 127 (N.Y: Philosophical Library, 1947).

the relatively few names for colours in the colour spectrum. 'Language is incomplete and fragmentary, and merely registers a stage in the average advance beyond ape-mentality. But all men enjoy flashes of insight beyond meanings already stabilized in etymology and grammar. Hence the rôle of literature, the rôle of the special sciences, and the rôle of philosophy:—in their various ways engaged in finding linguistic expressions for meanings as yet unexpressed.'[1]

The charge of vocabulary deficiency often takes a form which is easily confused with the ordinary dissatisfaction over the limitations or inaccessibility of our own vocabulary. We sometimes complain of 'being unable to find the right words', though when we do so we know how to go about effecting a remedy. The philosophic complaint is not at all an expression of frustration over not finding the words which are there for the choosing. The trouble is that *no* words are exactly the right words. They do not exist. Language is accordingly claimed to fall short, to lag behind both experience and conceptual thought. In studying the history of ideas we are asked to remember 'the struggle of novel thought with the obtuseness of language'.[2] Again, we are told that 'content cannot be communicated': language is incapable of conveying the ineffable in experience. No colour word, for example, ever conveys the precise colour experience, partly because what is unique in individual experience cannot be shared, partly because the specificity of experience always escapes embodiment in general terms, which we of necessity use. In the attempt to describe our experience we are in constant struggle with the coarse medium of expression. The claim that the words we have are deficient in power of expression, especially in expression of quality, suggests that if the gaps in language were filled we should have words capable of doing what the present ones cannot do. The type of grievance just expressed is not, however, to be assuaged by the invention of new terminology. No new word fills the need exactly.

Further, in those cases where a practical dissatisfaction is actually allayed by the introduction of new terms, the fact that new dissatisfactions are possible tempts one to a new and different type of complaint. In practice one sometimes finds that when certain linguistic gaps are filled further gaps are discovered, whence one

[1] A. N. Whitehead, *Adventures of Ideas* (1933), p. 291.   [2] *Ibid.*, p. 153.

comes to feel that however many holes may be plugged in the dike there will always be others. For example, suppose that a vague word like 'insanity' is replaced in psychiatric usage by a series of words which discriminate between the various types of mental disorder. These words again may need to be replaced by others. Whenever this kind of situation occurs it is natural to complain that the old language, which was felt to be adequate up to the time when new discriminations were needed, was actually inadequate all the while, because its words were neither precise enough nor numerous enough. It is like a meagre kit of blunt tools beside a complete kit of precision instruments. The trouble is that there is always the possibility of new and sharper precision instruments with which present instruments would compare unfavourably. One is then tempted to say no tools are really sharp enough since there could be still sharper tools which would be better; nor are there enough of them since a greater number would be more useful. And one is tempted to say a revised and augmented language is unsatisfactory for analogous reasons. It is in the same position with respect to the language of the future as the outmoded language now is with respect to it. It too has gaps and inexactnesses; we are merely not aware of them at present.

The existence of rudimentary languages alongside more highly developed ones gives additional force to the suggestion that every language has gaps which in a more highly developed language would be filled in. Looking back on the rudimentary language we attribute to it the lacks which, from our present vantage point, we should feel if we were forced to continue using it. Whenever the merits of the new symbolism are extolled, the rudimentary language suffers by invidious comparison. Thus one philosopher writes: 'The development of mathematics . . . shows that with new linguistic means new kinds of facts can be described. In a language possessing, say, five numerals and the word "many", even the simple fact that in a field A there are six more sheep than in a field B cannot be stated. The use of an arithmetical calculus permits us to describe relations which simply could not be described without it.'[1] Now of course it is quite true that one notation can express facts which another notation cannot. This is

[1] K. R. Popper, 'Why Are the Calculuses of Logic and Arithmetic Applicable to Reality?' (Symposium), *Arist. Soc. Proc.*, suppl. vol. XX (1943), pp. 58-59.

a matter of fact. But it can be turned into a matter of complaint, and one, furthermore, which leads to a complaint forever beyond remedy. It is natural to suppose that the poorer notation suffers from deficiencies that the richer notation makes good, and that such deficiencies existed even before the need for a new symbolism was felt. Now, if a given language which served its purpose for a period of time could at the same time be defective, there seems to be no reason for supposing other languages are not in the same position. Our attitude towards both rudimentary and more highly developed languages should be the same: if the one is defective, why not the other? The only difference between a language with which we are at present satisfied and one with which we are dissatisfied is that we have not yet discovered, in the first case, the inherent inadequacies which may very well exist. Our attitude towards less highly developed languages than our own is infectious: if, unlike a house intended to keep out rain but built without a roof, those languages could be deficient without our knowing it, then we seem to have a ground for dissatisfaction with every language. For all we know, every language may have gaps. And it is a source of dissatisfaction with every language that this doubt must remain. Such a dissatisfaction can never be removed, since so long as a new symbolism is unneeded there is no way of determining whether there are deficiencies or not.

There remains one further criticism, directed against natural languages, which should I think be classified with the 'philosophic' complaints just discussed. This is that natural languages are not constructed after the manner of formal systems: they have no rules that determine which sequences of symbols are meaningful sentences and not a sufficient number of rules for deciding in a great many cases whether one proposition is a consequence of others. In a formal system such rules are framed independently of any meanings the symbols may have. By contrast, in our ordinary language the rules of grammar will not decide, without recourse to the meanings of the constituent symbols, whether a given combination makes sense. Nor will formal transformation rules provide a complete list of consequence relations; for many consequence relations, such as that between 'This is a horse' and 'This is an animal', are not formal. Consequently, logicians often express dissatisfaction with the vernacular because it falls short of the model—of the consciously planned language of a logistic system. But is this a dissatisfaction which can, at least in theory, be remedied? If we were to adjoin to ordinary language a set of special rules to the effect that 'goodness is tastier than 10' does not make sense, etc., and a further set of rules telling us that '*x* is a horse' implies '*x* is an animal', etc., should we in this way achieve the ideal set by the model? There would be no disguising the fact that these rules differ from the usual formation and transformation rules. Disregarding the fact that there would be an astronomical number of them, would we be satisfied with the resultant 'system'? Should we have a formal system with formal rules, or a more explicit statement of what we already have—ordinary English, with some of the transformation rules functioning as rules for the use of individual words? Such a statement as ' "*x* is a horse" implies "*x* is an animal" ' tells us that we may not apply the word 'horse' in any case where we cannot apply the word 'animal'. And if we wish to call this a 'formal' rule, then we do so by courtesy only; and no one will be deceived into supposing we have what would ordinarily be called a formal rule. The complaint, then, that natural languages lack precise rules of formation and transformation seems, like the 'metaphysical' dissatisfactions canvassed thus far, incapable of being dispelled.

The claim that language is a clumsy vehicle never quite fitted to its task, that it is *intrinsically* unequal to the demands we make of it, has been contrasted as sharply as possible with the uncontested fact that language has certain defects which are difficult to overcome but which conceivably, and often in practice, are overcome. It was necessary to emphasize this distinction because on the surface the claim and the statement of fact look so much alike. Both appear to express regrets about imperfections of language, and the similarity between them is accentuated not merely by the use of exactly the same words in the expression of specific complaints but by a parallel delineation of possibilities of remedy. I have tried to show that the philosophic complaints against language, for all their similarity to ordinary complaints, are the sort which are never stilled.

I shall further try to show that they are pseudo-complaints, counterfeits of the genuine article. They correspond to the genuine complaints like the shadow of a man to the man; they have no substance. Philosophers who deplore the shortcomings of language create the impression that these are remediable by proposing various means of improvement. It must be admitted that it is usually not clear whether they are endeavouring to remove an ordinary dissatisfaction or are only going through the motions. I wish to maintain that if it is a philosophic dissatisfaction which they are attempting to remove, then the appearance that remedial steps are being taken is illusory. Attempts to silence philosophic complaints *must* fail. By analysis of what is demanded in order for each specific inadequacy to be corrected I shall try to show that the ideal of adequacy is not simply in fact impossible of attainment, but that it is logically impossible. What must be done in order to free language from philosophic criticisms cannot conceivably be done. And if this can be shown, it will thereby be established that the criticisms are spurious. No complaints over failures to overcome shortcomings are real complaints if success is ruled out by logic.

I shall first give an account of various philosophic attempts to correct language. Each attempt is foredoomed to failure, although each has the appearance of being a genuine attempt to overcome a genuine shortcoming. Consider first the attack made by philosophers on vagueness. At least two methods have been proposed for its elimination or diminution. One is the construction of ideal language systems; another is analysis. The first, of which the main proponents are the logical empiricists and certain logicians, creates a new symbolism, not to fill out the gaps in ordinary language, but to provide a model by means of which the reform of common syntax could be accomplished.[1] The second, of which Professor G. E. Moore is the primary exponent, aims at clarification of concepts; and this clarification has been claimed to effect a diminution of vagueness.

It is not entirely clear how the construction of artificial language systems is to contribute to the reform of common syntax, though the following has been offered by way of explanation: 'the syntactical property of a particular word-language, such as English . . . is best represented and investigated by comparison with a constructed language which serves as a system of reference.'[2] In the

---

[1] Y. Bar-Hillel, 'Analysis of "Correct" Language', *Mind*, Vol. |LV (1946), pp. 339–40.   [2] R. Carnap, *The Logical Syntax of Language* (1937), p. 8.

work from which this quotation is taken, Carnap did not attempt to establish this thesis, but one would expect syntactical reform to proceed by the elimination of such expressions as violate the rules for the construction of correct sentences. That there will be differences between a language which has 'just grown' and the formalized counterpart which replaces it is assured by the fact that 'in constructing a syntax and semantics for a natural language, say English, [a point is made of resolving] certain uncertainties vaguenesses, and inconsistencies, which are found in the existing (pragmatical) usage. . . .'[1] One would expect comparisons to be effected between the natural language and its formalization. At least it would be expected that similarities and divergences, for example, between the English usages of 'implies' and the single usage of this term in the interpreted system, would show up, even though not pointed out.

I think it is doubtful whether the construction of an artificial language with any considerable divergence from ordinary English would induce anyone to reform ordinary language to conform to it. In respect of certain imperfections in a natural language, e.g. ambiguity and inconsistency, it cannot be denied that the model language can serve a useful function. If in ordinary English one had occasion to construct sequences of symbols which according to the theory of types were nonsense, one would doubtless reform one's language. But in respect of vagueness, an exact formal language provides no cure whatever. Its exactness is lost when it is applied to the vernacular. For example, the model makes the term 'implies' relatively free from vagueness in the connections in which it functions. But when the term is placed within the vague contexts existing in English, the model turns out to be useless. The formalized language has nothing to offer which is in any way relevant to resolving the vagueness prompting such questions as 'Does "S has $50,000" imply "$S$ is rich"?' In fact, if a linguistic change is effected in such a way as to give an answer, it is the pressure of the practical need for a decision, not the example of a model language, which brings it about.

It is not part of the views of practicing philosophical analysts that language suffers from an *intrinsic* inadequacy. As the work of

[1] Alonzo Church, 'Carnap's *Introduction to Semantics*', *Philosophical Review*, Vol. LII (1943), p. 298.

Moore bears witness, it is unquestioned that language, even ordinary discourse, is always capable of satisfactory emendation. It is usually supposed that analysis yields an expression which is clearer than the original; and if it does this it yields a positive and practical satisfaction, undiluted by the hopeless dissatisfaction residing in philosophic complaints. It is when analysis is claimed at least to diminish vagueness[1] that one wonders whether this means is being used to allay an ordinary or a pseudo dissatisfaction. The latter would appear to be the case from the account given by Copilowish. For although he maintains that 'any borderline case may be resolved by means of an analysis and definition of the term',[2] he at the same time casts doubt on the possibility of fulfilling the promise he holds out. He admits that because the terms of the definiens are vague, the definiens must likewise be vague, so that our hope of diminishing vagueness in the definiendum lies in repeated analysis. However, 'we cannot assume an attainable limit to this process, even though we tend towards absolute precision as a limit. . . . [This] is perhaps not even theoretically possible'.[3] If it is not even theoretically possible to reach a goal, it is difficult to see what it means to say that we approach it, or even to say that a goal exists. The process of removing vagueness, if conceived as a process of approaching what is not theoretically attainable, is no process of *removing* vagueness. 'Removing vagueness', like 'approaches the horizon', describes nothing.

It seems to be undisputed that analysis of a general idea (or definition of a general term) has some merit, though it is difficult to say precisely what it is. I do not think it can be the removal of vagueness, or even the diminution of it. If an analysis is correct and if the definiendum is vague, it is hard to see how the definiens could be any less vague. For example, the definition of 'animal' as 'any member of the group of living beings typically endowed with sensation and voluntary motion' leaves it still undecided in certain cases whether a thing is animal or plant. If an analysis makes the application of a word sharp in cases where it was not sharp before, then it has not merely elicited features already contained in the meaning of the word; it has added something. The

---

[1] I. M. Copilowish, 'Border-line Cases, Vagueness, and Ambiguity', *Philosophy of Science*, Vol. VI (1939), pp. 181–195.
[2] *Ibid.*, p. 188. [3] *Ibid.*, pp. 187–88.

criteria for the word's application in these cases have not been analytically derived. They have been added, and analysis has *elicited* nothing. The only thing an analysis would seem capable of doing is to make our *knowledge* of the meanings of words non-vague. But this it could do only if the words were nonvague to begin with. Closer inspection of the foliage of a tree will show the leaves to be sharply outlined instead of blurred, as they seem to be from a distance, only if in fact they have sharp outlines. When the application of a word is genuinely vague, the close inspection we make of it in an analysis will only reveal its vagueness.

The fact that borderline cases still exist in the face of correct analytic definitions is evidence that continued analysis will not resolve such cases. In actual practice our means of coming to a decision about a borderline case is not to engage in a series of definitions. We not only do not continue with a series of definitions; we do not even go a few steps. Usually the resolution of borderline cases is effected *arbitrarily*, by settling on some feature of the analysans and ignoring others, or even by allowing some further feature not given in the definition to decide the issue. The decision to classify desmids as motile plants rather than as animals must have been made by virtue of some other feature than those listed in the above definition of 'animal'. In some cases a question about classification is settled without any appeal to definition. The classification of $\sqrt{2}$ and $\sqrt{-1}$ as numbers was justified once it was proved that every algebraic equation of nth degree has n roots, whence $x^2 = 2$ and $x^2 = -1$ would have to have roots. It might be claimed that this proof showed up analytic properties of roots, and hence of numbers, which were previously unknown. I should say this proof did not demonstrate an analytic connection between numbers and algebraic equations, but that *accepting* it as a proof constituted an extension of the meaning of the term 'root', whereupon the meaning of 'number' was likewise extended. It would have been awkward to divide algebraic equations into those having roots and those not, and much simpler to say some had rational roots, some real, and some imaginary. After choosing the simpler alternative it again would have produced an awkward asymmetry not to call these new roots numbers. The decision whether the negative numbers were properly to be called numbers was most likely settled in a similar manner, by reference to considerations of symmetry: if numbers can always be arrived at by the process of addition, one does not want to say the process of subtraction yields them only up to the point where zero is reached.

It is significant that continued analysis should be proposed as a means of resolving vagueness when there exists the simple expedient of making a decision. I think with this proposal the resolution of vagueness changes from a practical problem to one of those recalcitrant philosophic problems whose solution we shall always despair of. For the remedy for vagueness is conceived in such a way that the dissatisfaction must remain. Making a correct analysis looks like *finding* some feature which will settle the application of a term. But there is no discovering a feature, say, of being rich which would decide whether a man with $50,000 was rich. To elicit it by analysis would be to find a feature which is not there to be found, inasmuch as the conventional definition of 'rich' does not stipulate a minimum sum the possession of which makes one rich. Continued analysis would obviously not help. If it becomes necessary to come to a decision, then the only settlement will be an arbitrary one. For example, if a man were legally bound to give up two-thirds of his earnings when he became rich, and at no point would admit to being rich, a successful suit to compel payment would no doubt involve a court decision that part of the meaning of 'being rich' was to have, say, $50,000. And the court's decision would not be an interpretation of what the word already meant but of what the court decreed it was to mean in this case.

It cannot be denied that analysis does sometimes help in making a decision in a dispute. It may elicit a feature which we choose to emphasize as the deciding factor. That is, it may make explicit a feature not explicitly grasped before, which we select as the most important defining criterion. But the analysis does not in any way determine the importance we place on it.

That certain complaints against language are spurious but that they have a deceptive similarity to genuine ones, even in the matter of remedies for their removal, has I think been sufficiently established. I wish now to show the pseudo-character of each complaint, by showing that the improvement of language which would be required to allay the dissatisfaction is logically impossible. In each case we are apparently presented with an ideal which language falls short of. But it turns out that the attainment of that ideal is not possible even in theory; the improvement which seems to be sought is a self-contradictory will-o'-the-wisp, which there is no real chasing, but only the semblance of chasing.

Let us consider first the desire for a more adequate terminology which is expressed in the complaint that we cannot find the right words to say precisely what we mean. Sometimes a psychological blockage prevents our finding the right words, but what prevents the philosopher from finding the right words is that they do not exist. The philosopher's dissatisfaction is that no word in the existing vocabulary is exactly the right word. The obvious remedy would seem to be creation of new words to express what one intends. Whitehead's large-scale manufacture of new terminology looks to be this sort of remedy. He says: 'Every science must devise its own instruments. The tool required for philosophy is language. Thus philosophy redesigns language in the same way that, in a physical science, pre-existing appliances are redesigned.'[1] What philosophers do indicates that such redesigning of language has a twofold aim. One is to name new phenomena which philosophers claim to have discovered; the other is to enable us to express ideas of which we are aware but which are 'verbally unexpressed'[2] and moreover, in the present language, inexpressible.

The invention of symbolism to name new philosophic discoveries has an interesting feature worth remarking on. A new philosophic terminology for this purpose gives the impression of satisfying a linguistic need in a quite straightforward way; and its introduction is therefore not to be classified with attempts at linguistic improvement which are bound to fail. What philosophers do when they introduce such new words as 'sense-data', 'monads', or 'universals' appears to have its model in what scientists do when they become aware of an important phenomenon for which there is no word. One philosopher, for example, characterizes the analysis of 'I seemed to see a penny but there was none' as 'I sensed a penny-like sense-datum but it was not of a penny' as follows: 'The new notation is given in an attempt to reflect more adequately the form of the fact which the original sentence expresses; and it does so because it *names* an element not hitherto

[1] *Process and Reality*, p. 16.   [2] A. N. Whitehead, *Modes of Thought* (1938), p. 49 (New York: The Macmillan Co., 1938).

named.'[1] If philosophers do make empirical discoveries and for convenience give names to the entities discovered, it is quite proper to describe their invention of new terms as a straightforward provision for a linguistic need. What they do is then of the same order as what chemists do when they discover a new element. But the curious feature of their terminological revision is that there is no general agreement among philosophers as to whether it is needed—whether there *is* any new phenomenon named by the new name.[2] Discoveries claimed by philosophers differ in a puzzling way from those claimed by scientists. Disagreements over the existence of the purported facts, which all are in a position to examine, persist despite all 'evidence'.[3] The question about the introduction of philosophic terms for new discoveries thus seems to be, not whether one can fill a linguistic need by this means, but whether there is any need. The case is different with regard to the redesigning of language demanded by philosophers who claim to have no words for the ideas they wish to express.

It is a commonplace that a person who knows one language may find, when he learns another, that what is expressible in his native language is not always exactly expressible in the acquired one; something gets lost in the translation. Such a person is in a very different position from one who asserts, within his language, that no word is the right word for what he wants to say. His complaint suggests that what is needed is an adaptation of language so as to express those meanings which it is now too gross to express. To this end new words are required, since the old ones will not do.

Now, is it logically possible for a new word to be the right word for an idea? How will a new word, which so to speak comes naked, be the right word? To be the right word it must carry exactly the right meaning, whereas being new, it has, to start with, no meaning. It will have to be given its meaning in the way in which the unsatisfactory word was given its meaning: ostensively, by application to phenomena, or verbally, by being correlated with known words. But the new ostensive definition can do no more than the

[1] Helen Smith, in 'Symposium: Is There a Problem About Sense-data?' *Aristotelian Society Proceedings*, suppl., vol. XV (1936), p. 84.
[2] See G. A. Paul, *ibid.*, pp. 61–77.
[3] For a study which works out this kind of point in another connection, see M. Lazerowitz, 'The Existence of Universals', in *The Structure of Metaphysics*.

old one did; and if a verbal definition gives the word the *right* meaning, the meaning it *should* have, then there exist expressions in the language which do have exactly the right meaning, in which case there is no real cause for complaint.

But if the old words cannot be the right ones, then neither can the new ones, since they must be explained by the old ones. A tailor cannot hope to satisfy a customer who complains that the old fabric is no good by spinning a new fabric from the old threads. To introduce a new word by means of old ones is of course to do with the old words what was claimed could not be done. Any description of what would make an expression, which we do not as yet have, the proper one to express what we cannot now say would involve our actually having the proper words for expressing what we wish. It would appear, then, that 'finding the proper words because the old ones will not do' is but a pretended task. For what must be done is self-contradictory: invent new words to which the meaning we wish them to express is assigned, but to which that meaning cannot be assigned for lack of the right words.

Another closely related complaint, though a somewhat different one, is that language is not capable of expressing the ineffable in experience, that what we experience 'words cannot describe'. Communication of the concreteness of our experience is impossible, and for a variety of related reasons. One is that its specificity always escapes embodiment in general terms, another that words cannot unlock the door to an indvidual's private world. Only if language could 'embody what it indicates' would our experience be uncommicable: 'The art of literature, vocal or written, is to adjust the language so that it embodies what it indicates.'[1] But that such a state of affairs should be achieved is self-contradictory. For what would it be like for the experience indicated by a colour word to be incorporated in the language? Apparently the experience itself would be in the position of a word. But in that case the embodiment would function to indicate something beyond itself. It would then not be an embodiment, but a symbol—the original unsatisfactory substitute for the experience. The only meaning we can give to the expressed aim that what the symbol inadequately stands for should be *embodied* in the symbol is that what the symbol stands for should *replace* the symbol. This

[1] A. N. Whitehead, *Essays in Science and Philosophy*, p. 107.

means that it would take over its *representative* function. But to do so would be self-stultifying; for once what the symbol denotes takes over the rôle of denoting, the old complaint would reappear. It must reappear, since it is the representative, denoting function of the symbol that is complained against.

If we consider what would happen to a symbol, as contrasted with what it symbolizes, were it to embody what it indicates, we arrive at an equally paradoxical consequence: a symbol embodies what it designates only when it no longer designates. Suppose we require that terms describing experience be made less and less general until finally a point is reached where they carry in themselves what they indicate. At this point one would apparently not have a symbol at all, but the experience. An experience, not a symbol, would now be a constituent of the description, in which case understanding a statement about someone's experience would consist in *having* the experience. This is to say the symbol would incorporate its referent only by no longer referring to something beyond itself. But then it would no longer be a symbol. It turns out that the complaint against language is that a self-contradictory state of affairs does not exist: words do not function both as symbols to indicate a content lying beyond themselves and at the same time carry that content in themselves. This is scarcely a complaint.

It is sometimes urged that words are no better instrument for the communication of thoughts than they are of subjective experiences: 'although the dictionary or the encyclopaedia gives what may be called the official and socially sanctioned meaning of a word, no two people who use the same word have just the same thought in their minds'.[1] It is to be supposed from this statement of Russell's that a word is like an ill-fitting garment for the thought which it clothes, since it used to clothe so many different thoughts. A thought can only make an appearance to us in its verbal clothes, and in accordance with this view we must say there is merely an illusion, created by the repeated use of the same clothes, that the words dress one and the same idea.

But now is it not impossible that a word should have a socially sanctioned meaning and yet that no two people who use the word

[1] Bertrand Russell, *A History of Western Philosophy* (London: Allen & Unwin, 1945), pp. 50–51.

ever have that meaning in mind? How could one and the same meaning be attached to the word by society and yet no two of its members attach that meaning to it? That a word has such and such a meaning fixed by convention means that it is customarily used in social intercourse to express that meaning, whereas that no two people have the same thought corresponding to the same word entails that no two are giving the word its customary use. From Russell's claim it follows that no two people use the word in the way many people by custom use it, which is absurd. It therefore provides no reason for condemning language as unfitted to communicate thoughts.

It might be supposed that the invention of new symbolism is conclusive evidence of the inadequacy of the language to which it is adjoined, and that one would be justified in condemning such a language even before the need for further symbolism is felt. It is natural to view symbols of the form $a + bi$, for example, as additions made to the existing language of numbers for the purpose of filling in gaps which the language previously had. The situation is the same with rudimentary languages which a highly developed language seems to complete. Thus, the present language of arithmetic, in which we have the possibility of indefinitely writing numerals, seems to complete the language having the numerals from one to five and the word 'many'. That it is capable of expressing facts (e.g. that $6 > 5$) which the rudimentary language cannot seems properly to be ascribed to the superiority of a complete language over a fragmentary one.

Is this, however, a proper account of the difference between a simple and a highly developed language? And if it is, are we not forced to say that for all we know every language is incomplete? A counter-question is in order here: Incomplete with reference to what standard? Unless there exists a wider language of which a given symbolism is a part, we have no standard in relation to which it is incomplete. Further, even the fact that a symbolism L_1 is part of another, L_2 does not necessarily make L_1 incomplete, although it may be inadequate for certain purposes. The language of arithmetic can be said to be part of the language of real numbers; it lacks certain symbols and the rules for their usage. But although arithmetic is *inadequate* for certain purposes, e.g. for solving algebraic equations, it is not an *incomplete* arithmetic. No parts of it are *missing*, as there would be from a symbolism which purported to be our arithmetic but which lacked the operation 4 × 4. Taken by itself it is the whole language. It is completely unlike a dictionary with missing pages. Any inadequacy which at a given moment a *language* comes to have is not due to incompleteness. The classification 'incomplete' (and hence also the classification 'complete') is not properly applicable to a language. A symbolism which purports to be a language but which has missing parts can be called incomplete, but a language L_1 does not become incomplete when it becomes a part of L_2, because it does not purport to be L_2. It is a whole even though additions are made to it, since these additions do not supply missing parts. To repine that, for all we know, every language may be incomplete is to indulge in the absurd complaint that a whole language is perhaps not a whole language. Furthermore, it sounds as though a remedy may be needed, whereas there is no completing what is already a whole. We can add to it; but we cannot complete it.

It is natural, when we have the new language and look back at the old one, to read into the old one the inadequacy we should feel were we to continue using it in certain contexts. We assert that the rudimentary language cannot express certain relations among concepts which the more highly developed one can, as though this were a deficiency which is internal to it. Actually we are merely stating the fact that certain symbols, together with the rules for their use, are not part of it. And this is not like saying that certain cards are missing from the deck. It is like saying the deuces play no rôle in a game which uses a deck without them. This is not a defect. The game played without the deuces is not a deficient game, but a *different* one. Similarly, the game with 'one', . . . 'five', 'many' is simply a different one from that with 'one', 'two', and so on. The adequacy of the rudimentary language to the purposes for which it was constructed is in no way affected by the fact that the symbols '6', '7', '8', . . . do not occur in it and that 'many' plays a rôle in certain respects dissimilar to these. A language is in some ways like a map. A map that gives only the rivers of a certain territory and gives no detail of the mountains will be of no help to the mountain climber; but it is not thereby shown to have been inadequate before he needed a map for such a purpose. Similarly, there *was* no linguistic inadequacy before the need was felt which prompted introducing a more useful notation. A symbolism *cannot* be inadequate so long as it does the work it was designed to do. It cannot be criticized for not doing more than this. To say a language fails to come up to certain specifications when it was not constructed according to them is simply nonsense.[1]

I want now to consider the invidious comparison often made between our ordinary correct English and the model language of symbolic logic. The point of the comparison is not merely to cite the advantage, in fact the necessity, of a consciously planned syntax for a logistic system; it is evidently a criticism that English falls short of an ideal, and the criticism is made with the intention of reform. There is one general goal which I should suppose would determine the reformation of ordinary discourse: a reconstruction in the direction of exactness. To this end I should expect a basis to be laid for it in explicitly stated formal rules of formation and transformation, together with semantical rules assigning meanings to the expressions which are well formed, i.e. are in accordance with the formation rules. The result would be what Prof. Alonzo Church calls a formalized language, which he distinguishes from a logistic system only in its having an interpretation.[2] That is, to purely syntactical rules of formation and rules of inference, semantical rules are added. It is Church's view that there is no difference in principle between such a language and a natural language—though on this point logicians are disagreed. He wrote: 'The difference of any formalized language from a natural language lies not in any matter of principle, but in the degree of completeness that has been attained in the laying down of explicit syntactical and semantical rules and the extent to which vaguenesses and uncertainties have been removed from them.'[3] He illustrates his point by giving examples of such rules for a small segment of English. But the result is not quite English. For (1) its syntactical rules are 'less irregular, and logically simpler'[3] than those embedded in the complex language in use, and (2) 'the laying down of rules for a natural language, because of the need to fill gaps and to decide doubtful points, is as much a process of legislation as of

[1] For guiding ideas of the last two paragraphs I am indebted to lectures at Cambridge University by Dr L. Wittgenstein.
[2] 'The Need for Abstract Entities in Semantic Analysis', *Proceedings of the American Academy of Arts and Sciences*, Vol. 80, No. 1 (1951), p. 100.
[3] *Ibid.*, p. 106.

176

reporting'.[1] An instance of such a 'doubtful point' is counting 'The number of planets is round' as a sentence, which the few rules he gives allows. He observes that 'the advocates of a set-theoretic language may decide one way and the advocate of type theory another, but it is hard to say that either decision is the "true" decision for the English language as it is.'[2]

Carnap speaks in a similar vein of the 'meaning postulates' figuring in a language system, by reference to which he wishes to define the concept of analyticity. Whether, for example, one must include '$(x) . x$ is a bachelor $\supset \sim (x$ is married)' as a meaning postulate he says 'is not a matter of knowledge [that the concepts "bachelor" and "married" are incompatible] but of decision'.[3] The fact that the words 'bachelor' and 'married' are usually understood to designate incompatible properties might influence the decision, if one intended to reflect in the system some of the relations between the meanings of English words. Where the meaning is rather vague, as for example, that of 'raven', whether the author of a system includes '$(x) . x$ is a raven $\supset x$ is black' as a meaning postulate is arbitrary. 'It is . . . his task to make up his mind whether he wishes the predicates "raven" and "black" of his system to be used in such a way that the first logically entails the second. If so, he has to add the postulate . . . to the system, otherwise not.'[3] The resultant language system, call it L, will of course only approximate to the natural language; and the explication of the familiar concept of analyticity by means of the definition of 'analytic in L' will succeed as an explication only insofar as it agrees with the pre-systematic notion. But neither Carnap nor Church would judge a proposed criterion of analyticity by how closely it reproduces the pre-systematic concept. In connection with another question, namely, the question of settling on the criterion for deciding whether a given theory commits one to the existence of certain entities, Church writes: 'One important consideration in judging a proposed criterion of ontological commitment is how closely it reproduces the pre-systematically available notion of existence. But it is not profitable to press this test of correspondence with ordinary language beyond a certain

[1] *Proc. American Academy of Arts and Sciences*, Vol. 80, No. 1 (1951), p. 107
[2] *Ibid.*, p. 112.
[3] 'Meaning Postulates', *Philosophical Studies*, Vol. III (1952), p. 68.

degree of approximation. For ordinary language itself is not accurate beyond a certain point. . . . It is not a question of reproducing ordinary language but of reforming it.'[1]

I think it is evident that these logicians take ordinary language to be unsatisfactory because it is not 'Pythagorean'—not governed by rules precluding irregularities. A reformed English would presumably be something like the language of geometry, in which usage would be governed by precise rules. One would have to 'evade the manifold equivocacy of English words by selecting . . . just one meaning of each word mentioned'[2] or by signalizing all the different meanings. Presumably all meaning postulates would have to be stipulated explicitly. The result would be a language free from features which sometimes cause difficulty in ordinary contexts, such as ambiguity and vagueness. But it would not be English nor would it serve the purposes the natural language serves. In fact most of the things which make a natural language rich would have been squeezed out—poetic usage, metaphor, and even the use of language for which vagueness of concepts is a necessity of practice. For example, consider the definition of 'vitamin', cited from Webster by Dr D. B. Zilversmit in his article 'The Impact of Rigid Definitions on Scientific Thinking': 'A vitamin is an *organic* substance essential to the nutrition of most *animals* and some *micro-organisms*, acting in minute amounts on metabolic processes . . . not *ordinarily* synthesized or stored in the body in *large* quantities. . . .' The words italicized are obviously vague. Zilversmit notes that 'an expert knowledge of all the words or concepts used in the definition is not necessary',[3] specifically, the precise meaning of the word 'organic' or the precise borderlines between plants and animals. 'The definition is good', he says, 'because it avoids a sharp boundary. . . .' He goes on to show how such a loose definition would be useful to a person who wished to know whether thyroxin, which is produced by the thyroid gland, would best be defined as a vitamin. The utility of words whose boundaries are not exact is evident in more homely contexts; consider, for example, the word 'bald'. If the definition of a vague

[1] 'Ontological Commitment', Symposium. *The Journal of Philosophy*, Vol. LV (1958), p. 1012.
[2] 'The Need for Abstract Entities in Semantic Analysis', *Op. cit.*, p. 107.
[3] Reprinted from *Perspectives in Biology and Medicine*, Vol. VII (1964), p. 243.

word is to convey its actual meaning, its definiens must be as vague as the definiendum; otherwise the definition of a symbol with a different use, we might say a *new* term, is being offered. The word 'analytic', for example, is taken from pre-systematic contexts, and a definition of it given in an artificial (formalized) language may be guided by its usage in the natural language but will not be a definition of *that* word. The point of the definition of course is that it will enable us to decide cases to which it applies which previous usage left undecidable. At least one must suppose there are some purposes which a formalized language serves which a natural language does not. But a reformed language will not do what ordinary language does now—serve our ordinary needs and purposes. It is not clear whether the logician's complaint against ordinary language is that it is not a formalized language. If it is, then it is a logically impossible demand that the language which removes the complaint should do what the original one does.

In all the philosophic criticisms made against language we find operative what appears to be a perfectionist ideal. The case is the same with the charge that inexactness in language is responsible for vagueness. Here again, as I want to show, attainment of the ideal situation is logically impossible. Vagueness is a source of complaint only if there is a standard which the existence of this phenomenon shows language to fall short of. Now, the ideal is exactness, an exactness such that we can always discriminate verbally between things having ϕ and those not having it. Given that the thesis of Platonic realism is correct, that beyond language there exists a realm of universals, we seem to be provided with standards of exactness of which language falls short: 'The world of [universals] is unchangeable, rigid, exact, delightful to the mathematician, the logician, and the builder of metaphysical systems. . . .'[1] Universals, in contrast with the words by which we designate them, are precise: either ϕ or non-ϕ characterizes a given thing; there seems to be no sense in talking of vague universals. In fact a standard procedure for refuting the thesis that there are universals is to argue that common properties are not exact.[2]

It would appear from this that vagueness resides in our language and precision in what it inexactly designates. In accordance with

---

[1] Russell, *The Problems of Philosophy*, p. 156.
[2] See Locke, *Human Understanding*, Bk. III, ch. iii, 13.

the demands of logic, a thing must be characterized by either ϕ or non-ϕ. That is, logic declares the exactness of universals by the law of excluded mean: $(x) . \phi x \vee \sim \phi x$. However, when we come to specific instances of the law, e.g. x is a bush or not a bush, we find that the exactness supposedly possessed by the characterizing properties is not reflected in the language by which we designate them. With all information at hand we are unable to say whether a thing has either property. If we try to resolve our indecision by introducing a third category, 'perhaps ϕ', we find ourselves without any means of discovering whether what is *perhaps* ϕ is actually ϕ. A new indecision is replaced by the old. We are like a tailor who asks a customer to try on a suit, with the remark 'Perhaps this one fits you', but who is never in a position to say more than 'Perhaps it fits', even when the customer has it on. No matter how closely he looks he is never able to discover whether what perhaps fits does fit.

This analogy raises the question whether 'perhaps ϕ' makes any sense if there is no conceivable means of resolving our uncertainty into ϕ or non-ϕ. In the present situation we do not know what it would be like to come to this sort of decision. And this is to say that neither 'perhaps ϕ' nor 'actually ϕ' has meaning. The two are correlates, and if it is not logically possible to determine that ϕ applies, then the 'perhaps' loses its function. Without the means, even in theory, of being certain that a thing is ϕ, we have no logically possible goal of certainty of which we fall short in saying 'perhaps it is ϕ'. The view that vagueness resides in language and precision in what it designates suggests that universals are analogous to patterns which the tailor's scissors are too blunt to follow accurately enough to get an exact fit. But the analogy is misleading because the pattern, 'actually ϕ', cannot exist if 'perhaps ϕ' can never conceivably be supplanted by the definite knowledge that the thing either conforms or not to the pattern.

The demand that words have the precision of the characterizing properties they stand for, with its presupposition that we have in precise universals a standard with which language can be compared, can be shown to be logically unreasonable on somewhat different but related grounds. The assumption motivating the demand is that a word can be vague while the universal it designates is sharp. But is this logically possible? Since the universal is the meaning of the word, the assumption is that a word can have a vague application though its meaning is nonvague. But the application of a word is fixed by its meaning, so that the application could not be less sharp than the meaning.

It might be held that the demand that language be exact would be unobjectionable if it were divorced from reference to the existence of universals. But this is not the case. What would it be like for language to be free from vagueness? Does 'having no possible borderline cases' describe a possible situation? I think that it does not and that we have only the pretence of a standard in the demand that words be applicable in such a way as always to set off things having ϕ from those not having it. For it is always theoretically possible to construct cases which we are unable to classify as one or the other. Given any two things one can imagine one slowly merging into the other, and if this is the case, there will always be a point in the transformation at which the application of a word, or its negative, is undecided. If it is always possible in theory that there be such cases, then it is logically impossible that there be none such. So it could be no real condemnation of language to point to the presence of vagueness, just as it is no condemnation of an infinite series that it has no last term.

11

THE PROBLEM OF JUSTIFYING
INDUCTIVE INFERENCE*

I wish to begin with a matter about which, to quote Russell, 'none of us, in fact, feel the slightest doubt'.[1] I then propose to discuss doubts of that curious academic kind with which philosophers have challenged common sense, with a view to seeing through them clearly enough to find the way back to the common-sense, non-sceptical position. It is not intellectually satisfactory to indulge in the ordinary man's reaction of brushing aside these doubts as trivial or unreal. But it may be possible to cope with them without having to relinquish the common-sense position.

Consider the following quotation from Russell's *Problems of Philosophy*:

'We are all convinced that the sun will rise tomorrow. Why? Is this belief a mere blind outcome of past experience, or can it be justified as a reasonable belief? . . . If we are asked why we believe [this], we shall naturally answer, "Because it always has risen every day". We have a firm belief that it will rise in the future, because it has risen in the past.[2] . . . The problem we have to discuss is whether there is any reason for believing in what is called "the uniformity of nature".[3] . . . Do *any* number of cases of a law being fulfilled in the past afford evidence that it will be fulfilled in the future?[4] . . . When two things have been found to be often associated, and no instance is known of the one occurring without the other, does the occurrence of one of the two, in a fresh instance, give any good ground for expecting the other?[5] . . . If not, it becomes plain that we have no ground whatever for expecting the

---

* Reprinted from *The Journal of Philosophy*, Vol. XLIV, No. 10, May 8, 1947.

[1] *The Problems of Philosophy*, 17th impression, p. 94.

[2] Pp. 94–95.   [3] Pp. 98–99.   [4] P. 96.   [5] P. 101.

sun to rise tomorrow, or for expecting the bread we shall eat at our next meal not to poison us.'[1]

Russell makes clear that in raising these questions he is not suggesting we seek for a proof that these expectations '*must* be fulfilled, but only for some reason in favour of the view that they are *likely* to be fulfilled'.[1] In other words, he is asking for some justification of the inference that the sun is *likely* to rise tomorrow from the fact that it has done so, not of the sun's being *certain* to rise. The task of justifying an inference that something is likely is a more modest one than that of justifying the inference that it is certain. But if both inferences are felt to be in genuine need of justification, then the doubt directed against the weaker inference must be more drastic than that directed against the stronger. Obviously the doubt whether the repetition of concomitances or sequences of events makes a similar concomitance or sequence *probable* is of a more radical kind than the doubt whether it makes this certain. One might feel hesitant, for example, about claiming it was certain that aspirin would stop the present headache on the grounds that it had always provided relief, and not feel at all hesitant about claiming that these grounds made it at least probable.

Such assurance, however, does not for long preserve immunity against the progressive infectiousness of doubt. It is part of the natural history of doubt to spread. Hume raised doubts concerning our certainty of any inductive conclusion p. These can be, and in fact have been, extended to conclusions of the form 'p is probable'. The same sort of considerations which historically gave rise to the suspicion that even our most assured inductive conclusions are uncertain give rise equally to uneasiness whether *any* evidence could even make them probable. We see this in the progress of philosophers to the more extreme doubt, that brought against the legitimacy, in general, of conclusions of the form 'p is probable'. In this paper I shall be concerned with doubts of this kind.

It will be useful here briefly to indicate the sources of these in doubts originally raised as to the legitimacy of any inductive conclusion of the form 'p'. The main sources are two in number: (1) the doubt whether any number of cases of a conjunction of

_____
[1] *The Problems of Philosophy*, p. 96.

characteristics could make certain any proposition about its continued occurrence; (2) the doubt, even though some number could make it certain, whether one could ever know the number of cases had was sufficient. The first, stated explicitly by Hume, eventuated in the claim that evidence in the form of observations of which we are perfectly certain leaves the inductive conclusion uncertain, the reason being that they are not sufficient for its *deduction*. The fact that two characteristics ϕ and ψ have always been associated is not sufficient to deduce that they always are nor even that they will be in the next instance. To quote Hume:

'There can be no demonstrative arguments to prove, that these instances, of which we have had no experience, resemble those, of which we have had experience. We can at least conceive of a change in the course of nature; which sufficiently proves, that such a change is not absolutely impossible.[1] . . . We have no reason to draw any inference concerning any object beyond those of which we have had experience.'[2]

These comments apply equally to inferences that something is probable and are explicitly extended to them by C. D. Broad when he says, 'Now it is quite certain that, if my *only* premise is, "I have observed N ϕ's, and 100 per cent of them are ψ", there is no valid form of argument by which I can either prove or render probable the conjecture that 100 per cent of the ϕ's in nature are ψ.'[3] Thus the doubt whether any number of cases are adequate evidence for the truth of a conclusion p has grown into a doubt whether they are ever adequate even to render it probable.

And even though some number of cases could make it probable, we can still be uncertain that it is probable, since our source of uncertainty shifts to a doubt very similar to (2) above: the doubt whether any particular number of cases observed is sufficient. If one can doubt whether N cases make p certain, one can obviously doubt whether they make it probable. For example, do five cases of illness after sweet wine make it probable that the next instance

---

[1] *A Treatise of Human Nature*, Bk. I, Pt. II, sec. 6.   [2] *Ibid.*, section 12.
[3] 'Mechanical and Teleological Causation', *Proceedings of the Aristotelian Society*, Supplementary Volume XIV, p. 89.

of wine drinking will have such a sequel? Or does one need more cases to assure this? Suppose ten more cases were not so followed. Then we should be inclined to say our first five cases were insufficient to infer a probability. But if after our first five, fifty more cases were so followed, we should not know exactly what to say about our previous limited evidence. And no matter what number we mentioned, a question could be raised to throw the inference in doubt. Can we ever know that our evidence is sufficient to warrant 'it is probable that p'?

One further uncertainty about the conclusions of inductive arguments, which infects those of ordinary deductions as well, I wish to mention briefly but without elaboration, since it can be interpreted as an uncertainty about a special sort of inductive inference and its special features are not relevant in this paper. This uncertainty concerns, on the face of it, not the validity of inferring a conclusion from premises, but the premises themselves. According to Hans Reichenbach, no premises about physical objects or events could be certain, and hence nothing inferred from them could be. Only propositions of logic or about one's immediate experience are beyond doubt true. It is never absolutely certain, for example, that there is a die before me when I see it, feel it, bet upon it.[1] Sensory observation is subject to all sorts of error, and for that matter we may not even be sure that what our senses reveal is other than the material of dreams or hallucinations. Error lies, not in any judgment recording one's immediate experience, but in the inference one makes from it to the existence of a counterpart in the real world. Thus the evidential premise of an ordinary induction is in the position of an inductive conclusion from immediate experience. Any doubt about it will therefore be but a special case of doubt about inductive conclusions in general. Clearly Broad's sceptical doubt could be rephrased, as follows, so as to apply to inferences from immediate experience: Can one's immediate experiences, any number of them, ever make an evidential premise probable? This question has special features which give it an even more academic character than the similar question about inductions made from premises about physical objects and events. In fact one would not in ordinary circumstances raise the question whether it was *ever* certain a die was before one, let alone

[1] *Experience and Prediction*, p. 331 University of Chicago Press, 1938).

the question whether this was probable. The first kind of question I tried to deal with in my paper in *The Philosophy of G. E. Moore*,[1] treating it along lines developed by John Wisdom and Morris Lazerowitz. In this paper I shall ignore the special features of scepticism with respect to the senses and confine consideration to the general question: Given that we *know* premises which we take as evidence, can they or *any conceivable* premises make our conclusion probable?

This is but a variation on the old problem, 'Can inductive inference be justified?' It is not, however, my intention here to attempt a solution of this problem in the form of a detailed philosophical theory to the effect that probable inference can, or can not, be justified. The questions I should like to answer are quite different, questions which might properly be characterized as 'metaphilosophical': Why is there the philosophical problem of justifying such inferences? Is there any genuine problem? The latter question is of fundamental importance. In practice the necessity of justifying every inference, no matter how assured, never presents itself as a problem. Actuaries of insurance companies, after settling the question whether the statistical evidence warrants their probability judgment, would be shocked at the question whether any statistical information could ever justify any such judgment. In calling attention to such a fact, it is not merely that I want to suggest that inductive inference needs no justification, as I think it does not—for this is simply to contradict those who feel it does—but that I want to see if the philosophical problem will disappear when one sees how those who have attempted to solve it have conceived it. In what follows I shall take it that attempted justifications of inductive inference, even though in fact directed towards securing that the inference of *p* be legitimate, are equally relevant to securing the legitimacy of the inference '*p* is probable'. I have already indicated how doubts about the one can be or have been extended to the other, and I shall therefore treat attempts made so far to eliminate these doubts as directed towards securing a probability rather than a certainty.

As one looks through various attempts at justifying inductive inference in general, say those of Mill, Russell, Broad, it becomes clear what it is supposed justification would be like. This is that

---

[1] *The Library of Living Philosophers*, Vol. IV.

we should be able to know that p is probable, given that we know such facts as:

(1) that ϕ and ψ have always been associated

or

(2) that ϕ and ψ have been associated in a certain proportion of cases.

Quite a number of different kinds of inference have premises answering to these two general descriptions. From premises of type (1) we infer such conclusions as:

It is probable that illness always follows large quantities of drink. It is probable that illness will follow drink in the next instance.

And from premises of type (2) such conclusions as:

It is probable that continued throws of a penny will maintain for heads the observed proportion $\frac{1}{2}$.
The probability of lipoid pneumonia being fatal in this particular case is $\frac{9}{10}$.

In connection with such conclusions philosophers have admitted the force of Hume's criticisms. But then, being convinced that nevertheless they are sometimes justified in drawing inferences of this sort, they have gone on to seek the justification. Attempts they have made indicate that what they seek is some means whereby inductive inferences may be made *logically valid in form*, such that the premises *entail* the conclusion 'p is probable'. This would satisfy the condition that the conclusion be known once the premises are known.

Mill, Russell, and Broad have all, ostensibly, conceived their task to be that of supplying to the inference a premise to be conjoined with the empirical facts about concomitances, from which the conclusion follows. Mill, for example, writes: '. . . every induction is a syllogism with the major premise suppressed; or (as I prefer expressing it) every induction may be thrown into the form of a syllogism by supplying a major premise.'[1] What is to be supplied, he says, 'is an assumption involved in every case of

[1] *A System of Logic*, Bk. III, Ch. 3, sec. 1

induction,' and this is 'our warrant for all inferences from experience.'¹ Russell holds that 'All arguments which, on the basis of experience, argue as to the future or the unexperienced parts of the past or present assume the inductive principle. If the principle is unsound, we have no reason to expect the sun to rise tomorrow, to expect bread to be more nourishing than a stone, or to expect that if we throw ourselves off the roof we shall fall. All our conduct is based upon associations which have worked in the past, and which we therefore regard as likely to work in the future; and this likelihood is dependent for its validity upon the inductive principle.'² Broad, although he is unable to say precisely what premise conjoined with 'I have observed N ϕ's and 100 per cent of them are ψ' would justify him in conjecturing that 100 per cent of the ϕ's in nature are ψ, is in agreement that there must be some premise which does this.

The premise which Russell adjoins to the observational evidence, and which as regards unexamined cases he says 'alone can justify any inference from what has been examined to what has not yet been examined',³ is as follows:

'(a) The greater the number of cases in which a thing of the sort A has been found associated with a thing of the sort B, the more probable it is (if no cases of failure of association are known) that A is always associated with B;
'(b) Under the same circumstances a sufficient number of cases of the association of A with B will make it nearly certain that A is always associated with B.'⁴

This is the so-called 'inductive principle', as it applies to the probability of a general law. As I understand Russell, he takes this principle to play the rôle of a premise in every induction we make about universal concomitances. In order to exhibit this I set out the following inference, in which I make explicit every premise supposedly used in arriving at the conclusion 'p is probable'. For this purpose I need only part (b) of the inductive principle, and in particular a weakened form of it which I shall designate as (α):

(α) Under similar circumstances a sufficient number of cases of

¹ *A System of Logic*, Bk. III, Ch. 3, sec. 1   ² *The Problems of Philosophy*, pp. 106–07.   ³ *Ibid.*, p. 106.   ⁴ *Ibid.*, p. 104.

B accompanying A will make it probable that B always accompanies A.

(β) Under similar circumstances a sufficient number of cases of dry leaves burning when lit will make it probable that they always burn when lit.

(γ) In the past dry leaves when lit have burned a hundred times without exception.

(δ) A hundred cases with no exceptions are sufficient to make it probable that dry leaves when lit always burn.

Therefore, it is probable that dry leaves when lit always burn.

In practice when we infer such a conclusion as this we pass directly to it from (γ). But it will be admitted that (δ), to the effect that we have enough cases to render our conclusion probable, is implicit in this passage. Russell seemingly wants to hold that without (β)'s being true we could not assert (δ). That is, unless there is such a thing as a number of similar cases being sufficient to make it probable that dry leaves burn, no number mentioned would tend in the slightest to do this. (α), as we see, is simply the *form* of this general premise (β), and we must have it if we are ever to have a general premise for any other argument than this one.

As this example indicates, I have taken it that according to Russell finding a justification for an inductive inference consists in finding the premises necessary to make it logically valid, that is, in supplying enough premises to throw it into the form of a deduction. Among these are the inductive principle, and its special instance (β). It will be recalled that those who suppose inductive inference requires justification demand it shall be such that one can *know* the conclusion 'p is probable'. A simple step to securing this is to exhibit it as the conclusion of premises which are such that if they are certain the conclusion is also. Any deduction satisfies this condition. But this is not sufficient. If the conclusion is to be known, then the premises must be also. And, curiously enough, this according to Russell is precisely what is impossible. The inductive principle, premise (α), he says is 'incapable of being proved by an appeal to experience'; 'we can never use experience to prove the inductive principle without begging the question'.[1] Hence we must simply accept it 'or forgo all justification of our

[1] *The Problems of Philosophy*, p. 106.

expectations about the future'.[1] Now it is clear that if a particular inductive conclusion is in doubt *only because* it is doubtful whether any number of cases renders any proposition probable, then one does not justify the conclusion by *assuming* that they do. Nothing is gained by using as a premise what is in doubt. For if one is to establish the conclusion one must know the premises are true. Expressing an inductive argument in the form of a deductive one by supplying the requisite premises thus provides a spurious kind of comfort.

Further, a closer examination of the sequence of propositions, (α), (β), (γ), (δ), makes it very puzzling what function Russell expected (α), or (β), to serve in establishing the conclusion (p is probable'. For this conclusion follows from (γ) and (δ) without the help of anything further. In addition (α), and its special case (β), appear to be singularly empty tautologies. (β), for example, states that a sufficient number of cases of dry leaves burning when lit will make it probable they always do. The natural question is 'sufficient for what?' and the natural answers is given in the following paraphrase of (β):

If the number of cases of dry leaves burning when lit is sufficient to *make it probable* that they always burn, then it is probable that they do.

(α) permits of a similar paraphrase. It is clear that the addition of these necessary propositions to (γ) and (δ) will in no way help to deduce the conclusion. In fact as the use of truth-tables shows, the conjunction of a necessary proposition p with any contingent proposition q, or set of such, will have no more deductive fertility than the contingent proposition alone: $p.q. \equiv .q$. So giving our inductive argument a deductive form can not in this case be described as consisting in the addition of premises ((α) and (β)) without which the conclusion could not be inferred. On the basis of this account, the relevance, let alone the importance, of the inductive principle in a particular inference is very doubtful.

I think some account of this principle remains to be given.[2] I have pointed out that neither (α) nor (β) is a proposition with the

---

[1] *The Problems of Philosophy*, p. 106.

[2] What follows by way of analysis of it I owe in large part to discussions with M. Lazerowitz.

help of which the conclusion is deduced. That is, their rôle is not like that of the general premise of a syllogism, e.g. 'All men are mortal', without which the conclusion, 'Socrates is mortal', can not be inferred. Suppose now for purposes of comparison with our inductive inference we conjoin to the familiar syllogism the proposition

(θ) If all men are mortal and Socrates is a man, then Socrates is mortal.

and that to this we add

(ω) If all a is b and x is a, then x is b.

The adjunction of (θ) and (ω) to the premises of the syllogism is of no help in deducing 'Socrates is mortal'; the premises alone are sufficient for this. (θ) and (ω) are both necessary, and hence could not help establish an empirical conclusion. However, the fact that (θ) is necessary is the same as the fact that 'Socrates is mortal' may be deduced from the two given premises. And the fact that (ω) is necessary is what is meant by saying this syllogistic argument is valid in virtue of its form. (θ) and (ω) are not premises, but *rules* according to which deductions are made, (ω) being the general rule of which (θ) is the special instance.

Now there is some analogy between the rôle of (ω) and the rôle of (α), the inductive principle. If we put (α) in the form

If for some specified number N, N cases of association of A and B occur and if these are sufficient, then it is probable that A and B are always associated,

it appears, not as a premise, but as giving the *form* of the inference

(γ) Dry leaves when lit have burned one hundred times without exception.
(δ) One hundred cases are sufficient.
Therefore, it is probable dry leaves always burn when lit.

A similar thing was pointed out by C. N. Whiteley in his paper in *Analysis*,[1] where he maintained that the inductive principle expres-

[1] 'On the Justification of Induction', *Analysis*, Vol. 7 (1490), p. 69.

ses the form common to particular inductive arguments. Unless the form is valid, the particular inductive argument can not be. The same, of course, characterizes (ω), the form of the syllogistic argument cited. The difference is that whereas everyone would grant that (ω) is the rule according to which 'Socrates is mortal' is validly deduced from its premises, it is not as clear, and philosophers such as Broad are ready to challenge, whether (a) is the rule according to which inductive conclusions are inferred. For one thing, the hypothesis of (a), 'If for some number N, N cases . . . are sufficient', implies the possibility of *some* number of cases being sufficient, by itself, to render a proposition probable. And this is what Broad denies.

Of course (a), as stated, is undeniable: If some number N of cases occur and are sufficient to make p probable, then p is probable. It can, however, be restated so as to free it of its trivial appearance. In the following form (a) does not look as certainly, nor as trivially, tautologous:

A sufficient number of cases of association of A and B make it probable A and B are always associated.

'A sufficient number' seems to denote any of a sequence of numbers having a lower limit, so that (a) might be replaced by:

Some number of cases of association of A and B makes it probable they are always associated.

Here we have the proposition which Broad claims is certainly false, since according to him it is insufficient for making any proposition probable *merely* that there should be N cases of association without exception. Yet one feels inclined to agree with C. Lewy that in accordance with the English usage of the word 'probable' this is a necessary proposition, so that to assert the observational premises of certain inductions and deny that the conclusion is probable is a self-contradiction.[1] 'Some number of cases makes p probable' looks to be strictly analogous to the necessary proposition, 'Some number multiplied by 2 equals 14'. These two propositions can be instructively compared. The function on which the latter is con-

---

[1] 'The Justification of Induction', *Analysis*, Vol. 6 (1939), pp. 89–90.

structed, namely, '$x \times 2 = 14$', is such that it has a necessarily true value, '$7 \times 2 = 14$'. Is it similarly the case for the function 'x cases make p probable'? If it is, and if in the inductive inference we have used as an example, 100 is a value rendering it tautologous, then our premise (δ), that one hundred cases are sufficient to make it probable that dry leaves always burn when lit, plays no rôle in deducing the conclusion. This can be deduced from (γ) alone, that dry leaves when lit have been found to burn one hundred times without exception. 'One hundred cases make it probable that dry leaves always burn' would not be needed for passing from (γ) to the conclusion any more than 'All squares are four-sided' is needed in passing from 'This is a square' to 'This is four-sided'. A necessary proposition, to reiterate what was said before, can never be a *premise* with the help of which an empirical conclusion is deduced. But of course if a given proposition of the form 'x cases make p probable' is necessary, then the conclusion 'p is probable' follows necessarily from the empirical evidence. And our necessary proposition functions as a rule according to which we deduce it.

Now it is quite obvious that whatever the analogy between 'Some number of cases makes p probable' and 'Some number multiplied by 2 equals 14', the lack of analogy is equally obvious, and it is this which vitiates Lewy's contention against Broad. The function '$x \times 2 = 14$' has but one tautologous value, whereas 'x cases make p probable', if it has any tautologous values, will have many—all those from some number N on. And the difficulty is that we do not know at precisely what point the function becomes tautologous, if it does so. This is merely another way of putting the uncertainty expressed in the question, 'How can one know the number of observed cases is sufficient?' One knows by inspection precisely when one has found the value which makes '$x \times 2 = 14$' necessary. But one does not know by inspection whether the empirical evidence entails 'it is probable that p'.

It is doubtless this fact which is responsible for the feeling that inductive inference needs justifying. Usually this justification has been conceived as a matter of supplying, not a validating rule, but some general empirical premise. At least there is some problem about induction which supplying this is supposed to solve. This problem is, I believe, not 'How can any number of cases render anything probable?' but some other problem which, even though solved, would leave the question about cases unanswered. I shall try to support this claim in what follows, for this is not the accepted view about what is gained by supplying a general premise about the constitution of nature. Broad, for example, holds that in order to know a conclusion of the form '*p* is probable' it is necessary that we know some premise of this sort. In general his view is that inductive arguments all involve a premise to the effect that there is in nature constant causal determination and something like 'loading' in favour of one alternative rather than another, and that in order for this to be the case nature must answer to the principle of limited variety.[1] Very roughly, this principle is that nature is not infinitely complex—that every object and event analyzes into a limited number of elements and hence that a limited amount of variety is possible from combinations of these elements. Again very roughly, what would be secured if the general empirical premise were true is that nature obeys simple causal laws.

Now my thesis is that this concern that nature obey simple causal laws is a concern that it be possible for us to make inductive inferences at all, not that it be possible to *know*, once the conditions for making an inference are satisfied, that any given probable conclusion is validly inferred. That is, there are two questions, 'What would justify us in making inductive inferences, i.e. what would make it possible to do this?' and 'What would justify, in the sense of "validate", the conclusion "*p* is probable"?' Broad has, I think, answered the first question while supposing himself to have answered the second. He makes a premise about nature a requisite for deducing the conclusion, whence we could not know '*p* is probable' without knowing this premise. I want to consider briefly what the consequences are if the premise about nature is false. I am not certain, but I believe that if nature is not of such-and-such a constitution inductive inference would not be possible. And in this case we should have no problem of validating an inductive conclusion. The problem as to what validates an inductive conclusion can arise only if it is possible for inductive inferences to be made.

From a number of statements about nature which have been cited as premises of inductive inference I shall select a few typical

[1] 'The Principles of Problematic Induction', *Proceedings of the Aristotelian Society*, Vol. XXVIII, p. 45.

ones and see what their falsity entails. Usually, to put it vaguely, it has been held that nature must be uniform, that the law of universal causation must operate. Now, it is not sufficient that the law that every event has a cause and similar causes have similar effects hold. As Russell said, 'it is not the reign of law but the reign of *simple* laws which is required'.[1] But now for what is it not sufficient, for what is the reign of *simple* laws required? Both Venn and J. M. Keynes have provided an answer which supports my contention that the premise about nature which is being sought is one which assures the *possibility* of making inductions. Keynes says[2] that if every configuration of the universe were subject to a separate and independent law and if every difference in bodies led to their obeying different laws—in other words, if it were false that nature is under the reign of simple laws—it would still be the case that nature was uniform and causation sovereign; but prediction would be impossible. If inductions are to be made at all, nature must not be like this. Nor must it be such that though every event is causally determined no causal law has more than one instance in the history of the universe. As Venn points out,[3] induction could not take place in such a world either. Here the reason we should not be justified in inferring '*p* is probable' would simply be that we could not start to make any inference. We should not have any observational premise about repeated concomitances.

The point is clearer if we consider the consequences of falsifying the premise Mill cited as being a warrant for every induction. According to Mill it is a necessary condition for proving any inductive conclusion that nature be uniform. By the uniformity of nature he meant that there are in nature such things as parallel cases—that it is sometimes the case that what is true of one instance of ϕ is true of all instances. In other words, some generalizations hold in nature, or there are uniformities in nature. Let us suppose there are no uniformities in nature, simple or otherwise. In this event two situations are possible: (1) that no characteristic occurs with any other in accordance with any law—that is, that there are no constant conjunctions of any characteristics, but that each occurs with absolutely any other; (2) that there are some repeated

---

[1] *The Analysis of Matter*, p. 232.
[2] *A Treatise on Probability*, p. 249 (London: Macmillan & Co., 1929).
[3] *Empirical Logic*, pp. 96–97 (London: Macmillan & Co., 1889).

concomitances and sequences but that their repetition is not universal. In the first case we clearly have a suspension of the principle of limited variety. In such a world the amount of possible variety would be unlimited. In fact there could not even be what Broad has characterized as 'natural kinds'—groupings of characters which constitute such recurrent entities as humans, horses, trees, etc. Were a malignant demon to scramble up such a world, it would be one in which no inductions could be made. For one thing, there would not be human beings to make them. In fact it is doubtful whether what is being described here is even a conceivable situation. As Isaiah Berlin points out,[1] in the extreme case where no character ever occurred more than once, we should have no general terms to refer to it, and such a chaos could not even be talked about let alone inferred from.

However, the case is different if there are some repetitions of sequences or characters, even for relatively short periods of time. Suppose that for some centuries there has been that constant conjunction of characters which constitutes mankind, and that other conjunctions of characters are repeated for a couple of generations. Is inductive inference possible? First of all, if we *knew* it to be false that there were any universal conjunctions we should of course never say it was probable that ϕ and ψ were always associated. However, if it were false that there were uniformities, but because there were some repetitions and recurrences it was not *known* to be false, we could and would still make probable inferences. We should have the same kind of evidence which we now have, the sort expressed in premise (γ), namely, in one hundred cases without exception dry leaves when lit have been found to burn. What we do in establishing the probability of a special uniformity is to make an inference from observed repetitions. Of course if our ancestors told us that things had been different in their day we should be uncertain whether it was probable the next instance of ϕ would be ψ or that all future instances of ϕ would be ψ. And if ϕ and ψ were never observed in conjunction again we should not say it was probable ϕ would be associated with ψ in the next instance. In fact after a time we should most likely say it was improbable.

[1] 'Induction and Hypothesis', *Proceedings of the Aristotelian Society*, Supplementary Volume XVI, p. 99.

Exactly how much repetition there must be before we draw probable inferences I do not know, but certainly in a world where there was very little we could not draw them. For we should lack the observational premise, e.g. 'One thousand cases have been found without exception . . . etc.' And we should need this for inference regardless of what other premise might be needed. The point I am trying to make here is that the question as to what nature must be like before we are justified in making any inductions at all, i.e. what it must be like to have proper observational premises, is different from the question whether, given the observational premises, we are justified in drawing a conclusion from them.

I want to return now to this latter question. The fact that philosophers feel that there is a problem here shows some sort of dissatisfaction. To say what this dissatisfaction is, when we in fact do not for a moment feel uncertain that, for example, the sun will rise again and the springtime come, is to answer *our* question, Why is there the philosophical problem of induction? It seems to me this is a question which ought to be asked. For this need of justifying inductive conclusions never is felt in any ordinary circumstances. Our behaviour shows this: We are willing to bet that 1, 2, 3, or 4 will come up on a fair die, as against 6. We never become fearful that the laws of nature will be suspended, so that we hesitate to plant a garden on the grounds that the sun may never shine again. And yet, despite this, we feel challenged by the question, 'Are you warranted in supposing it probable the sun will shine again?' as we are by the question, 'Are you warranted in supposing it probable that virus A is responsible for the illness of all these guinea pigs?'

Certain linguistic analogies between questions and doubts philosophers express and questions and doubts of the scientist or ordinary man are, I think, responsible for our feeling the challenge. Either the questions and doubts give vent to some dissatisfaction or they positively create it. It is clear that the request that a scientist justify a particular inductive conclusion and the request that inductive conclusions in general be justified bear at least a verbal analogy to each other. And the doubt expressed in 'She loved you today and yesterday, but have you any good reason to suppose that she will love you tomorrow?' is analogous in the same way to the seeming doubt expressed in 'Yesterday, and for many years before that, things which were dropped fell; but have you any good reason to suppose the law of gravitation will continue to operate tomorrow?'

Further, there is close enough analogy between inductive inferences and deductive ones that questions whether an inference is warranted seem to be such as could be settled. In a deduction it is always possible, even though sometimes difficult, to determine whether a conclusion is validly drawn. And when it is, it is a misuse of language, i.e. self-contradictory, to assert the premises and deny the conclusion. The linguistic pattern of inductive arguments is very similar to that of deductive ones, and there are some cases in which it definitely seems a misuse of language to assert that a conjunction has been repeatedly observed and then to deny the probability of its occurring in a fresh instance. One would feel that a person who said 'I have known thousands of cases, and no exceptions, of people being burnt when they touched a hot stove, but it is not probable that I shall be burnt the next time I do it', or 'The penny has come up heads a million times straight, and never tails, but it is not probable the penny is unfair', was somehow misusing language—that he didn't know the use of the word 'probable', and was saying something self-contradictory.

Now despite all these analogies there are equally obvious lacks of analogy. To ignore these is to fail to see that questions and doubts which the sceptic has about induction are but pantomimes of questions and doubts which are genuine. For example, to ask of a scientist whether his evidence is sufficient to warrant a particular inductive conclusion is to ask a useful question to which certain procedures he commonly engages in are relevant by way of answer. Should he be made unsure by the question, he will reconsider his evidence, and, if satisfied, will reiterate his probability judgment, and, if not, will experiment further. By further tests he could, for example, increase or decrease the probability that a particular virus induced illness in his guinea pigs, or he might even disestablish the probability judgment previously arrived at. But now the question, 'Are any empirical facts evidence for any conclusion "p is probable"?' is not one to which any testing procedure is relevant. Nor is it useful to ask it. For it does not create a doubt which in any way affects our behaviour.[1] We don't become uncertain, in virtue of *this* question, of the conclusion of which we were certain.

However, the sceptic's comment, 'You must admit that the fact that a law has operated in the past is thin reason for expecting it to continue', manages somehow to be convincing. The main reason for this I believe to be the following: Despite the fact that some inductive arguments closely parallel deductive ones, so very many do not. The sceptic's emphasis on the lack of parallel makes us intellectually uncomfortable even with regard to those inferences we previously felt sure of. For example, we all feel that there would be something peculiar in saying 'I have a million favourable cases and no unfavourable ones, but still p is not probable'. This seems to be a misuse of language. But even here we are not as sure there is an entailment relation between the observational premise and the conclusion 'p is probable' as we are in the case of deductions which are valid in virtue of their form. This uncertainty I believe arises from the fact that we can think of innumerable cases where one doesn't know whether to say the inductive conclusion follows or not. Suppose that one hundred cases of my drinking coffee at night were followed by sleeplessness, and that this did entail the probability of my spending a sleepless night next time, would fifty cases entail it, or twenty-five, or ten? There is no way whatever of deciding this. And the indecision about the special inference spreads to all inference, despite the obvious lack of analogy, already cited, between the genuine question, 'Have I sufficient evidence to warrant this inference?' and the question, 'Have I ever sufficient evidence to warrant any inference?'

It is one of the features of a philosophic problem that we feel puzzlement and yet not of a kind which in any way alters our behaviour. Here we have an instance. In practice we do not doubt that we are in general justified in making inductive inferences— though we all grant that sometimes we are not; and yet certain considerations produce an academic dissatisfaction with inductive inference in general which makes us try to justify it. This justifica-

[1] See 'Moore's Paradox', by M. Lazerowitz, in *The Philosophy of G. E. Moore*, for a discussion of the academic character of a similar philosophical doubt; also 'Philosophical Perplexity', by John Wisdom, *Proceedings of the Aristotelian Society*, Vol. XXXVII, pp. 78–79.

tion is conceived as a matter of finding a means whereby, being certain of the observational premise, we can be certain that p is probable. I want to say that the remedy for the dissatisfaction we are made to feel about inductive inference is misconceived. If this can be shown then it will be clear why there is the philosophical problem about inductive inference. I shall begin by tracing the dissatisfaction and the attempt to allay it.[1]

Let us begin by comparing ourselves with an imaginary tribe of beings who are unwilling to call any proposition probable unless supported by a million cases. Such beings would doubtless complain over seldom being able to establish any probability. But would their situation be like our own? Consider the following inference. From this we shall see how dissimilar our situation is, and why the dissatisfaction, which made Broad say no number of cases by itself could make p probable:

Three cases of drinking coffee at night were followed by sleeplessness. Therefore, it is probable that drinking coffee at night is always so accompanied.

Now suppose coffee was drunk at night fifty more times without any unpleasant sequel. This would make us say that our first three cases were insufficient to establish the probability of coffee's causing sleeplessness, that is, that it is false that the observational premise implies the conclusion. It might then be argued that if three cases wouldn't necessitate p's probability, would seven, or eight, or ten? Can one case ever make the difference between the implication's being false and its being necessary? And even though we agreed with Lewy that some number of cases would make the implication necessary, and even agreed on some particular numbers which did this, we should soon find ourselves in the position of being unable to decide, as we diminished the number of cases, the precise point at which the implication became non-necessary. It is an impressive fact that on substituting consecutive values in the function 'x cases makes p probable' we derive a numerically ordered sequence of propositions with regard to which there is no reason for saying any one is necessary and its immediate predecessor is not. Apparently Broad is so impressed by this fact that he is

[1] In this I am indebted to discussions I have had with M. Lazerowitz.

willing to deny that any of them is necessary, which is to deny that any number of cases make p probable. We are in a much worse position, seemingly, than the people who must find a million supporting cases before they can infer a probability. We do not know exactly how many cases we need. The sceptic makes us feel that we should. In these circumstances it is natural to conceive our task as *finding* either a premise to conjoin with the evidence from which 'p is probable' would follow, or a rule which inductive inference must conform to if valid. I have tried to argue that what is being sought is a rule or rules, since a premise about nature secures something else.

Now what would such rules do? Clearly what they do in deductions—provide criteria for determining whether the arguments are correct. This means providing exact criteria for the use of the word 'probable', *criteria fixed by the number of cases*, such that from a definite number of cases it can be known that 'p is probable' follows. If such were found we should know which values of x in 'x cases make p probable' yielded something necessary. Whenever the premise involved one of these numerical values we should know it entailed the conclusion just as we know that 'this is square' entails 'this is four-sided' because we know 'all squares are four-sided' is necessary.

Finding such rules would certainly provide us criteria for correct inference. But now where should one look for them? Let us consider what Aristotle did in formulating rules for valid deduction. He examined arguments accepted as correct and derived the rules from them. What is the case with inductive inference? Here, even in those instances when no one doubts that the conclusion is warranted, inspection doesn't yield the rule it conforms to. Now a rule is merely the abstract form of a class of inferences already accepted as correct. But if no rule is found in the inferences themselves, is there a rule? Aren't these our only source for the discovery of rules? If examination yields no rules than our inability to find them is simply due to there not being any. This is, I think, what is not seen by those who demand some justification for induction. They conceive justification as consisting in finding what is hidden, and that if one fails no inference can be known to be valid.

The dissatisfaction with inductive inference which prompts the quest for a hidden principle which justifies it arises from the following commonplace: that instead of certainty that '*p* is probable' follows from the empirical facts, in case after case there is indecision. One does not know whether the evidence is sufficient, nor how to test whether the evidence is sufficient. If we look at the English usage of the word 'probable', we see that 'Some number of cases makes *p* probable' does give the appropriate context for probability statements; that is, it is a sort of rule for the use of the word 'probable'. But it does not tell us specifically with *what number* of cases we may use the word. It provides no exact rule, no rule that specifies the precise minimal number of cases from which 'it is probable that *p*' *follows*. The complaint is that an inexact rule is no better than no rule at all.

It thus turns out that the apparent dissatisfaction with not being able to find rules is in reality a dissatisfaction with the linguistic fact that there are no exact rules. The philosopher's complaint is quite unlike that of the people who find it difficult to establish a probability because they require for this a million cases. Their language contains a definite rule for saying when a proposition is probable. The philosopher's complaint is that ours does not. We do not know at what precise point a given proposition becomes probable, for in our language this has not been decided. That is, we have no fixed criteria in our language for saying whether an inductive argument is correct. The pair 'probable', 'not probable' are vague in much the same way 'rich' and 'poor' are. When a man has only a penny to his name and when he has a million dollars we are certain of the application of the terms 'rich' and 'poor'. But for a whole set of values in between we do not know what to call him. And it is this fact that makes it tempting to argue that no man could be rich since the difference between being rich, poor, or any state in between, could not be in the having or lacking one penny. It seems that there should be some sharp dividing line between these states, some point at which it is proper to apply the one term and not the other. Similarly with the term 'probable'. For a whole middle range of values of *x* in 'If *x* cases . . . occur, then *p* is probable' we do not know whether it follows that *p* is probable or not. To know this requires knowing which values when substituted in the function yield something necessary, and this has not been decided. Nevertheless it seems that there should be some point at which the function becomes necessary, before which it is not.

There *should* be such a point—that expresses exactly the dissatisfaction about inductive inference. The complaint that we do not in given cases know whether we can validly infer that p is probable appeared to be the complaint that we had *found* no rules to which valid inductive inference conformed. The remedy of this situation would be had when these were found. But this puts the philosopher's dissatisfaction in a misleading way: as though it were over the inability to find rules rather than over the lack of them. The fact is that nothing is hidden. If to justify induction we must look for rules according to which one correctly deduces 'p is probable', we are looking for what does not exist. But if the feeling that induction needs justifying is merely the feeling that there *should be* rules of this sort then the means of remedying the lack is not to be described as finding them, but as making them. To ask that the criteria for the word 'probable' be more exact than they are, that there be a sharp line between correct and incorrect inductions as there is amongst deductions—this is a way of urging that exact rules be made up in such a manner that in being certain of the observational statement we can be certain of 'probably p'. This is, of course, to urge a modification of our language. And to do this is to express a dissatisfaction with it. Here I think we have our answer to the question, 'Why is there a problem of justifying inductive inference?'

I can not here go into whether this urge to modify the language so as to remedy what appear to be its inadequacies is justified. But I will point out that if we try to eradicate the vagueness of the word 'probable' we should most likely want hundreds of rules, and all of them would appear quite arbitrarily formulated. For example, we could make it a rule that fifty or more cases of dry leaves burning when lit made it probable they always would burn, and that twenty-five or more cases of sleeplessness following coffee at night made it probable it always would follow. And so on. We should want a rule for each inference. And in no case would there seem to be any special reason for accepting the rule. Why should twenty-four or forty-nine cases be insufficient—why should an inference from these not be necessary while an inference from twenty-five or fifty cases would be? Undoubtedly if such rules were accepted philosophers would find them the source of a new problem. Their complaint would in these circumstances be against the excessive sharpness of the word 'probable' instead of its excessive vagueness. The new dissatisfaction would arise from the *arbitrariness* of the rules rather than the lack of them.

It would seem that the word 'probable', like the word 'rich', is for the purposes of ordinary life as sharply defined as we want it; and even philosophers have shown no real interest in sharpening the criteria for its application else they would have tried to still their dissatisfaction by the only means open to them, namely, by specifying such criteria. All this indicates that present usage is satisfactory, otherwise we should have what we do not now have, precise criteria fixed by the number of cases. Once this is admitted, the need to justify probable inference disappears. At this point we have returned to the common-sense position.

12

THREE ASPECTS OF MOORE'S
PHILOSOPHY*¹

It is reported that a Chinese who came to Cambridge commented on his philosophical pilgrimage as follows: 'I came to Cambridge to study philosophy with Professor Moore, and what I learned was something about the English language.' The aspect of Moore's philosophical activity which these words suggest is nowadays perhaps the one uppermost in the minds of Moore's critics and of all the subsequent school of analysts to whom Professor Brand Blanshard attributed 'that preoccupation with language which is one of the most curious aspects of the current philosophy of analysis'.² There are, however, other aspects of Moore's doing of philosophy which have also acted as powerful determinants of the direction philosophy has taken, perhaps the most familiar being his defence of common sense. This defence of common sense had as a by-product, very probably not consciously intended by Moore, a defence of ordinary language. It may not be possible consistently to interpret the work of his lifetime as directed to both of these ends at once, but it is undeniable that various philosophers have interpreted it as directed to one or the other and sometimes to both. Either interpretation is plausibly supported by placing different constructions on the technique Moore made use of, namely, analysis. With this technique for clarifying concepts, i.e. for clarifying the meanings of words, Moore's name has come to be associated—not because he made important use of it for the first time in the history of philosophy, for in fact many historical figures have used it, but because through him the technique of analysis became very explicit and was used by him in a characteris-

* Reprinted from *The Journal of Philosophy*, Vol. LVII, No. 26, December 22, 1960.
¹ This is a revised version of a paper read at a meeting in memory of G. E. Moore, Columbia University, January 15, 1959.
² 'The Philosophy of Analysis', *Proceedings of the British Academy* (1952), p. 63.

ESSAYS IN ANALYSIS

tic way. The defence of common sense, the defence of ordinary
language, the clarification of concepts—each in its way has had an
enormous influence on philosophy in the English-speaking world.
I should like to comment on each, and thereby to attempt to do
at this memorial meeting in honour of Professor Moore the kind
of critical philosophical study for which he has set the standard.

Moore's role as the great refuter is so familiar that one is likely
to forget the basic purpose of his refutations. Moore conceived
philosophy as having a positive task, namely, 'to give a general
description of the *whole* of the Universe, mentioning all the most
important kinds of things which we *know* to be in it . . .';[1] and he
thought what he called the Common Sense view on these matters
to be true and hence views in contradiction to it false. Moore
commented that 'what is most amazing and most interesting about
the views of many philosophers, is the way in which they go
beyond or positively contradict the views of Common Sense: they
profess to know that there are in the Universe most important
kinds of things, which Common Sense does not profess to know of,
and also they profess to know that there are *not* in the Universe
(or, at least, that, if there are, we do not know it), things of the
existence of which Common Sense is most sure'.[2] Some of the
views which go beyond Common Sense Moore is not concerned
to attack, and in fact certain of his own accounts of what there is
in the Universe certainly are of this kind. But the point not to be
lost sight of is that his refutations of other views about the Universe
are intended to leave the field to Common Sense.

It is worthwhile characterizing more exactly the views which go
against Common Sense, i.e. which go against those beliefs men
have had 'almost as long as they have believed anything'[3] and
which have not changed with our progress in knowledge. In the
case of all these views it is natural to express them negatively, as
asserting that something does *not* exist, that something is *not*
known, that something is *not* as it appears. Bradley says that
material objects are not real, Hume that no one can know that
they exist, Parmenides that they merely appear to undergo change
but in fact do not. And some of these metaphysicians, in condemning the sense world as mere appearance, are in the position

[1] *Some Main Problems of Philosophy* (1953), p. 1 (London: George Allen &
Unwin, 1953) [2] *Ibid.*, p. 2. [3] *Ibid.*, p. 3.

206

of the proponents of negative theology, who can only say of the real what it is not. Bradley's claim of a suprasensible Whole, in which the self-contradictoriness of its predicates is resolved, Hume's account of genuine knowledge, which it is logically impossible for sense-evidence to achieve, certainly go beyond the views of Common Sense; but at the same time they are destructive of the views of Common Sense, without making any clear positive claim. They might be characterized as negative metaphysics, the philosophical counterpart of the *via negativa*.

From a number of Moore's writings it is clear that he thought these views were factually false, and he used analysis in his characteristic manner to try to show them to be false. His disagreement with the negative metaphysicians might be called a family quarrel, a disagreement between brother metaphysicians over what is the true state of affairs. He at no time took them to be saying nothing at all. Although the claims of logical positivists were well known to Moore and appeared at a time when he was at the height of his philosophical activity, he did not subscribe to the thesis that the statements of these metaphysicians were pieces of literal nonsense. In fact, in lectures I attended in 1934-35 he criticized Professor A. J. Ayer for saying metaphysical sentences have no meaning at all while defining them by the kind of meaning they have (i.e. as asserting something unverifiable). Ayer held that 'A good example of the kind of utterance that is condemned by our criterion as being not even false but nonsensical would be the assertion that the world of sense-experience was altogether unreal . . . it is plain that no conceivable . . . observations could have any tendency to show [this].'[1] Moore on the other hand, set out a criterion for concluding to the falsity of a metaphysical proposition, not to the literal meaninglessness of the sentence expressing it.

I want to say something about this criterion and the technique by which he made use of it. The criterion is to the effect that any view which implies either the falsity or self-contradictoriness of a belief of Common Sense is itself false or self-contradictory. The criterion can be construed as a double criterion, one as a means for defending ordinary language, the other as a means for defending Common Sense. But for the moment let us consider its use to

[1] *Language, Truth and Logic*, 2nd edition (1948), p. 39.

ward off attacks on the truth of common sense beliefs, i.e. of such beliefs as 'There are in the Universe a great number of material objects',[1] that the earth has existed for many years past, that there are other human beings than oneself, each of whom, like oneself, has had various experiences. Now the technique by which Moore made use of this criterion involves what he called 'translation into the concrete'. He made this process explicit in his treatment of the view that Time is unreal when he suggested that one 'try to translate the proposition into the concrete, and to ask what it *implies*. . . .'[2] 'Time is unreal' he translated into 'There are no temporal facts', and this implies that nothing ever happens, has happened, or will happen. Similarly, to consider, for variety's sake, a different philosophical view, 'Physical objects are unreal' implies that there are no objects external to our minds. And if we try to think what this 'really comes to, [we] at once begin thinking of a number of different *kinds* of propositions, all of which plainly must be untrue . . .'[3] if physical objects are unreal. It will not be true that the earth exists, or the mountains on it, or human bodies, or any other animate bodies. The falsity of all these propositions is implied by 'There are no external objects' in the same way as 'There are no blue things' is implied by "There is nothing coloured.' As is well known, Moore ostensibly brings the logical consequences of the theory—what it implies—into confrontation with the facts: the claim that there are no hands, for example, into confrontation with the fact he makes evident to everyone by holding up each of his two hands and saying, 'Here is a hand'. Translated into the concrete, the theory can be seen to imply the falsity of what everyone knows to be true, and hence must itself be false. And it is sufficient proof, according to Moore, of the common-sense belief that there are external objects to exhibit a pair of hands.

Moore made it clear in his 'Reply to My Critics'[4] that he took 'There are external objects' to be an empirical proposition, and of course its negation as well. In fact the statement 'There are no external objects' he supposed could express both an empirical

---

[1] *Some Main Problems of Philosophy*, p. 3. [2] *Philosophical Studies* (1922), p. 209 (London: Routledge & Kegan Paul, 1922). [3] *Ibid.*, p. 209.
[4] *The Philosophy of G. E. Moore*, Library of Living Philosophers, Vol. IV (1942).

proposition and the non-empirical one that 'There are external objects' is self-contradictory,[1] presumably on the ground, which to me is questionable, that ' "p" is self-contradictory' entails that 'p' is false, i.e. that ' "There are external objects" is self-contradictory' entails that 'There are external objects' is false. One would expect a refutation of the one sort of proposition to differ radically from that of the other. It is possible that Moore's refutation of 'There are no external objects', with its avowed aim of defending a belief of Common Sense, may not be what it has been taken to be. An interpretation has been placed on his argument which throws it into a very different light, an interpretation which makes out Moore's translation into the concrete to be defending not a common belief, but ordinary language. Some of Moore's earlier contemporaries had charged him with begging the question, pointing out that anyone who maintained that there are no external objects would also maintain all that it apparently implies, that there are no hands, no mountains, no animate bodies, no earth. A Bradleian, or a sceptic, would refuse to accept the proof Moore gave of external objects by exhibiting a pair of hands, on the ground that it assumes the thing in question. The charge of circularity would effectively stalemate the argument, interpreted as an attempt to refute a factual claim about the world. In order to maintain that Moore's argument *is* a refutation, some other construction had to be placed on it and also on the Bradleian claim against which it was directed. This Professor Norman Malcolm attempted to do.[2] He maintained that 'the essence of Moore's technique of refuting philosophical statements consists in pointing out that these statements *go against ordinary language*'.[3] Malcolm interpreted negative metaphysicians as not disagreeing with Common Sense over any empirical facts but rather as disagreeing over the language used to describe those facts. He supposed them to be attacking Common Sense for what they consider improper forms of speech, their own language being a more correct way of speaking.[4] If a negative metaphysician who asserts 'There are no external objects' is claiming that it is improper language to say 'There are mountains', then I think Malcolm was right in saying

---

[1] *The Philosophy of G. E. Moore.* p. 672.
[2] 'Moore and Ordinary Language', *The Philosophy of G. E. Moore.*
[3] *Ibid.*, p. 349.   [4] *Ibid.*, pp. 350–53.

that it is his claim, not ordinary usage, which is erroneous. And *if* what Moore does in his proof is to remind us that it is correct to describe some states of affairs by 'There are mountains', then he has sufficiently refuted a person who says it is not.

Now there is something puzzling about the thesis, perhaps no longer held by Malcolm but nevertheless interesting on its own account, that the negative metaphysician is misdescribing the use of language. It is just as absurd that he should hold ordinary usage to be incorrect while knowing it is correct as that he should hold common sense beliefs to be false while knowing the facts which make them true. In either case he makes an incredible mistake. And something even more puzzling has been pointed out by Professor Morris Lazerowitz in his paper 'Moore and Philosophical Analysis', namely, 'how the two kinds of mistake [about usage, and about non-linguistic matter of fact] could be made *in the same utterance.* . . . [For] in making a linguistic mistake a philosopher is not mistakenly denying matter of fact, and in mistakenly denying matter of fact he is not making a linguistic mistake'.[1] The point of Moore's translations into the concrete cannot be to correct Bradley's use of the *term* 'physical object' by showing him that the factual belief expressed by 'physical objects are unreal' is false.[2] It therefore appears that his refutations cannot be construed as having to do two jobs at the same time, to defend the truth of common sense beliefs and to defend the propriety of ordinary language. It can indeed be argued that despite appearances to the contrary they do have one of these two tasks, the defence of ordinary language, but not if this defence rests on Malcolm's charge that philosophers are misdescribing it. The defence will take an entirely different form. Moore's work does, I think, constitute a defence of the language of Common Sense. One of its undeniable consequences has been its enormous influence in holding philosophers to the use of ordinary language and in making a use in conflict with it a criterion for repudiation of a view. But that it should do this presents a puzzle: How can his translations into the concrete, i.e. his making explicit the implications of *propositions* and *concepts*, be construed as having a bearing on the use of *expressions*?

[1] *Studies in Metaphilosophy* (1964), pp. 211–12.
[2] See similar point, *ibid.*, p. 212.

Let us consider what the analysis of a concept is taken to come to. In his 'Reply to My Critics' Moore stated that analyzing a concept is not the same thing as defining a word,[1] although in the first lecture of his which I attended in 1932 he said that analysis of concepts is resolved into something very like the definition of words and that 'in a strictly limited sense' the analysis of a notion is identical with the definition of a word. To make use of Moore's example, clearly it is incorrect to say ' "Brother" means male sibling' and 'A brother is a male sibling' are identical, since one is an empirical linguistic statement and the other is not. But it is also undeniable that in defining the word 'brother' one has analyzed the concept *brother* which the word stands for. Furthermore, the words used in the expression of the analysans name the criteria for the application of the word which denotes the analysandum, and this is what any sentence correctly expressing a complete analysis does. So there is a close connection between the analysis of a concept and the use of an expression, and further, between a correct analysis and correct usage. Another way of showing the connection is given by Lazerowitz' account of sentences of the form 'It is logically impossible that $\sim p$', which are equivalent to ' "p" is necessary'.[2] The fact that the English sentence 'It is logically impossible for there to be a brother who is not a male sibling' expresses a necessity implies that the phrase 'brother but not a male sibling' has no use in English to describe any creature. If it did, then it would describe something which would falsify the necessary proposition the sentence expresses. This fact about the way language is used prevents the sentence from saying anything falsifiable. And anyone who understood a given sentence expressing a necessary proposition would know a fact about the use of words.

Now among the philosophical views Moore was concerned to refute are those which assert the unreality of physical objects, selves, etc., the ground for these assertions being that the concepts *physical object*, *self*, etc. are self-contradictory. This nonempirical ground Moore takes as implying that propositions expressed by such sentences as 'The earth has existed for many years past' and 'There are other human beings than myself' will always be false. And whether or not Moore made it explicit, this ground also

[1] *The Philosophy of G. E. Moore*, pp. 664-65.   [2] *Op. cit.*, pp. 198-99.

assures a linguistic fact about terms occurring in such sentences: if the concepts *physical object* and *self* are self-contradictory, then concrete physical-object terms or terms referring to persons will be self-contradictory. Hence, expressions ordinarily used to describe a thing or person will now describe nothing at all, as no self-contradictory expression has a descriptive use. Bradley's view could with apparent plausibility be taken to imply that many everyday expressions have no use. But although it is sometimes the case that we do not know an expression to be self-contradictory, clearly an expression which in everyday speech has an application, whether to things, states of affairs, or persons, cannot be self-contradictory.

For Moore to maintain against a philosopher that a certain concept is not self-contradictory is in effect to argue that in the language in which the philosopher expresses himself the word denoting the concept has a use. Looked at verbally, translations into the concrete show that certain words do not lack application. But as already remarked, negative metaphysicians are perfectly familiar with facts about the usual applications of words and can hardly be supposed to be misdescribing language. It has been maintained that Moore's seemingly empirical refutations, which he expressed in the idiom used to refute factual claims rather than in that used to attack linguistic claims, are actually linguistic countermoves against attempts to change the language of Common Sense. I do not want to develop or argue for this thesis which has been explicated in detail by Professor Lazerowitz in the paper previously cited. The thesis, in addition to justifying the claim about Moore's work that it urges preserving the linguistic *status quo* and opposes idle innovations in ordinary language, has the merit of escaping the difficulty in the two most natural claims about his work: that it shows a belief about the world which contradicts Common Sense to be false, that it shows a philosopher's claim about linguistic usage to be mistaken. And it resolves the puzzle I set out earlier in supposing that it defends at one and the same time both the truth of common beliefs and the propriety of ordinary language. Moore's work is instead construed as urging that ordinary language not be changed. 'The propositions which he lays down as truisms . . . are not statements of fact as to what exists and what things are, but examples of the kind of everyday utterance which are not to be tampered with by metaphysically inclined philosophers under the guise of making . . . analyses.'[1]

It seems to me that Moore's refutations, effected by translations into the concrete, are much more convincing when taken as arguments whose import is linguistic than when taken as defending a factual truth. I call attention to the two divergent interpretations to which Moore's work lends itself, as opposing those theories about reality which go against commonsense beliefs, and as opposing the linguistic correlates of such theories, to make clear what it is that has changed the direction of philosophy. The one interpretation has eventuated in the resurgence of philosophical realism, the other in meta-philosophical studies of philosophers' language.

There is a third contribution which Moore's work has made to philosophy, and which I shall mention briefly because of a somewhat different direction philosophy has taken recently. Moore stated, and by practice implied, that analysis is one of the proper businesses of philosophy.[2] Inevitably this involves the close examination of the usage of expressions. In virtue of the kind of philosophical work on systems of metaphysics and ethics current when Moore began to write, it was natural that Moore's attention turned to certain expressions of key importance in the statements of these positions. When he belaboured philosophers for 'the attempt to answer questions, without first discovering precisely *what* question it is which [they] desire to answer',[3] he had in mind questions about such concepts as *good* and *right*, and he accordingly examined the uses of the terms 'good' and 'right'. Moore's analyses were always anchored in an obvious way in philosophical positions. Recently the work of certain philosophers has moved away from such anchorage, the result being a type of lexicography whose relation to the solution of philosophical problems is unclear. But there can be no doubt that attempts, for example, by Professor J. L. Austin, to clarify the meanings of nearly synonymous terms has its impetus from Moore's earlier attempts at analysis. Possibly this is a third direction into which Moore's thought will turn philosophers. That it had already turned some of them away from negative metaphysics and that it has produced a school devoted to the defence of ordinary language is clear.

[1] *Op. cit.*, p. 213. [2] *The Philosophy of G. E. Moore*, p. 676.
[3] *Principia Ethica* (1922), p. vi (Cambridge University Press, 1922).

13

MOORE'S 'PROOF OF AN EXTERNAL WORLD'*

In his 'Proof of an External World', read to the British Academy,[1] Professor Moore is concerned to establish the proposition 'that there exist things external to our minds'. Certain sceptical philosophers appear to doubt the truth of this proposition, and hence Moore, although he does not doubt it, considers it a matter of some importance 'whether it is possible to give *any* satisfactory proof'[2] of it, and if it is possible, to produce one. If no proof can be given then one is left the alternative of claiming to know this without proof or of being forced, as Kant thought, to accept the existence of things outside us 'merely on *faith*'.[3] In this paper Moore gives an argument which he considers 'a perfectly good proof',[4] and which if conclusive would remove what Kant characterized as a scandal to philosophy—the scandal of being unable to counter anyone's doubts with a proof. The proof Moore gives he asserts to be a good one, provided he knows what is asserted in its premise.[4] And he claims he does know this.

The proof consists in proceeding from the assertedly known premise, 'Here is a hand', to the conclusion which logically follows from it, 'there exists a thing external to us'. It is analogous to a very common form of argument, viz. to that in which an existential assertion is established by pointing out a specific instance. One proves that there is an officer of the law in a given village by pointing out the local sheriff, that there is a coin in the collection plate by pointing out a penny. 'That (pointing) is a

---

* Reprinted from *The Philosophy of G. E. Moore*, Vol. IV, The Library of Living Philosophers, edited by P. A. Schilpp (Open Court Publishing Co.).
[1] Annual Philosophical Lecture, Henriette Hertz Trust, *Proceedings of the British Academy*, Vol. XXV, 1939. [2] *Ibid.*, p. 275.
[3] *Critique of Pure Reason*, Preface to Second Edition, B xxix, note. (Kemp Smith's translation.)
[4] 'Proof of an External World', *Proc. British Academy*, Vol. XXV, p. 298.

sheriff of village K' entails 'There is an officer of the law in village K' and 'There (pointing) is a penny in the collection plate' entails 'There is a coin. . . .' In the same way Moore points out a hand (i.e. a physical object, i.e. as he explains, an object to be met with in space[1]), and from this it follows that there is an external object. 'Here (pointing) is a hand' entails 'There exists a hand', which entails 'There exists an external object'. This proof he says fulfills conditions which we require to be fulfilled in order for a proof to count as rigorous[2]: the premise is known to be true, it is different from the conclusion inferred from it, it logically implies the conclusion.

It is clear that Prof. Moore considers the proposition, 'There are external objects', to be an empirical one. It follows from a proposition which is established by empirical evidence, viz. the evidence of the senses. One has merely to show two hands and one has established that there are external objects. But though Moore thinks this proof is conclusive he is well aware that the sceptic will not be satisfied.[3] The latter's dissatisfaction arises from requiring a proof of what Moore has not tried to prove and which, according to Moore, needs no proof because it is known without proof.[4] Now the sceptic requires a proof of what Moore has not tried to prove, namely, the *premise*, 'Here is a hand', because he considers that its truth cannot, as Moore claims, be *known*, any more than the truth of what follows from it. Moore's proof will not answer the sceptic if the latter is as ready to question the truth of such premises as that of the conclusion, and if, as the sceptic certainly would hold, it is the truth of such premises about which he is in doubt. If the sceptic were to admit that there were hands but deny that there were objects external to us, then and only then would Moore's proof be a refutation. It would be shown that 'being a hand' entails 'being such as to be met with in space', which in turn entails 'being external to us'. But to a sceptic who is quite willing to admit that 'being a hand' entails 'being an external object', Moore's proof will not be to the point.—It will not refute his claim that it cannot be known there are hands.

It is characteristic of philosophical controversies that 'refutations' of a theory so often fail to appear conclusive to the propoun-

---

[1] 'Proof of an External World', *Proc. British Academy*, Vol. XXV, p. 295.
[2] *Ibid.*, pp. 297–98. [3] *Ibid.*, p. 298. [4] *Ibid.*, pp. 299–300.

ders of it. And this is not due to any incapacity to follow the 'refutations'. In connection with the controversy under consideration it is my purpose to investigate why neither Moore's 'refutation' nor any 'refutation' will serve to convince the sceptic, and why no argument the sceptic produces will seem conclusive to Moore. This will require investigating what it is each wishes to do and what argumentation for establishing one conclusion or the other comes to.

It is misleading to say Moore's proof will not succeed in dispelling the sceptic's doubt about the existence of hands; for this suggests that some other proof—one, say, in which he was made to touch as well as to see hands—would succeed where this one fails. We shall see that this is not the case at all. It is also entirely misleading to take the sceptic's dissatisfaction as indicating that Moore is easily convinced there are external objects, while he, the sceptic, is very hard to convince. We have only to see that no possible amount of further evidence would alter the sceptic's claim about the limitations of our knowledge, to see that any other proof of the kind described would be as unacceptable as the one propounded. For consider the sceptic's response to attempts at convincing him: Suppose one said, 'See, here is a hand'. The sceptic would reply, 'I can only know that I seem to see a hand. For all I know no external object may be there at all. I could be dreaming or having an hallucination.' Suppose then one made him touch one's hand. The response would be the same. And the use of *all* his other senses in connection with appropriate objects would evoke the same response. The curious thing about this attempt to convince him is that both he and his opponent differ with respect to whether they know, when both are in possession of precisely the same information. In saying, 'See, here is a hand', Moore's experience differs in no important respect from that of the sceptic. And the experience of each is of the kind which serves, under ordinary circumstances, to justify one's claim to know. For example, no detective, on being shown an incriminating letter his sleuths had hoped to find, would say, 'I can still only believe there is such a letter'. He would dispute his sleuths, in case he lacked confidence in them, only so long as they had seen the letter and he had not. But he would say that he knew there was such a letter as soon as he had seen what they saw.

In the argument between Moore and those philosophers who say they doubt the existence of hands, he and they both are being shown a hand, and Moore would have information which they lacked only if during the time the hand was shown they had been seeing nothing at all—e.g. had been suffering from psychic blindness. Under such circumstances there would be such a thing as new evidence when the blindness passed, which evidence would be supplemented by touching the hand, pressing it, pinching it, etc. All possible sensory evidence taken together would be said to justify one's claiming to know there was a hand. But in the circumstances in which the sceptic is described as disagreeing with Moore neither one of them is blind. And although both are in a position to see, touch, and feel the hand, and although both are in possession of equally good apparatus for receiving visual and tactual sensations, the sceptic would maintain against Moore that neither he nor Moore knew a hand to exist. He would maintain this no matter what further senses were brought into play. That is, he would preclude the information given by all the senses together from constituting testimony sufficient for proof, so that there would be no such thing as sufficient evidence in comparison with which the testimony of any one sense would be incomplete evidence. All evidence will be incomplete. This is why any attempt at 'proof' by appeal to the senses will be unacceptable.

The sceptic's claim that one can never know, but only believe, that external objects exist suggests that though the evidence furnished by the senses is insufficient to give us knowledge it is evidence of such a sort as to warrant belief. In that case he should be able to say what evidence now lacking would be sufficient to give us knowledge. It might well be that no human being is at present able to come into possession of such evidence, but if evidence is relevant to establishing the existence of external objects he should be able to state what evidence would satisfy him. But now what evidence *could* establish the existence of external objects if the evidence of all the senses together cannot? What is lacking? The sceptic cannot say, because he cannot say what *in addition* to feeling, seeing, tasting, etc., is to be done in order to establish the existence of external objects, i.e. what in addition to doing the 'ordinary' things. Surely nothing is lacking if nothing in addition to what we ordinarily do in getting to know, even when we are being most cautious, can be described. It is thus not the case that the sceptic is super-careful, hard to convince, that he requires more evidence than it is practicable for anyone to produce. For if he were merely *hard* to convince, it is conceivable that evidence should be produced which would overcome his resistance. It does not make sense to speak of convincing him when nothing additional to what we call 'convincing a person' can be described.

The peculiarity of the sceptic's claim that no one has or can have knowledge of the existence of external objects although no conceivable evidence for establishing their existence is lacking, becomes clear on contrasting it with: 'No one can know who committed the sabotage since all witnesses, the criminal included, died in the explosion'; or by contrasting 'No evidence is sufficient for establishing the existence of external objects' with 'No evidence submitted is sufficient for establishing the identity of the criminal'. It is clear that 'No one can know who committed the sabotage' is an empirical statement, justified by the empirical fact that all witnesses are dead. 'No evidence submitted is sufficient for establishing the identity of the criminal' is also an empirical statement, true, say, because of the ineptitude of the sleuths. And being empirical, we know what it would be like for each of these to be false. We could describe conditions under which we should know who committed the sabotage, and we could describe what kind of additional evidence would be sufficient for establishing the guilt of a suspect. But when the sceptic says no one can know that external objects exist, he cannot describe what prevents him from knowing, what obstacle stands in his way. Nor can he describe what kind of thing he would need to know in order for evidence for the existence of external objects to be complete. He cannot because he wants to say that *there are no describable circumstances* in which anyone could be said to know that external objects exist. This comes to saying that 'no one knows external objects exist' *cannot* be falsified, that is, that it is *not an empirical assertion* about our ability to know. His assertion does look very much like empirical assertions such as 'I cannot know there are mountains on the far side of the moon', which is true because of certain obstacles (which I can describe) which I lack the ingenuity to overcome. But the fact that no empirical justification can be given for the sceptic's assertion and that there is no way of describing how one could get to know external objects exist shows it is not at all like this. This fact shows, rather, that the sceptic is arguing for the *logical impossibility* of knowledge and not for any empirical fact. He is arguing that any such statement as 'I know there is a dollar in my purse' is logically impossible, and hence that 'I do not know there is a dollar in my purse' is necessarily true.

But now it is hard to suppose the sceptic is arguing that such propositions are necessarily true when it is plain that as language is ordinarily used they are not: 'I do not know there is a dollar in my purse' makes an assertion about me, and 'I do know there is a dollar in my purse', far from being self-contradictory, as it would be if the former were necessary, makes another assertion about me. The sceptic is aware that language is at present so used that each of these statements describes what could be the case. What then does his argument come to? When the sceptic points out that 'the senses might be deceiving one—one might be having an hallucination', he cannot be *showing* 'I do not know hands exist' to be necessary. For our present language is such that it is not necessary. Yet it is clear from what has been said previously that the sceptic cannot be urging the truth of an empirical statement: His avenues of information are equally as good as Moore's, information of the same kind is before them both, with no relevant facts lacking, and yet he holds in opposition to Moore that neither this information nor any information provided by the senses could constitute proof that there is a hand. Now if the sceptic is not showing either that his claim is logically necessary or that it is as a matter of fact true, he must have some other reason for adducing the consideration about the possibility of sense-deception. There still remains the alternative of adducing this to show that 'no one knows of the existence of hands' *should be* necessary. Can this be what the sceptic intends? Of course it is plain that he does not *say* 'no one knows that hands exist' should be necessary. He argues as if it were necessary, and as if he were calling attention to considerations which make this clear. That this procedure conceals what he is actually doing will I think become plain by examining, as a first step, what follows from 'the sentence "s" expresses a necessary proposition'.

Consider the statement, ' "There are no round squares" expresses a necessary proposition'. This entails that the phrase 'round squares' has no possible application. Similarly, consider the italicized in the following: 'The sceptic argues as if *"no one knows that hands exist" expresses a necessary proposition.*' This is to argue as if 'knowing hands exist' had no application. Certainly the sceptic, in urging that under no describable circumstances could one be said to know any kind of external object exists, behaves as though the phrase in question was actually not used to apply to anything. It is clear of course that it does have a use in present language, just as it is clear that 'no one knows hands exist' does not express a necessary proposition. It is also clear that the sceptic is not making a simple mistake which could be pointed out by calling attention to these two linguistic facts. Moore quite rightly takes issue with the sceptic, but their dispute is not to be settled merely by showing the sceptic that he is using language incorrectly. The sceptic knows that 'knowing hands exist' has use, and that 'no one knows there are hands in the world' is used to express something which can be *either* true or false. He is holding that they *should not* be so used, only he does not say so explicitly. He is holding that 'no one knows there are hands' *should be* necessary, only he conceals this beneath the indicative form of his expression. The sceptic asserts that no one knows hands exist as though this *already* were a necessary truth. But actually what he is doing is making a disguised proposal that it be accepted as a necessary truth.[1] And in doing this he is proposing, or recommending,[2] that certain expressions in our language be deprived of their use, i.e. that certain expressions shall have no sense. 'Knowing there are hands', 'knowing there are coins', etc., will not make sense, although 'believing there are hands' will. In pointing out that one's senses might be deceiving one, the sceptic is urging what he considers a good reason for revising present language. The revision would consist in discarding the use of such expressions as 'I know there is a tree in the garden' to assert empirical facts.

Moore's attempt to establish the existence of external objects shows that he conceives the sceptic to be doing something quite other than I have stated here. If my view of what the sceptic is doing is correct it is obvious why no argument Moore brings

[1] Pointed out in discussion by M. Lazerowitz.
[2] John Wisdom, 'Philosophical Perplexity', *Proc. Aristotelian Society*, Vol. XXXVII, p. 71.

forward will provide an answer to him. Because the sceptic is proposing a revision of language, no facts either about one's mental capacities or about correct linguistic usage will shake the conviction with which he asserts that no one can have knowledge. The kind of argument Moore gives by way of an answer indicates that he supposes the sceptic to be in fact doubting whether there is an external world. He produces empirical evidence which if conclusive should dispel that doubt. I want now to consider what Moore's argument comes to, whether he is doing what he seems to suppose he is doing (namely, establishing the truth of an empirical proposition, 'There are external objects'), and why the considerations the sceptic brings forward fail to alter Moore's contention that he knows.

The point of Moore's argument would seem to lie in producing the rational conviction that there are external objects. It is obvious that it is the sceptic and not the ordinary man who is to be convinced, since the ordinary man needs no convincing. Yet his argument is the sort used to convince the ordinary man of the existence of something *in question*, e.g. a dime in a box. A dime is pointed out in order to establish that a thing of that sort exists. But as for the further step in the argument, namely, the inference of 'There is an external object' from 'There is a dime', it could not *convince* the ordinary man of the existence of an external object since this would not be *in question*. And had it been in question, as it supposedly is in the case of the sceptic, pointing out a dime would by no means serve to convince him that there is a coin there. If the existence of external objects is in question, then calling attention to a visual experience no different in important respects from many past experiences which the sceptic has precluded from constituting proof will not convince him. The force of Moore's argument lies in its analogy to an ordinary empirical argument for establishing to the satisfaction of the ordinary man the existence of something in question. But in fact it is a sort of linguistic pantomime of such an argument, lacking analogy with it in essential respects: Proving that an external object exists by showing that there is a coin in a box is like proving there is a tree in the process of proving that there is a treasure hidden under the tree. Pointing out a dime in a box can settle an argument about the existence of a coin because pointing calls attention to a thing with features differentiating this thing

221

from things of other kinds. But can one 'point out an external object' and thereby settle any question about whether there is a thing of that kind? If one can by pointing out either a dime or a coin establish the existence of a coin, it looks as though one could establish the existence of an external object by pointing out either a coin or an external object. For the classification 'external object' seems merely the most general term of the series, 'dime', 'coin', 'external object', that is, it seems to be a name for a kind of thing, only a more general name than 'coin', just as 'coin' is a name for a kind of thing, only a more general name than 'dime'. But is 'external object' a general name? Can one 'point out an external object' as one can any kind of thing?

These questions can be settled by comparing the phrase 'external object' with a term about which there can be no doubt it is a general name, viz. 'coin'. Suppose one wished to teach a person the word 'coin'. One would point out a number of things to which this term applied, and also some to which it did not, for example, tax tokens. The teaching would consist in calling attention to features which this kind of thing had and in some cases to features had by other things from which it was to be distinguished. One could urge the person to make sure the thing was a coin and not a tax token by looking closely. Whether the person learned the word 'coin' would be tested by asking him to carry out the orders, 'Bring me a coin', 'Bring me a tax token', etc. Obviously he could fail to carry out these orders by bringing some other kind of thing than what was asked for. Consider now teaching someone the phrase 'external object'. The difficulty would be that one could not *point out* anything to him which was not an external object. One could not urge him to look more closely to make sure the thing was an external object and not some other kind of object. Nor would one explain what kind of object was in a box by telling him there was an external object in it. Further, the order, 'Bring me an external object', has the peculiarity that anyone who brought one anything at all could not fail to carry it out. Carrying out the order would provide no means of testing whether the person had learned the use of 'external object'. We have not provided for the possibility of making a mistake, and hence there is no way of testing whether we have taught him. In fact there is no way of teaching him if there is no possibility of testing whether he has learned what we have taught. These considerations show, it seems to me, that 'external object' is not a general name for some kind of thing, designating features distinguishing that kind of thing from some other kind. One can only bring something which this names if one can fail to bring it. If this is the case then one cannot *point out* an external object, so that no argument about the existence of external objects could be settled by 'pointing out an external object'.

This shows that Moore's proof is not analogous to an ordinary empirical argument for establishing something in question. There is no possibility of directly establishing that there is an external object since 'external object', unlike 'coin', is not a general name for some kind of thing. The force of Moore's argument lies in its obvious similarity to proving there is a coin in a collection plate by pointing out a dime. So soon as one sees that the existence of external objects is not to be established by the same empirical methods serving to establish the existence of a coin because of the lack of analogy between 'external object' and 'coin', his proof loses force. If 'There is an external object' is to be established at all, it will be only because one has established something from which it follows. It *cannot* itself be established in the way the antecedent of the entailment is. By contrast, in pointing out a dime one could establish directly either that there was a dime, or what is entailed by this, that there was a coin. One would not have established the existence of a coin *only* because one had established the existence of something from which its existence follows. The existence of a coin can be established by pointing out a coin, but the existence of an external object cannot be established by pointing out anything.

The lack of analogy between 'There is a coin' and 'There is an external object' with respect to proof has its counterpart in a lack of analogy with respect to disproof. There is no possibility of disproving, by any of the methods employable in disproving that there is a coin in the plate, that there is an external object. If someone were to question whether there was a coin in the plate, one could disprove that there was either by showing him that there was nothing at all in the plate or by showing him that every object in the plate was a button. But if someone were to question whether there were external objects, could one show empirically that there were no objects at all? Philosophers who have tried to prove that there are no external objects have made no pretence of using empirical methods to do so, attempting to show that there *could be* no external objects, i.e. that it is logically impossible that there should be. Further, it is clear that one could not, by way of disproof, show anyone that one had been mistaken about the object before them both (as one could with the coin) and that the object was in fact not an external one. This is impossible for the same reason that it is impossible to carry out the order, 'Bring me an object which is not an external one'. The phrase 'object which is not an external one', like 'external object', is not a general name for a kind of thing.

Even though pointing out an instance of a kind of thing will not establish 'There is an external object' because 'external object' is not a name for a kind of thing, it might seem that as long as this proposition is entailed by one which is so established, it would itself be established indirectly. This will be seen not to be the case by examining the entailment, ' "There is a dime" entails "There is an external object",' and comparing it with ' "There is a dime" entails "There is a coin",' or by comparing the two necessary propositions, 'A dime is a coin', 'A dime is an external object'. To hold that 'A dime is a coin' expresses a necessary proposition entails holding that anything which is a dime satisfies all the criteria for applying the word 'coin'—criteria such as 'being a piece of metal', 'being stamped by public authority', 'being made for use as money', etc. It is to be noted that these criteria distinguish this kind of object from other kinds, so that producing an object satisfying these criteria will make it true that there is an object of this kind and will falsify the opposite assertion. Now what, different from this, is being said in saying that 'There is a dime' entails 'There is an external object', or that 'A dime is an external object' is necessary? From what has been said above about the phrase 'external object' I think it will be clear that holding 'A dime is an external object' expresses a necessary proposition does not entail holding that anything which is a dime satisfies all the criteria for applying the phrase 'external object'. For this phrase is not used to apply to any kind of thing. One will therefore not have established the existence of anything of the kind 'external object' in producing a dime. Nevertheless Moore is doing something very important, with reference to the sceptic's claim, in asserting such entailments as ' "There is a dime" entails "There is an external object".' An analysis of 'being an object external to all our minds' shows the importance of what he is doing. Each of the terms of the following list, some of which are equivalent to each other, gives a partial analysis of this concept: 'being such as to be met with in space', 'being an object of possible experience', 'being such as could be perceived', 'being accessible to one or more senses', 'being such that one mind could perceive it at two different times or that more than one mind could perceive it at the same time'. It will be noted that all of these involve the notion of possibility. 'A dime is an external object' will mean in part 'A dime can be perceived', 'A dime can be seen, or felt . . . or . . .', 'A dime can be perceived by two different persons', etc. The possibility asserted is obviously a logical possibility. And if 'A dime is perceived by two persons' expresses something logically possible, then it makes sense to say 'A dime is perceived by two persons'. The above list provides then, not criteria for applying the phrase 'object external to all minds', but criteria for its *making sense* to say certain things about dimes, hands, and other things for which it would express something necessary to say they were external to all minds. Moore's statement that 'There is a hand' entails 'There is an external object' calls attention to criteria for applying 'external object words', so that if a thing of a given kind is an external object it follows that such expressions as these make sense: 'Smith and I both saw the thief', 'I found a gold piece in the box', 'I heard the lion and later saw it', 'The suit I saw today was the same one I saw yesterday', etc. It is clear that if these expressions make sense, then one knows what it is like for what they express to be true. Now what they express implies the existence of a thief, a gold piece, a lion, a suit, respectively. So if one knows what it is like for them to be true, one knows what it is like for 'There exists a thief', '. . . a gold piece', '. . . a lion', '. . . a suit' to be true. And if one knows what it is like for these to be true, it makes sense to say 'I know there is a thief is true', etc. Thus Moore, in calling attention to the entailment between 'There is a hand' and 'There is an external object', calls attention to criteria for the use of such words as 'hand', 'dime', and the like, and in doing this shows that in English it makes sense to say 'I know there is a dime in the box'. That is, Moore's argument (although it does not establish the truth of an empirical proposition about the existence of a kind of thing, external objects) has as a consequence that it is *logically possible* to know there are coins in a box. We recall that the sceptic argued as if it were logically impossible.

Of course Moore appears to have attempted something quite different from showing the logical possibility of having knowledge. For to show this is not to show any matter of fact. Moore seems to assert that as a matter of fact he knows there is at least one external object. Throughout, he gives the impression of defending common sense against the sceptic (who at times likewise appears to be asserting a matter of fact about what we can or cannot know). Yet his defence of common sense consists in 'proving' a proposition which is not a commonsense belief. (Compare 'There are external objects' with 'There is cheese in the refrigerator'.[1]) And he tries to allay doubts which are not commonsense doubts: that external objects exist does not come in question in the way the existence of a treasure does. And then it turns out on close examination that his attempted proof of 'There is an external object' is not at all analogous to 'There is a coin in the plate', which it should be if it were to prove what he intends. He has, however, countered the sceptic's claim that it *cannot* be known there are hands. For it follows from what he has said in the course of his argument and in his analysis of the notion 'external object' that 'knowing there is a hand' expresses something logically possible.

Now to say that 'knowing there is a hand' expresses something logically possible is to say this expression makes sense. As language is ordinarily used it is clearly true that this expression and others like it do make sense. And that this is true can be seen independently of any argument. The importance of insisting, as Moore has done, that one can know there are hands, lies in what the sceptic has done. It will be recalled that the sceptic argued as though such expressions as 'knowing there are hands' had no application, that is, did not make sense. He argued this although he knows they do in fact make sense, doubtless using them himself under ordinary circumstances to express something. This being the case it will not settle the dispute for Moore to show the sceptic he is using language incorrectly. For as was argued earlier, the sceptic is *recommending* that it be correct to say only that one

---

[1] Cf. Wittgenstein's remark that the philosopher of Common Sense 'is not the common-sense man'. *The Blue Book*, p. 48.

believes there are hands and incorrect to say one knows this. Moore's argument constitutes an insistence on retaining present usage—on retaining 'know' as well as 'believe' to preface statements about physical objects. It is the sceptic's recommendation which makes Moore's insistence relevant. And though Moore never expresses his argument against the sceptic as an argument concerning the sense of phrases such as 'knowing there are hands' (nor even as an argument concerning whether knowing of the existence of hands is logically possible), it is the great merit of Moore's position that it makes one see, by calling attention to ordinary usage, that the sceptic's linguistic recommendation is objectionable. This merit appears upon examining the consequences of accepting his recommendation:

The sceptic, in proposing as necessary 'no one knows of the existence of any external object' is in fact proposing that ordinary language be changed, so that under no circumstances shall it be correct to say that I know there is a button in the box, but only that I believe this. Now how is the usage of the word 'believe' affected by this recommendation? The sceptic himself does not say, but there are obviously only two courses open to him: to insist that no change in its present usage is necessitated, or to recommend a modification of its present usage so that it would mean what we now mean by either 'know' or 'believe'. Let us consider these alternatives in turn. Were the sceptic to maintain that the usage of 'believe' is unchanged by his recommendation about the use of 'know', while depriving it of a correlate functioning in the way 'know' at present does in connection with propositions about external objects, he would involve himself in contradiction. As the word 'believe' is ordinarily used it functions as a contrast term to 'know'. We say such things as: 'I believe it's true, but I wish that I knew', 'I believe she's innocent, but I shall pretend I know it', 'I used only to believe there was a buried treasure. Now I know it'. With the sceptic's revision of language no such contrast would be possible since it will not make sense to say one knows such a thing. Can the word 'believe' then retain its present usage if it is deprived of its correlate 'know'? It is clear from the following consideration that it cannot and that the sceptic would involve himself in contradiction were he to maintain that it did: As indicated by the above instances of the correct usage of 'believe', saying that one believes something entails the logical possibility of knowing what is only believed. Thus the sceptic could not without contradiction hold that 'believe' retains its ordinary use and at the same time hold that knowing that external objects exist is logically impossible.

He does not in fact commit himself to this contradiction since he has not committed himself at all on the usage of the term 'believe'. And he could escape it either by introducing into language a new word functioning as 'know' now does in such statements as 'I know there's a chair in the next room', the word 'believe' at the same time retaining its present usage, or by extending the usage of 'believe' so that it would function both where we now use 'believe' and where we now use 'know'. In either case his position would be as objectionable, for another reason, as it would be were he to deprive 'believe' of any correlate functioning in the way 'know' does and at the same time insist that no change is necessitated in its usage. For suppose he were to introduce another term 'x' functioning as 'know' does, so that 'I believe there's a chair in the next room' would entail the logical possibility of 'x-ing' there is a chair. It is clear that this notation does exactly what the old one did—no more, no less—and that it is therefore completely pointless to introduce it. The same obtains were the sceptic, upon eliminating 'know' as a preface to empirical propositions about external objects, to extend the usage of the term 'believe' so that it would function both where we now use 'believe' and where we now use 'know'. It is clear that this notation in which a new term 'believe' takes over the function of both 'know' and the present term 'believe' has no advantage whatever over the old one. If anything, it has a disadvantage, in that what is meant when one says 'I believe Smith is in the next room' might not be clear. 'Believing' this will mean either knowing it or merely believing it, and unlike pun words, the context of 'believe' will not indicate which meaning is intended. It would be natural to eliminate the ambiguity by using 'believe' where we now use 'know' and 'merely believe' where we now use 'believe'. Such a notation would contain in itself the seeds of the sceptic's discontent with the old notation. It might give rise to exactly the considerations which moved the sceptic to desire revision in the first place, so that the sceptic might now insist that one should say one 'merely believes' there are external objects. In any case if the sceptic's revision of the language with respect to 'know' were to have as a concomitant the introduction of a new term to do what 'know' does or the extension of the usage of 'believe' to achieve this, it is clear that there would be no point whatever in making it.

It is the great merit of Moore that by calling attention to the present usages of 'know' and 'believe', he leads one to see that none of the courses open to the sceptic with respect to the term 'believe' is unobjectionable. He makes one see that present language is adequate to express all we want to express, despite there being circumstances in which we cannot answer the question, 'Do you know there is a rat in the room or do you only believe it?'

Consideration of this kind of question is what leads the sceptic to suggest revision of the language. It is the fact that there are no criteria distinguishing sharply between veridical experience, illusion, hallucination, and dream experience which the sceptic uses to justify his holding one can never know that hands, say, exist. Since there are circumstances in which we ask ourselves, without knowing the answer, 'Am I dreaming? Am I having an hallucination?' the sceptic feels justified in asking, 'How can you know in *any* circumstances that you are not dreaming or having an hallucination?' He points out that dream experiences can be exactly similar to those of waking life, that every veridical experience can be exactly duplicated by an illusory one, i.e. that there are no criteria, no marks, for distinguishing in all cases the one from the other. The possibility of confusing one kind of experience with the other is sufficient to show that there are no clear distinctions between them. The sceptic then uses this fact as substantiation of what appears to be an *hypothesis*: 'You might in the case of all experiences be dreaming or having an hallucination'. But this is no hypothesis such as, 'You might have appendicitis'. He means to say that it is logically possible that one is dreaming when one has the kind of experience one claims to have in waking life and that it is therefore logically impossible to know that one is not dreaming. Now if it is logically impossible to know one is not dreaming, the phrase 'knowing one is not dreaming' makes no sense. The same holds for 'knowing one is not having an illusory experience'. Further, 'S does not know he is not dreaming' and 'S does not know he is not having an illusory experience', will now express something necessary and will lose their use to express empirical facts. The sceptic of course knows that in ordinary language 'S knows he is not dreaming' and 'S does not know he is not dreaming' both equally have a use to express matters of facts, and hence he can be understood as recommending that they should not.

The kind of reply Moore gives to the sceptic, even though not intended as an objection to a 'recommendation', is in fact a flat rejection of it. To the sceptic's claim (1) that one does not know there is a hand before one, and to his reason for holding this, (2) that one can never know one is not dreaming, Moore replies: (1) 'How absurd it would be to suggest that I did not know it, but only believed it, and that perhaps it was not the case!'[1] and (2) 'I have conclusive evidence that I am awake.'[2] The importance of these replies of Moore's lies in their conjunction with his admission that he cannot *prove* what the sceptic insists must be proved before one can know any fact about hands: the premise, 'Here's a hand', from which 'There is an external object' follows. Moore concedes that this premise cannot be proved, since 'in order to do it [he would] need to prove for one thing, as Descartes pointed out, that [he was] not dreaming'.[2] Nevertheless, he denies forthrightly that this is any reason for saying one does not know. 'I can know things, which I cannot prove.'[2] And among the things he claims he can know without proof is that here is a hand. Further, since he claims to have 'conclusive evidence' he is awake (even though he cannot say what all the evidence is, as he would be required to do were he to prove it), this also must be a thing he can know without proof.

The difference between Moore and the sceptic, and the importance of Moore's answer, lies in what each says about the impossibility of proving one is not dreaming. When Moore admits that he cannot prove he is not dreaming he is calling attention to the same fact the sceptic used to persuade one that one should not say one knew of the existence of hands. This is that there are no *sharp* criteria for the application of the terms 'dreaming', 'not dreaming', 'having an illusory experience', 'having a veridical experience'. The sceptic in demanding a proof of 'Here's a hand' as a condition

---

[1] 'Proof of an External World', *Proc. British Academy*, Vol. XXV, p. 296.
[2] *Ibid.*, pp. 299–300.

of saying one knows such a thing is requiring the exhibition of sharp criteria for distinguishing between dream and waking life. 'Know' and 'prove' would thereby have an interchangeable usage. By contrast, what Moore in effect goes on to say is that the lack of sharp criteria is no reason whatever for saying one can never know one is not dreaming or having an illusory experience, that the fact that there are some criteria for the application of these terms, even though they are not such as to distinguish sharply in all cases between dream and waking life, is sufficient for holding one can know there is a hand before one. To require that in every conceivable circumstance we should say we believe rather than know this, because we sometimes cannot answer the question, 'Do you know there is a rat in the room or do you only believe it?' is like requiring us to say we never know when to use the word 'heap' because we cannot say exactly how many grains are required; or when to use the word 'bald' because we cannot say how many hairs are the maximum; or when to use the word 'fowl' because we cannot say exactly the number of months required to make a chicken old enough to count as a fowl.

It is clear that Moore is in effect insisting on retaining conventions already established in the language about the usage of the words 'know' and 'believe', and that the consequence of what he says is the preservation of the linguistic *status quo*. He has not himself shown the pointlessness of the sceptic's attempted revisions of language, for he has not seen clearly what the sceptic is doing and consequently has not shown what he is doing. But in calling attention to ordinary language (and Moore is constantly calling attention to what is correct) he takes us the first step toward seeing what the sceptic is doing and that what he is doing is pointless. For reminding one of how language is ordinarily used is a way of making one feel there is something absurd about what the sceptic propounds. When the sceptic says one cannot know there is a hand before one, Moore exclaims, 'How absurd it would be to suggest that I did not know it, but only believed it, and that perhaps it was not the case!'[1] His reply is like that of the ordinary man who does not allow himself to become entangled in a philosophical dispute— it dismisses the sceptic's conclusion by contradicting it but without countering his argument. The great importance of such a reply is

---

[1] 'Proof of an External World', *Proc. British Academy*, Vol. XXV, p. 296.

to make one feel as the ordinary man feels, as though there is something ridiculous about it. The mere contrast between ordinary language and the language of the philosopher was sufficient to make Hume say, '. . . and when after three or four hours' amusement I . . . return to these speculations, they appear so cold, and strain'd, and ridiculous, that I cannot find in my heart to enter into them any farther.'[1] It has been Moore's rôle in philosophy to shock philosophers who tend to become oblivious to this contrast into a realization of it. Because he is himself a great philosopher, Moore can succeed in this, whereas the ordinary man's remarks would have no influence. For the ordinary man can so easily be lured into talking in the same way. Moore *in doing philosophy* constantly holds ordinary language before one, so that one is made to feel, not only upon returning to one's views but while philosophizing, that they are 'strain'd and ridiculous'. Once one feels this one has taken the first step toward seeing why—toward seeing that a 'rectified' language only says in another way what ordinary language does. Our language is such that when we philosophize, certain considerations constantly tempt us to revision, while considerations which would make us see our language needs no revision and is adequate to express all we want to say, are discounted and forgotten. We are tempted to think that the sceptic weaves a verbal material which is much finer than the coarse fabric of ordinary discourse. But in forcefully reminding us of current usage, Moore sets us on our way to seeing that like the imposters of the tale of The Emperor's New Clothes, the sceptic is weaving nothing at all, and that in fact the Emperor is naked.

---

[1] *A Treatise of Human Nature*, Bk. I, Pt. IV, Sec. VII.

14

FACTUAL, MATHEMATICAL AND METAPHYSICAL INVENTORIES

Proposition[1] of Wittgenstein's *Tractatus* reads: 'The world is everything that is the case'. But what does 'everything' cover? Apart from its generality, its reference to the world, the question would seem to be clear and unambiguous enough, and to have a straightforward answer. Under 'everything' we should list trees, buildings, human beings, animals, etc. However, when a philosopher asks the question 'What is there in the world?', something more than this kind of simple-minded, commonplace answer is expected. In G. E. Moore's opinion the attempt to answer it is of first importance. He wrote: '. . . it seems to me that the most important and interesting thing which philosophers have tried to do is . . . to give a general description of the *whole* of the Universe, mentioning all the most important kinds of things which we *know* to be in it.'[1] In part, what makes the question important and interesting is that it presents some sort of difficulty, as is evidenced by the fact that philosophers have for centuries divided on what kinds of things there are—whether there are material objects, minds, relations, properties, numbers, propositions, facts, or only some selection of these, or even none at all. The divergence of opinion is very different from that occurring in a disagreement over whether there are people or gold deposits within a certain region, or over whether there are primes between 2000 and 2031. The difference between the disagreements parallels the difference in the kinds of tasks undertaken by the census taker, the miner, the mathematician, on the one hand, and the metaphysician on the other. The metaphysician keeps a ledger of reality and unreality, of what exists and what does not exist, which would seem to rule out many run-of-the-mill inventories. Thus, if according to his ledger there are no material objects, a warehouse inventory is ruled out; if there are

[1] *Some Main Problems of Philosophy*, p. 1.

no relations, then one can spare oneself concern over the relatives who are to benefit under one's will, etc. Yet we all recognize that in fact warehouse inventories, censuses of cities, existential proofs in mathematics are made without regard to what the metaphysician's ledger records as real. The metaphysician is not consulted. Questions as to how many people there are in a city or how many cars come off an assembly line or how many primes there are within a given sequence of numbers may have conflicting answers; but it is known in a general way how to decide between answers. The situation is very different with regard to existence-questions and answers in metaphysics; it is in fact so different that the doubt arises whether metaphysical statements refer to the world at all. Indeed, the suspicion arises whether the metaphysician has set himself a task of inventory which is only the semblance of a task. In this essay I shall maintain the impossibility of such an inventory, not because the task is beyond our powers but because there is no task.

It would seem that to say there are things, properties, numbers, facts, etc. is to state what there is in the universe, and that like other existence-claims it should be possible to ascertain whether they are true. To maintain that it is impossible to ascertain their truth suggests the presence of a logical or psychological obstacle. In both the *Notebooks* and *Tractatus* Wittgenstein characterized *thing, fact, function, number*, etc. as 'pseudo' or 'formal' concepts, to contrast them with what he called 'proper' concepts, declaring that the sentences '1 is a number', 'M is a thing', 'There are *n* objects' are senseless.[1] He said: 'To ask whether a formal concept exists is nonsensical. For no proposition can be the answer to such a question.' (4.1274).[2] It is clear that according to his early writings there could be no deciding the correct answer to such a question, not because its answer poses insuperable difficulties but because there is no question.

In this essay I do not wish to maintain that such questions are nonsensical. But I do want to argue that the answers do not state what there is in the universe. I shall try to show that in a round-about way they are verbal rather than factual in import. In support

---

[1] *Tractatus*, 4.1272, and *Notebooks, 1914-16*, p. 108.
[2] From the translation by D. F. Pears and B. F. McGuinness (London: Routledge & Kegan Paul, Ltd., 1961). This translation is to be used throughout.

of this claim I call attention first of all to differences and similarities between three types of existence-statements: (*a*) those asserting a fact which might be otherwise, (*b*) existence-propositions of mathematics, and (*c*) metaphysical propositions stating the existence of the most general categories of things. Their similarity is of course obvious. In particular, the last two kinds have as their verbal model statements of the kind (*a*)—such statements as record, for example, the contents of a drawer, a warehouse, a gallery, an archaeological excavation. There seems merely to be a difference in the boundaries within which things of each kind are located—in the case of (*a*), spatio-temporal, in the case of (*b*), neither spatial nor temporal, in the case of (*c*), universe-wide, or without boundaries. That persons and artifacts are discovered by a different organ of the mind than are irrational roots or propositions seems as inconsequential a difference as the difference in boundaries within which discovery is made. All are discoveries in the cosmic warehouse. The functions '*x* is a young person', '*x* is an irrational root of $x^2 = -2$', '*x* is an attribute' seem on the same ontological footing and merely to take different sorts of values, and the statement that there exist values of these functions seems to use 'exist' in the same way. To claim that metaphysical sentences differ so radically from existential sentences of everyday life and mathematics that they do not tell us what there is, challenges both of these apparent facts.

On the face of it, their relation to contingent statements and to the necessary existential statements of mathematics appears to be that of the more general to the more specific. The impression that this is so is strengthened by seemingly unobjectionable entailments between specific existential statements of classes (*a*) and (*b*) and the general existential statements of (*c*). In fact a metaphysician might argue for the truth of existence-statements of the most general class (*c*) by adducing some such entailments as the following. (Take '→' to mean 'entails'.)

1. There are rickshaws in Shanghai → There are rickshaws → There are things
2. There are rickshaws in Shanghai → There are rickshaws → There is the property of being a rickshaw → There is a property
3. There are prime numbers between 10 and 15 → There are prime numbers → There are numbers

4. That there are planets is a fact → There is a true proposition → There is a proposition.

And the existence of properties might be argued as follows: If there were no property of being a tree, for example, there could be no instances of it—no trees. But since there are trees there is at least one property. These entailments make the proof of metaphysical statements about what there is seem very simple indeed.

We know, however, at least in the case of the long standing controversy over the existence of universals, that entailments which are asserted above to have the existence of universals as their consequents are continuously subject to challenge. According to Prof. W. V. Quine these consequents 'follow from the point of view of a conceptual scheme' whereas 'judged within another conceptual scheme an ontological statement . . . may be adjudged false'.[1] In other words, one can perfectly well admit there are rickshaws while holding it to be false that there is the attribute of being a rickshaw. So far as I can see, 'the conceptual scheme by which one interprets all experiences',[2] to which 'one's ontology is basic',[2] is either just the ontology under debate or else presupposes it logically. To say the existence of universals follows from 'casual statements of commonplace fact'[2] according to one conceptual scheme and not according to another is a simple denial that it follows from these casual statements alone, and provides no reason against its being held to follow. The puzzle is why it cannot be settled once and for all whether it follows or not. I think the question whether an entailment holds remains unsettled because it is unclear what the sentence 'There are universals' asserts, if indeed it asserts anything. So the similarity of 'There are things', 'There are attributes', 'There are numbers', etc. to 'There are rickshaws in Shanghai' and 'There are primes between 10 and 15' must be matched by differences which create an obstacle to coming to a decision on these matters. Quine writes: 'Our acceptance of an ontology is, I think, similar in principle to our acceptance of a scientific theory.'[3] If a survey of the differences among these sentences leaves them with only an outward, verbal similarity, Quine's claim may seriously come in question, and what, in truth, there is may appear not to be a question at all.

[1] 'On What There Is', in *From a Logical Point of View*, p. 10 (Harvard University Press, 1961).   [2] *Ibid.*   [3] *Ibid.*, p. 16.

One important fact of difference which bears on the continuing indecision concerning the entailments 1–4, and stands in the same need of explanation, should be noted at the start. This is the fact that existential statements of metaphysics, unlike commonplace factual statements and unlike statements of mathematics, have their truth-values chronically in dispute with no prospect of a settlement. Admittedly, we may be a long time discovering the truth-value of 'There are other inhabited planets' and of 'There are three consecutive 7's in the development of π'. But in the first case we could describe getting to know which truth-value it had, and in the second, even though we might not be able to describe getting to know this without being able to describe the proof, we should at least be in agreement, once a proof was produced, regarding what its truth-value is. The difficulties standing in the way of discovering the truth, or falsity, of factual and mathematical statements are quite different from each other, but in the case of neither sort is one presented with the puzzling features peculiar to the difficulties of discovering that it is true, or false, that there are in the universe things, or relations, or propositions, or numbers. One cannot specify what the obstacles are which prevent reaching a decision. For example, one finds a philosopher who denies that there are things unable to say under what conditions he would be constrained to allow that there are. And similarly a philosopher who denies the possibility of knowing they exist is unable to say what would have to be done in order to acquire this knowledge. Again, could one say what would show the proposition that there are numbers to be false? and how would one show it to be true in the face of a philosopher's challenge? Quine writes: 'When we say, for example, $(\exists x)(x$ is a prime $.\ x > 1{,}000{,}000)$, we are saying that *there is* something which is a prime and exceeds a million; and any such entity is a number, hence a universal.'[1] Suppose a philosopher denies that there are universals?

Metaphysical propositions differ from factual and mathematical propositions not only in the respects that they are in permanent dispute and in want of any specification of what would be required to determine their truth-values. They differ also in respect of their so-called proofs and disproofs, though here metaphysical propositions are more akin to mathematical propositions than to factual

---

[1] 'The Reification of Universals', in *From a Logical Point of View*, p. 103.

propositions. Traditionally, metaphysicians have presented arguments for and against existence-claims which resemble arguments in mathematics. F. H. Bradley, for example, argued that it is self-contradictory that things, properties, and relations exist. But unlike proofs of self-contradictions in mathematics, his arguments gain no general acceptance and at the same time are not shown, by those who reject them, to be guilty of any generally acknowledged logical misstep. A commonsense philosopher like Moore who retorts that since he knows he had breakfast before he had lunch he knows that a temporal relation, and hence a relation, exists, does not point out an error in the argument. And presumably Bradley already knows that such expressions as 'breakfast before lunch', '3 < 4', etc. are not self-contradictory expressions in current English. Despite his argument, he continues to use specific relation-words exactly as does Moore, and it is doubtful whether he could be made to feel, by Moore's translations into the concrete, that consistently with his view the word 'before' is in the same position as the phrase 'related to'. One gains the impression that in his eyes this phrase has been shown to be self-contradictory and hence without use in descriptive phrases but that his argument leaves untouched the use of specific relation-terms, like 'less than' and 'before'. Thus he could agree with Moore that he had had breakfast before lunch and deny the reality of relations. Similarly, philosophical mathematicians might agree that 'There is a prime number between 4 and 6' expresses something true while dividing on the existence of numbers.

It would appear that what one might call category concepts occurring as the entire predicate of existence-propositions have a quite different function, if they have a function at all, from specific concepts, or 'proper' concepts, as Wittgenstein called them. Evidently differences between these concepts are responsible for the differences just cited between metaphysical propositions and others. It will be useful, then, to compare the terms 'related to' and 'before', 'quality' and 'colour', 'number' and 'prime number', 'thing' and 'rickshaw', with an eye to their differences. Wittgenstein denied that the first term in each of these pairs is a generic name.[1] 'Red', to use W. E. Johnson's terminology ,is a determinant under the determinable 'colour', and 'scarlet' is a determinant

[1] From lecture notes taken by Alice Ambrose, 1934–35.

under the determinable 'red'; but the behaviour of the category concepts puts in question whether 'colour' is a determinant under the determinable 'quality', and 'rickshaw' a determinant under the determinable 'thing'. It is natural to suppose they are. To say that the concepts denoted by these words are related as the more generic to the more specific is another way of saying that 'There are rickshaws' entails 'There are things' and that 'There are shades of red' entails 'There are qualities'. Whether these are entailments is just the question at issue. At any rate, supposing they are entailments, the further question is whether they figure in demonstrations of the contents of the universe.

That these concepts are not related as the more generic to the more specific is suggested by various considerations. Take first the concept *thing*, which appears to be the most general of the concepts in the series, *rickshaw, conveyance, thing*. The word 'thing' seems to be a general name, only more general than 'conveyance', just as 'conveyance' is a general name, only more general than 'rickshaw'. Several considerations indicate that this way of looking at the terms is mistaken. First, teaching the use of the word 'thing' is not at all analogous to teaching the use of either 'conveyance' or 'rickshaw'. One could explain these latter by pointing to things to which each applied, and also to some to which they did not; for example, 'rickshaw' does not apply to carts or sleds. And one could test a person's understanding by asking him to point out rickshaws and conveyances. Obviously the learner could fail the test by pointing out some other kind of thing. We should know he had failed to understand 'rickshaw' if, for example, he pointed to a sedan chair or a gig, i.e. if he pointed to other species of things falling under the genus *conveyance*. This is the kind of mistake a person could make who failed to differentiate properly among *kinds* of things to which the word 'rickshaw' sensibly, even though falsely, applies. These considerations about teaching the use of the word show what the function of a generic name is, namely, to distinguish among kinds of things.

Consider now a person learning the word 'thing', and the type of mistake he could make, as contrasted with a person learning the word 'rickshaw'. A person who pointed to a gig and said 'That's a rickshaw' would make the mistake of assigning a false value to the variable in the function 'x is a rickshaw'. He could also make a mistake if he had an hallucination, or pointed to a shadow or a mirage, where hallucination, shadow, and mirage were all similar to a rickshaw. But a mistake of this kind is entirely different. It would consist of failing to distinguish appearance from reality, whereas the mistake of a person who pointed to a gig would consist in not distinguishing properly among kinds of conveyances. The expression 'x is a rickshaw' might be said to have two ranges of significance, which one could characterize as its 'reality' range and its 'appearance-reality' range. The one would comprise rickshaws and other kinds of real objects, the other, rickshaws and delusive rickshaw-appearances. There are thus two kinds of situation in which 'rickshaw' would have the function of a generic name to set off objects within its range of significance from others. But this is not so for 'x is a thing'. 'Thing' functions like a generic name to set off things from appearances, but not to distinguish among *kinds* of things. Nothing within its 'reality' range of significance could fail to be a thing. That is, all sensible substitutions on 'x' in the expression 'x is a thing', save for demonstratives designating shadows and the like, would yield something true. Unlike 'x is a rickshaw', there would be no possibility of assigning, from its reality range, a false value to the variable. The kinds of mistake a person being taught the word 'thing' could make are thus limited to mistaking appearances for reality. And this difference sets off 'thing' from proper concept words like 'rickshaw'. Of course these two are alike in that one could so far fail to understand both as to take them to apply to processes, events, qualities, relations, or numbers. If one cited any of these and said 'That's a rickshaw' or 'That's a thing' one would in each case utter nonsense, as English is at present used. But the difference between the two is that barring such mistakes or a confusion of reality and appearance, there is no other mistake a person being taught the word 'thing' could make.

This difference between the category concept *thing* and concepts like *rickshaw* shows up in a difference in the verifications of the existential generalizations of 'x is a thing' and 'x is a rickshaw'. Since both antecedent and consequent of the entailment 'x is a rickshaw $\rightarrow$ x is a conveyance' have within their reality range of significance both true and false values, both success and failure in establishing their existential generalizations are possible. This is a feature of any empirical verification. But compare the entailment 'x is a conveyance $\rightarrow$ x is a thing'. Within the reality range of the antecedent there are both true and false values, but within that of the consequent there are only true ones. There is nothing within this range which could fail to be an instance of the concept *thing*, which is to say that by choosing from this range one could never fail to establish that there are things. It is doubtful whether we should call a procedure which could not fail empirical or that we should say we had established anything by it.

The lack of analogy between 'There is a conveyance' and 'There is a thing' with respect to establishment has its counterpart in a lack of analogy with respect to disproof. It is clear what we could not, by way of disproof of 'There are things', show someone that he was mistaken about each of the objects within the reality range of 'x is a thing' (as we could with 'x is a conveyance')—we could not urge that they were in fact not things. A philosopher like Bradley, who wishes to prove that things are unreal, makes no pretence of using empirical methods to do so. Instead he attempts to show that it is logically impossible that there should be things. I think the difference between the two kinds of concepts, the category concept *thing* and generic concepts like *conveyance* and *rickshaw*, is the source of the differences (*a*) between establishing the existence of conveyances and the existence of things, which is not paralleled by a difference in establishing the existence of rickshaws and the existence of conveyances, and (*b*) between disestablishing the existence of conveyances and of things, which is not paralleled by a difference in disestablishing the existence of rickshaws and of conveyances.

Let us see whether any similar considerations hold in the case of existentials involving the category concepts *number*, *quality*, *relation*, *proposition*. Take first the sequence *even prime number*, *prime number*, *number*, of which *number* appears to be the most general concept. Consider the method for determining whether something is an instance of each sort. Numbers are obviously what we should test, i.e. only numbers fall within the range of significant application of these concepts. It is clear in the case of the first two concepts what calculations we should make in order to determine whether a number was an even prime, or a prime. But it is also clear that no similar calculation is involved in determining whether

31, say, is a number. '31 is an even prime', '31 is a prime', and '31 is a number' are on a quite different footing, in the following respect: whereas the denial of the first two results in a necessary truth and a necessary falsity, resp., the denial of the third is an absurdity of language. Its denial is on a par with pointing out a chair to someone and saying 'This chair is not a thing'. This consideration connects with two considerations which are analogous to those pointed out in the case of the concept *thing*: First, a person could be taught the use of the terms 'even prime' and 'prime' by citing numbers to which these words applied and numbers to which they failed to apply, but in teaching the word 'number' one could not cite anything, within its range of significant application, which was not a number. This is to say that the word 'number' does not serve to distinguish amongst kinds, as do 'even prime' and 'prime'. It does not single out a species from a genus. One can say it singles out a logical type from others; but this is to say that 'x is a number', unlike 'x is prime', does not have true and false values, but only true and nonsensical ones. Second, the method of establishing either that there is an even prime or that there is a prime among the integers is irrelevant to establishing what we are here supposing to be entailed by them, that there is a number. For as long as one is confined to the range of significance of 'number' one cannot cite anything to which the word 'number' fails to apply. Its truth-range and its range of significance are the same.

I think the situation with respect to the concepts *quality, relation, proposition* is in important respects analogous. To throw into doubt whether these category concepts are generic concepts, to which others are related as more specific to more general, one has but to consider such sequences of concepts as *scarlet, red, quality; nearness, relation; true proposition, proposition.* Suppose in these sequences the appropriate entailments hold: a is scarlet $\rightarrow$ a is red $\rightarrow$ a has a quality; a is near $b \rightarrow a$ is related to b; p is a true proposition $\rightarrow p$ is a proposition. One could explain the application of 'has the quality scarlet', 'has the quality red' by pointing to scarlet things and to red things. 'Scarlet' and 'red' both distinguish things which are scarlet, or red, from those which are not. But in explaining what it is to have a quality there would be nothing one could point to of which 'having a quality' was a distinguishing feature. For there could be nothing that fails to have a quality.

Similarly with relations. 'Being near to' could distinguish the objects *a* and *b* from the objects *a* and *z*. But 'being related to' could not distinguish any pair of things from any other pair. This is to say that *quality* and *relation* do not have the usual function of generic concepts. A further disanalogy with proper concepts shows up when one considers the differences in testing whether something is red or has a quality, whether two objects are near each other or are related. Similar disanalogies to those canvassed for the concepts *quality* and *relation* obtain in the case of the category concept *proposition* in contrast to *true proposition*. Only propositions fall within the range of application of these concepts, and it is clear that whereas there is a test for a proposition's being a true one, there is no test for 'There are other inhabited planets' being a proposition.

Differences between category concepts and others show up when one tries to represent them in another notation than English, the notation of logic. In the *Tractatus* Wittgenstein wrote: 'Formal concepts cannot, in fact, be represented by means of a function, as concepts proper can.' (4.126). 'Wherever the word "object" ("thing", etc.) is correctly used, it is expressed in conceptual notation[1] by a variable name. For example, in the proposition, "There are 2 objects which . . .", it is expressed by "$(\exists x,y) . . .$". Wherever it is used in a different way, that is as a proper concept-word, nonsensical pseudo-propositions are the result. So one cannot say, for example, "There are objects", as one might say, "There are books". And it is just as impossible to say, "There are 100 objects", or "There are $\aleph_0$ objects". And it is nonsensical to speak of the *total number of objects*. The same applies to the words "complex", "fact", "function", "number", etc. They all signify formal concepts, and are represented in conceptual notation by variables, not by functions or classes (as Frege and Russell believed).' (4.1272). In the *Notebooks* he refers to 'There are *n* things' as a pseudo-proposition, which 'shews in language by the presence of *n* proper names with different references' 'what it tries to express'.[2]

---

[1] The German words translate literally as 'conceptual notation', rather than as 'logical symbolism' (C. K. Ogden's translation Harcourt, Brace and Co., 1922); but in the context it is reasonably clear that Wittgenstein is referring to Russell's logical notation. [2] P. 20e.

In connection with these statements there are two points which need to be made. One point is that it is not intended that translatability into the notation of logic is to be taken as a test of the sense or nonsense of a corresponding English expression, but rather that peculiarities which show up in the logical notation highlight the peculiarities of English. The other point is that the notation of logic, in particular the quantifiers, may, and in fact does, leave open the matter in dispute between philosophers, namely, the status of existential sentences involving category words. To consider the second point first, quotations above from Wittgenstein make it clear that he takes such sentences to be nonsense. On the other hand, Quine takes quantification in certain contexts to commit one to an ontology, that is, to the truth of certain existence-statements. It would appear, according to him, that one is committed to holding that things, propositions, classes, attributes exist if individual variables, propositional variables, class variables, and functional variables are quantified over. He says: 'To be assumed as an entity is, purely and simply, to be reckoned as a value of a variable . . . this amounts roughly to saying that to be is to be in the range of reference of a pronoun. . . . The variables of quantification, "something", "nothing", "everything", range over our whole ontology, whatever it may be; and we are convicted of a particular ontological presupposition if, and only if, the alleged presuppositum has to be reckoned among the entities over which our variables range in order to render one of our affirmations true.'[1] The 'criterion of ontological commitment [is]: an entity is presupposed by a theory if and only if it is needed among the values of the bound variables in order to make the statements affirmed in the theory true.'[2] To say that a theory T 'presupposes an entity' is to say that T entails the existence of that entity. Clearly Quine takes it to be either true or false that such an entity exists. That is, he takes the indicated entailment in such a statement as '$(a)(\exists\beta)(x)(x\epsilon a . \equiv . x\epsilon\beta)$: →. There are entities over which a, β, and x range' to hold. And even though a schema such as $(x)Fx \equiv Fx$ involves no quantifier $(\exists F)$ . . ., to say that this schema is valid involves 'an appeal to classes'.[3] For this is to say that the schema is true 'for all values of its free (but bindable) variables under all assignments of classes as extensions of the

[1] *From a Logical Point of View*, p. 13.   [2] *Ibid.*, p. 108.   [3] *Ibid.*, p. 115.

schematic predicate letters'.[1] He adds: 'By treating predicate letters [or class letters] as variables of quantification . . . we precipitate a torrent of universals . . .'.[2] Though some schemata involving quantifiers over classes and attributes can be re-expressed as schemata free from commitments to classes or attributes, and although validity in first order quantification theory can be redefined by reference to rules of proof which Gödel has shown to be complete, there remain, according to Quine, schemata in class theory and in elementary number theory (like $(\alpha)(\exists\beta)(x)$ . . .) which will not reduce to schemata devoid of quantified class variables.[3] It is an extremely curious fact that on the matter of what is entailed by a statement containing bound variables there should be such a divergence of opinion. Quine takes it as inescapable that certain occurrences of bound (class) variables 'convict [us] of an ontological presupposition'. But he admits that Carnap's 'attitude is . . . that quantification over abstract objects is a linguistic convention devoid of ontological commitment'.[4] And Wittgenstein no doubt would have denied in the *Tractatus* that there is such a presupposition, on the ground that the phrase 'existence of numbers, classes, etc.' makes no sense.

It is curious also that Quine makes no objection to supposing the quantifiers $(\exists x)$ . . . and (x) . . ., which he reads as 'There is some entity x such that . . .' and 'Each entity x is such that . . .'[5], presuppose the existence of 'individuals'. What is puzzling is not merely the divergence of opinion, between him and Wittgenstein, over whether the phrase 'existence of individuals' makes sense, but that he makes no attempt to represent an ontological presupposition in logical notation. What happens when one tries to translate 'There are individuals', 'There are attributes', etc. into logical notation is an indication of the difference between these category concepts and generic concepts. 'There is at least one individual', which is proved in *Principia Mathematica* as proposition 24.52, i.e. $(\exists x) . x\epsilon$ V, involves the function $x = x$, a property which according to Russell is possessed by everything'.[6] (' V' is defined as the class $\hat{x}(x = x)$.) It is interesting also that such a proposition could occur

---

[1] *From a Logical Point of View*, p. 115.   [2] *Ibid.*, p. 123.
[3] See discussion, *Methods of Logic*, pp. 227–28.
[4] *Methods of Logic*, p. 208. (New York; Henery Holt, 1959)
[5] *From a Logical Point of View*, p. 102.
[6] *Principia Mathematica*, p. 216. $(x) . x = x$ is proved as proposition 50.53.

amongst the propositions of logic—that it should count as valid.[1] Of '($\exists x$) . $x = x$', which one might take to express 'There is at least one thing', Wittgenstein said in the *Notebooks* that 'it might be understood to be tautological since it could not get written down at all if it were false'.[2] And yet he was constantly unsure whether it, or its negation $\sim (\exists x)$. $x = x$, was a proposition at all.[3] Thus, 'Can we speak of the class $\hat{x}(x \neq x)$ at all?—Can we speak of the class $\hat{x}(x = x)$ either? For is $x \neq x$ or $x = x$ a function of x?'[4] Furthermore, 'Supposing that the expression "$\sim (\exists x)$. $x = x$" were a proposition, namely (say), this one: "There are no things", then it would be a matter for great wonder that, in order to express this proposition in symbols, we had to make use of the relation ($=$) with which it was really not concerned at all.'[5] Is there a way of saying in the logical notation, 'There are things'?

If one does not attempt to express it solely in the notation of logic, the natural treatment of 'There are things' is as the existential quantification of the function 'x is an individual'. Analogously for the statements 'There are attributes', 'There are numbers', 'There are propositions', etc. That is, it is natural to treat the terms 'individual' (or 'thing'), 'attribute', etc. as predicates, like 'book', 'prime', etc. But this is misleading, because it slurs over the important difference between the concept *thing*, or *individual*, and generic concepts. As has already been pointed out, 'x is an individual' does not have both individuals and non-individuals within its reality range of significance, unlike 'x is a book', whose range of significance comprises both books and non-books. Any values other than individuals yield nonsense when substituted for 'x' in 'x is an individual'. A similar point is imbedded in the following from the *Tractatus*: 'There are certain cases in which one is tempted to use expressions of the form "$a = a$" or "$p \supset p$" and the like. In fact, this happens when one wants to talk about prototypes, e.g. about proposition, thing, etc. Thus in Russell's *Principles of Mathematics* "p a proposition"—which is nonsense —was given the symbolic rendering "$p \supset p$" and placed as an hypothesis in front of certain propositions in order to exclude from

---

[1] See Russell's discussion of the way in which the logical primitives guarantee that 'there is something', *Principia Mathematica*, pp. 226, 335.
[2] P. 11e.   [3] See *Tractatus*, 5.5352.   [4] *Notebooks*, p. 16e.
[5] *Ibid.*, p. 47e.

their argument-places everything but propositions. (It is nonsense to place the hypothesis "$p \supset p$" in front of a proposition, in order to ensure that its argument shall have the right form, if only because with a non-proposition as argument the hypothesis becomes not false but nonsensical, and because arguments of the wrong kind make the proposition itself nonsensical.)' (5.5351).

What are we to say of the expressions 'p is a proposition', 'x is an individual', 'N is a number', 'ϕ is an attribute', 'R is a relation', and the existential quantifications of these? Certainly they do not appear to be nonsensical. But if not nonsensical, must one then admit that the values of the functions will constitute the items in a cosmic inventory? Is this the alternative? What must one conclude from the differences between 'p is a proposition' and 'p is true', 'x is an individual' and 'x is red', 'ϕ is an attribute' and 'Jones has ϕ', 'N is a number' and 'N is prime'? I have argued that the fact that the range of significance of the category functions and their truth-range are identical shows 'individual', 'attribute', etc. not to be generic concepts. The bearing of this on the possibility of listing what there is in the universe has now to be examined. I shall assume that the existential sentences 'There are individuals', 'There are numbers', etc. make sense. But I shall argue that their import is so different from factual existential statements like 'There are cougars in Arizona' and from mathematical statements like 'There are primes between 10 and 15' as to preclude our supposing they declare the existence of things in the cosmos. We need to look again at these three types of statements.

With regard to factual statements like 'There are cougars in Arizona' it is clear that they make no reference to any verbal fact. It may be remarked that if the sentence 'There are cougars in Arizona' expresses something true, the expression 'cougar in Arizona' applies to an instance of the concept *cougar*, and if it expresses something false, 'cougar in Arizona' fails to apply to anything. But in neither case does the sentence make a declaration about this expression, either overtly or covertly. I think it will become evident that the other two types of statements do not have this complete removal from verbal fact. Philosophers have sometimes distinguished existential statements of mathematics from factual statements by saying either of two things: (a) that the word 'existence' in mathematical statements means something different

—that mathematical entities have a different kind of existence from cougars and the like, or (b) that 'existence' means the same in the two contexts but that the entities said to exist are different.[1] Distinguishing between factual and mathematical existence-statements has sometimes been treated as a matter of deciding which characterization is the proper one. Philosophers who dispute over the two characterizations evidently share the assumption that, as in the case of factual propositions, the existence or nature of a kind of objects—abstract rather than concrete, is in question. The assumption implies that mathematical propositions, like factual propositions, are in no way verbal in import. But it seems to me that the necessity of propositions of number theory, say, which so radically differentiates them from factual propositions like 'There are cougars in Arizona', depends just on some fact about the use of words.

Consider such a statement as 'There is no greatest prime'. It is like the non-necessary statement about cougars in that it does not mean the same as a statement about a verbal fact. That is, it is not synonymous with any statement referring to words or phrases. 'There is no greatest prime', unlike ' "Brother" means male sibling' which mentions the word 'brother', does not mention the phrase 'greatest prime'. Yet what one knows when one sees that 'There is no greatest prime' expresses a necessary truth is exhausted by one's knowing that 'greatest prime' does not have a descriptive use. The fact that this sentence expresses a necessity derives simply from the use assigned to terminology—mathematical usage precludes the English phrase 'greatest prime' from describing any number. By contrast, no fact about the use of the descriptive term of such a sentence as 'There are no dinosaurs', which expresses a contingent truth, precludes the term from applying to anything. To know this matter of fact about the word 'dinosaur' is to know something in addition to knowing the usage of 'dinosaur'. That 'dinosaur' does not apply to anything is assured by a non-linguistic fact, to be determined by observation of the world. The word has a descriptive use and so *could* apply to an animal; but it does not,

[1] Quine says in *Methods of Logic*, p. 198: 'When the Parthenon and the number 7 are said to be, no distinction in the sense of 'be' need be intended. The Parthenon is indeed a placed and dated object in space-time while the number 7 (if such there be) is another sort of thing; but this is a difference between the objects concerned and not between senses of "be".'

and this in no way affects the use assigned to it. One cannot similarly say, as English is used, that 'greatest prime' could have an application but that an inspection of numbers bears out the fact that it does not. We can form the self-contradictory expression 'greatest prime', but once we have a proof that there is no greatest prime we know that the phrase has no conceivable application. What I am saying here is not that the sentence 'There is no greatest prime' *means* that 'greatest prime' has no use, but that in knowing it expresses a necessary truth this is the fact that we know; and there is no further fact to know. That is, to know that the sentence 'There is no greatest prime' expresses a necessity is just to know the empirical linguistic fact that 'greatest prime' has no use to describe a number.[1] The point is perhaps clearer in the case of necessary propositions for which no proof is required, like 'There are no round squares'. To show someone that it is true one does not ask him to survey geometrical figures. Instead one appeals to criteria for the use of the words 'round' and 'square'.

Since we wish to compare both existential and non-existential propositions of metaphysics with outwardly similar contingent and mathematical propositions, it will be useful to complete our account of mathematical propositions by exhibiting the linguistic character of existential propositions, in contrast with the non-existential ones just cited. For to do this is less simple than to indicate the verbal import of 'There is no greatest prime' or 'There are no round squares'. Consider the sentence expressing the necessary truth that there is a prime between 10 and 15. When we know that this sentence expresses a necessity, with what verbal fact are we acquainted? First of all, that the expression 'prime between 10 and 15' has a use to describe at least one number. But something more than this needs to be said in order to distinguish the fact that this sentence expresses a necessary truth from the fact that the sentence 'There are cougars in Arizona' expresses a contingent truth. For it might be said that in knowing these two facts one knows there are objects which the expressions 'prime between 10 and 15' and 'cougar in Arizona', resp., describe. Further, it might be said that in each case a non-linguistic fact, established

---

[1] For an elaboration of this treatment of necessary propositions see M. Lazerowitz' 'Logical Necessity' in *The Structure of Metaphysics*, esp. pp. 270–72; and 'Methods of Philosophy' in *Studies in Metaphilosophy*, pp. 46–56.

by observation, informs us that these expressions have application. The difference, of course, is that criteria for the use of 'prime between 10 and 15' informs us that the expression applies to a number and observation informs us that there is an animal to which 'cougar' applies. Explication of this difference will I think show up the verbal import of the proposition that a prime exists between 10 and 15.

Consider the translation into quantifier notation of the sentence 'There is a prime between 10 and 15': '$(\exists x)$. x is a prime . x is between 10 and 15'. The fact that this sentence expresses a necessity is equivalent to the fact that some sentence resulting from substitution on 'x' in 'x is prime . x is between 10 and 15' expresses a necessity. This is to say that within the language of numerals at least one numeral, 'a', is so used that 'a is prime and between 10 and 15' expresses a necessity. Take 'a' to be '11', and consider the fact that '11 is prime and between 10 and 15' expresses a necessity. What do we know in knowing this fact? That the criteria for the use of the component expressions prevent the expression '11 and not both prime and between 10 and 15' from having a use. What is logically impossible cannot, even in theory, have instances, and since '11 and not both prime and between 10 and 15' expresses a logical impossibility, knowing this fact comes to knowing that it has no theoretical application. And this is precisely what we know in seeing that '11 is a prime between 10 and 15' expresses a necessary truth. To say the necessary proposition expressed by the sentence 'There is a prime number between 10 and 15' has verbal import only is to say that in knowing that some specification of the sentence 'a is prime and between 10 and 15' expresses a necessity we know a fact about the use of a numeral.

Something should be said here in answer to the contention that a non-linguistic fact, namely that 11 is a prime between 10 and 15, established by an examination of numbers, informs us that the phrase 'prime between 10 and 15' applies to something. I have argued that the proposition '11 is a prime and between 10 and 15' is verbal in import. But suppose my claim is countered by the claim that inspection of numbers between 10 and 15 assures us that the phrase 'being prime' stands for an internal property of two of them—just as inspection of animals shows that 'being a cougar' stands for an accidental property of at least one animal. This counterclaim suggests the idea that numbers are objects, that 'being a number' is a generic name for them, and that 'prime between 10 and 15' is a description setting off one class of objects from another class. It is clear that at this point we have arrived at metaphysical positions, namely, that numbers are objects and that they exist. We turn now to an investigation of these and other propositions of metaphysics, both existential and non-existential, to determine whether they are such as to assert what there is, or is not, in the universe. I wish to argue that they are, like mathematical propositions, verbal in import. They are like mathematical propositions in this respect but yet are different.

Two differences are apparent at once. One is that they are all somehow idle. 'There are numbers' has no rôle in any number theory proof. And 'There are attributes', 'There are relations', 'There are propositions', 'There are things' are not the kind of sentences one would utter in anything but a 'philosophic moment'.[1] Likewise for their negations. The second difference is that two philosophers can dispute, without hope of coming to a decision, over whether there are such entities as numbers, attributes, relations, etc. while both are in the presence of the same facts and neither is blind, either psychologically or physically. This latter fact indicates not only that their statements are unlike assertions within mathematics, for which arguments adduced have a finality about them. It also indicates that the dispute is not empirical, that is, that the metaphysical propositions are like those in mathematics. Philosophers who deny the existential metaphysical claims under discussion here either refuse to accept the entailments of which they are consequents (e.g. that there are rickshaws entails the existence of things and of the attribute of being a rickshaw, or that there are primes between 10 and 15 entails the existence of such entities as numbers), or else they refuse to accept the truth of the entailments' antecedents. (For example, some philosophers object to G. E. Moore's 'proof' of an external world on the ground that it begs the question: they may grant that 'Here is a hand' entails the existence of an external object, but not accept that here is a hand.) It is interesting that those who deny existence-claims in metaphysics (a) refuse to accept any evidence in support of those claims, (b) argue demonstratively for their own claims. That is,

[1] G. E. Moore's phrase.

they proceed as though their views were *a priori*. In assessing the status of these views let us consider first those which deny the existence of certain categories of things, as their treatment presents fewer difficulties. Because they each occur within the context of general philosophical positions which dictate rather different arguments in support of them we cannot go into the detail of each view. But certain similarities will appear which bear on my claim that they are verbal in import.

Consider first Bradley's claims that there are no things, no qualities, no relations. These are made within the context of a philosophical position according to which things, qualities, and relations have the status of appearances. We leave aside for the moment the matter of their status in order to highlight the important fact about what appear at first to be empirical claims, the fact namely, that the arguments for them are *a priori*—directed to showing that the concepts *thing, quality, relation* are self-contradictory. The procedure is similar to the proof that there is no greatest prime, and we may justifiably assume that Bradley intends his statements to express necessary truths. We can therefore treat the propositions he asserts in the same way, as comparable propositions in mathematics, i.e. as having only verbal import—to use Prof. J. N. Findlay's expression, as 'reflecting' usage.[1] But do these metaphysical proposition in fact reflect usage? As a matter of English, the sentence 'There is no greatest prime' expresses a necessity; linguistic conventions being what they are, 'greatest prime' has no use. But it is obviously false to say that the words 'thing', 'quality', 'relation' have no use. Although they are not generic names for a thing or quality or relation, as are 'house', 'red', or 'north of', it is undeniable that in English they can be conjoined with 'proper' concept words without literal nonsense resulting. To know that 'There are no things, no qualities, no relations' expresses a necessity we should have to be knowing that 'thing', 'quality', 'relation' are deprived by current conventions of any function. But there are no such conventions, and of course a philospher who utters these sentences knows this.

If, then, his sentences express neither a necessary proposition nor an empirical one, and at the same time are not nonsense, what are his arguments in ended to do? The explanation is I think that

[1] 'Can God's Existence Be Disproved?', *Mind*, Vol. LVII, p. 182.

set out by M. Lazerowitz:[1] this that his arguments are persuasive devices, devices unrecognized by the philosopher who uses them, for altering present language in a non-workaday way. A metaphysical argument purports to demonstrate a necessary truth, but since present linguistic conventions prevent the sentence concluding the sequence of proof-sentences from doing what it purports to do, the argument can plausibly be taken to have another purpose: to induce one to accept other conventions. Wittgenstein wrote in the *Blue Book*: '[The philosopher] is not aware that he is objecting to a convention. He sees a way of dividing the country different from the one usual on the ordinary map. He feels tempted, say, to use the name "Devonshire" not for the county with its conventional boundary, but for a region differently bounded. He could express this by saying: "Isn't it absurd to make *this* a county, to draw the boundaries *here?*" But what he says is: "The *real* Devonshire is this". We could answer: "What you want is only a new notation, and by a new notation no facts of geography are changed.'[2] As Quine remarks, 'What there is [does not] depend on words'.[3] But the illusion that the existence of something is being asserted or denied or debated can depend on words. And a demonstration charged with no logical flaw can indeed create the illusion that some question is being settled about what should be listed in a cosmic inventory.

The use of words in a natural language is not so precisely circumscribed as to rule out their employment in argumentation eventuating in the most startling conclusions, for example, that the concept *relation* is self-contradictory. How in particular this is effected has to be ascertained afresh for the argumentation for each 'view'. The point I wish to make is that the sentence expressing a view, though it fails to assert a necessity, in purporting to do so has verbal import nonetheless. In the case of those metaphysical sentences which are advanced as if they express the necessary falsity of some existential proposition, the desired linguistic effect is evidently to preclude from use some word or phrase which now has a function. To argue that things, qualities, and relations *cannot* exist has the effect of producing reasons for linguistic revisions.

---

[1] See especially 'The Existence of Universals' in *The Structure of Metaphysics* and 'Moore and Philosophical Analysis' in *Studies in Metaphilosophy*.
[2] P. 57.   [3] *From a Logical Point of View*, p. 16.

The concluding sentence of the sequence of sentences used in setting out a demonstration fails, because of actual usage, to express a necessity; but in a revised language it would express one, and the point of the proof can be to justify *taking it* to express a necessity rather than showing that it does express a necessity. Such a revision would have no practical appeal. For the language in which words are so used that the sentence 'There are no things, qualities, or relations' expresses a necessity would be one precluding the use of 'thing', 'quality', 'relation' in existence-sentences. The revision can be made less drastic by doing what Bradley did: On a linguistic level, he assures the continued use of these words in appearance-sentences[1] in assigning to things, qualities, and relations the status of appearances. In effect what he does is to stretch the use of 'appearance' to apply to whatever thing-, quality-, and relation-phrases normally apply to. So the use of the latter is contracted rather than rejected altogether. The belief the metaphysician has that he has shown things, qualities, and relations to have the status of insubstantial appearance is an illusion produced by his unconsciously redrawing linguistic boundaries.

When Moore objects to Bradley's views and in defence of common sense opposes it with the claim that things and relations exist, it is most natural to take him to be asserting a plain matter of fact, even though it would be unnatural to assert such a thing in any ordinary circumstances. But construed as a reply to Bradley's position that they *cannot* exist, i.e. as a counter to a purportedly necessary proposition, the matter appears otherwise. Moore's claim has on the verbal level the effect of preserving the linguistic status quo. To see this it is useful to make the supposition that 'There are things', 'There are qualities', 'There are relations' assert empirical propositions and examine the character of the sentences resulting from substitution on the functions 'x is a thing', 'ϕ is a quality', 'R is a relation'. If the propositions asserted by the original sentences are empirical and non-verbal, the propositions asserted by 'This (say, a house) is a thing', 'This (say, red) is a quality', 'This (say, north of) is a relation' would serve to substantiate them. I think it must be admitted that the only circumstance under which the first proposition would be non-verbal

[1] For this thesis and its elaboration see M. Lazerowitz' 'Appearance and Reality' in *The Structure of Metaphysics*.

in import is that in which it serves to inform someone that he is not seeing a shadow, or a mirage, or having an hallucination. In such cases the word 'thing' would function like a generic name to set off objects within its range of significance from others. But if a philosopher were to justify his claim that there are things, qualities, and relations by asserting 'A house is a thing', 'Red is a quality', 'North of is a relation', clearly each of the statements he makes is necessary. And this tells us something about the logical character of the propositions they are supposed to support: they, also, will be *a priori*. The necessity of his supporting statements is guaranteed by the linguistic fact that in the sentences expressing them the words 'house', 'red', 'north of' have as part of their meanings *thing*, *quality*, *relation*, resp. And this is what knowing that 'A house is a thing', etc. express necessities amounts to. The status of philosophical existential propositions which are used to counter the Parmenidean denials now becomes easier to assess. If the propositions supposedly supporting them are verbal in import, then 'There are things, qualities, and relations' must likewise be verbal in import. For propositions whose sole informative force is verbal could not support propositions informing us about what there is in the world. Within the context of a dispute in which one of the disputants asserts the self-contradictoriness of the concepts *thing*, *quality*, *relation*, to insist that there are things, qualities, and relations has the effect of urging that the words 'thing', 'quality', 'relation' retain the use they already have in English.

Existence-claims about numbers, attributes, relations, and propositions, when made by a Platonist, require a somewhat different treatment than existence-claims a commonsense philosopher makes in denying the view that the world of appearances is unreal. A philosophical assertion that something exists has to be investigated in relation to what is being denied. In the case of the Platonic position, the objection is that abstract entities do not exist. This indicates that the Platonist is understood to assert certain objectionable entailments, of which some 'casual statement of commonplace fact' may be the antecedent and an objectionable metaphysical statement the consequent. Consider the assertion that the proposition 'There is a prime greater than 10 and less than 15' is necessarily true. The Platonist would maintain that this entails the existence of a proposition, of an attribute, of at least one number, and of a relation, and that the existence of each of these entails the existence of an entity, one which is abstract rather than concrete. That is, 'Propositions, attributes, numbers, relations are entities' is held to be necessarily true. Nothing will induce the Platonist to admit to the non-existence of a world of universals which, according to him, he clearly perceives by the eye of the mind. The fact that other philosophers fail to report such a finding in no way shakes him.

But of course if the sentence 'Propositions, attributes, numbers, etc. are entities' did express a necessary proposition then in point of English usage 'entity' could be used wherever 'proposition', 'attribute', etc. are used, just as 'sibling' can be used wherever 'brother' is used. It is obvious that the phrases 'true proposition', 'personal attribute', 'prime number' are proper English, whereas 'true entity', 'personal entity', 'prime entity' are not. Hence the philosopher who holds that 'Numbers are entities' states the essence of numbers, that it expresses what is undeniably because necessarily true, commits himself to a false proposition about English usage—unless the point of his claim is taken to be something else: to say, not that 'entity' does in fact classify numbers, but that it should. A revised language, in which 'Numbers are entities' expresses a necessity would do what is desired, classify numbers as entities. When the Platonic view that numbers have being is challenged by the rejoinder that numbers are scratches on paper, we may take the exchange as a family quarrel over what kind of entities they are, whereas as language is now used it is not a fixed convention that 'entity' describes numbers at all. The Platonic philosopher redraws the boundaries of the word 'entity'—extends it, and by this linguistic manoeuvre creates the illusion that he is asserting the existence of things not hitherto noted. Russell observed: 'Seeing that nearly all the words to be found in the dictionary stand for universals, it is strange that hardly anybody except students of philosophy ever realises that there are such entities as universals'.[1] His comment is made in the language of factual record, and the style of speaking is an important factor in creating an atmosphere which makes it difficult not to think the existence of something is being asserted. Although, as Quine remarked, what there is does not depend on words, the use of

[1] *The Problems of Philosophy.* 17th Impression, p. 146.

256

words to induce a new classification can produce the illusion that a *correct* classification of what exists is being made. Occam's injunction against the multiplication of entities can be interpreted as an injunction against creating the illusion, by language, that the existence of entities is being asserted. Language cannot create entities; but a philosopher can so use it that its point appears to be the factual assertion that something exists, whereas its point is verbal, not factual.

If what I have said about the import of existential and non-existential propositions of metaphysics is correct, then the disputes about them, and their 'proofs', have been misconceived. It is clear in general that if a statement is verbal in import it gives us information about a language but tells us nothing about the world to which the language is used to refer; it tells us nothing about what there is in the world.

INDEX

Acquaintance, 128, 130, 131, 137
  and inference, 130, 132
  and objects named, 132, 136
Analysis
  conversion, 22–3, 24
  as explication, 106, 118, 145, 147,
    167–8, 205–6, 211
  linguistic, 147
  logical, and atomism, 123, 124, 130,
    135
  and usage explication, 147–8, 211
Analyticity, 177–9
Appearance
  delusive, 67
  and reality, 122, 125, 240
A priori necessity
  and entailment, ch. 6
  nature of, 88–9, 93–4, 99, 218
  theories about
    conventionalism, 69, 72, 74–5, 86
    Mill's view, 41, 43
    Platonism, 72, 74, 75
A priori statements
  application to fact, 41, 44, 52
  as dependent on choice of language,
    85–8
  and experience, 48–58, 218
  and experiential statements, 29, 81,
    90, 101, 153 ff., 218
  and factual information, 41, 69, 77,
    95, 248
  features of, 18, 41, 43, 50, 218
  their function as rules, 44–8, 54, 71
  as treating of symbolism, 46, 51, 71,
    74–5, 86, 153 ff.
  verbal correlates of, 18, 82, 83, 211,
    219–20, 249
  and verbal information, 74, 81, 82,
    86, 153 ff., 211, 219, 248–50, 252,
    253
Aristotle, 124, 135, 201
Atomic facts, 131–2
  and their constituents, 123–5, 130–2
  and structure of ideal language,
    139–40
Augustine, St, 107

Austin, J. L., 213
Ayer, A. J., 74 n., 133, 155 n., 207

Bar-Hillel, Y., 165 n.
Berkeley, George, 126–7, 128, 143,
  146, 147, 149–51
Berlin, Isaiah, 196
Bernays, P., 157 n.
Beth, E., 157 n.
Black, Max, 151–2
Blanshard, Brand, 205
Bradley, F. H., 146, 206, 207, 209,
  212, 238, 241, 252, 254
Bridgman, P. W., 66 n.
Broad, C. D., 42 n., 184–5, 187, 188,
  192–4, 196, 200–1

Calculation, and experiment, 48
Cantor, Georg, 20, 60 n.
Carnap, Rudolf, 88, 143, 165–6, 177,
  245
Category-words
  as general names, 78–80, 222–4,
    238 ff.
Cayley, George, 73
Church, Alonzo, 26–8, 35–9, 176–8
Copilowish, I. M., 167
Courant, Richard, 70, 74

Democritus, 129
Descartes, René, 22, 70, 71, 122, 124,
  143, 145, 230
Descriptive phrases
  analysis of, 137
  contrasted with names, 137
  as symbols for constructs, 136

Empirical propositions
  compared with arithmetic proposi-
    tions, 41–3
  as entailing necessities, ch. 6
  as having evidential support, 218–9,
    241, 251
Entailment
  and logical necessity, ch. 6
  and strict implication, 91–2

258

GEORGE ALLEN & UNWIN LTD

London: 40 Museum Street, WC1

Auckland: PO Box 36013, Northcote Central, Auckland N4
Bombay: 15 Graham Road, Ballard Estate, Bombay 1
Barbados: PO Box 222, Bridgetown
Buenos Aires: Escritorio 454–459, Florida 165
Calcutta: 17 Chittaranjan Avenue, Calcutta 13
Cape Town: 68 Shortmarket Street
Hong Kong: 105, Wing On Mansions, 26, Hancow Road, Kowloon
Ibadan: PO Box 62
Karachi: Karachi Chambers, McLeod Road
Madras: Mohan Mansions, 38c Mount Road, Madras 6
Mexico: Villalongin 32-10, Piso, Mexico 5, DF
Nairobi: PO Box 4536
New Delhi: 13–14 Asaf Ali Road, New Delhi 1
Ontario: 81 Curlew Drive, Don Mills
Rio de Janeiro: Caixa Postal 2537–Zc-00
São Paulo: Caixa Postal 8675
Singapore: 36c Prinsep Street, Singapore 7
Sydney, NSW: Bradbury House, 55 York Street
Tokyo: P.O. Box 26, Kamata

LECTURES ON PHILOSOPHY
G. E. MOORE
Edited by CASIMIR LEWY

G. E. Moore lectured at Cambridge every year from 1911 until his retirement in 1939. These lectures were often attended by philosophers from different parts of the world, and they were one of the chief means by which he extended his influence on the philosophical thought of his time. Dr Lewy has now edited a selection from some of these lectures. They discuss problems in epistemology, in philosophical logic and in the methodology of philosophy. They contain ideas which Moore did not publish elsewhere, and they should be of unusual interest to students of analytic philosophy.

THE DISCIPLINE OF THE CAVE
J. N. FINDLAY

These lectures are the First Series of a course of Gifford Lectures whose Second Series will be given in December 1965–January 1966 and will be entitled *The Transcendence of the Cave*. The Second Series will continue the theme of the First Series and will be essential to its complete understanding.

The lectures make use of the Platonic image of the Cave to emphasize the fact that men feel their familiar experience to be full of many and strange restrictions, and to involve puzzles and discrepancies which they do not even see the possibility of solving and removing. Deep-set philosophical perplexities of this sort can be seen as arising out of the misunderstanding and meaningless abuse of ordinary ways of thinking and speaking. But they can equally be seen, in the Platonic phrase, as 'drawing us towards being', providing an apagogical proof of the 'absurdity' of ordinary thought, speech and experience except as modified and supplemented in ways which may point altogether beyond it. What may be called a mystical and otherwordly element, and a graded series of experiences in which it is enjoyed, may therefore need to be introduced into or rendered explicit in all our experience, action and diction, not as some gratuitous modification or addition, but in order to give a viable sense to the most commonplace human utterances and activities. The presuppositions of such a manner of reasoning of course involve much fundamental criticism and revision of contemporary conceptions of language, logic and meaning and of their relation to experience and to the teaching of the use of words.

The method of the lectures involves some use of a method akin to the descriptive, phenomenological method of Husserl, as well as a method akin to the dialectrical, revisionary method of Hegel. The lectures will also draw for inspiration on Platonist, Neoplatonist, Scholastic, Buddhist and other sources.

GEORGE ALLEN & UNWIN LTD